Graphic
Designer's
Essential
Reference

MARKET CONSULTING

We see it, too.

Botanus autem est nunc et
semper ex in gloriosa equam
erat. Lorem ipsum dolor sit
ametiscing elit. Nam aclectuis
eget telus fringila feugiat.

Fund Portfolio   Company Profile   Client Area

...simply clean,
...ize—with the science
...organic botanicals

NUTRIA

Bath and Body System

FISKE
MARKET CO
INVESTING
YOUR PER

Revive and Conquer

Don't simply clean, but catalyze — with the science of organic botanicals

How do y
see yours
living in th
twenty yea

Botanus autem est nunc
et semper ex in glorioe

Vestibulum vel euismou
lacus. Mauris volutpat
sui neque tincid unt elit
sceler isque artix magn
ificat duis autem summa

FISKE

Market Consulting

Investing from
your perspective.

MULTISYMPTOM
24-HOUR COLD REMEDY

RELAXIMIZE
DAY AND NIGHT

Revive and conquer.

Don't
simply
clean, but
catalyze—
with the
science of
organic
botanicals

FISKE
MARKET
INVESTIN
YOUR PER

Science
makes the
difference

Nutria
Bath and Body System

How
see

Graphic Designer's Essential Reference

*Visual Elements, Techniques, and
Layout Strategies for Graphic Designers*

Timothy Samara

BEVERLY MASSACHUSETTS

ROCKPORT PUBLISHERS

First published in the United States of America by Rockport Publishers
A member of Quayside Publishing Group
100 Cummings Center
Suite 406-L
Beverly, Massachusetts 01915-6101
Telephone: (978) 282-9590
Fax: (978) 283-2742
www.rockpub.com

....

ISBN: 978-1-59253-743-3
Digital edition published in 2011
eISBN: 978-1-61673-877-8

The content in this book originally appeared in the book *The Designer's Graphic Stew* (Rockport Publishers, 2010)

Cover and book design, book photography, and illustrations by Timothy Samara.

Photographic components of some illustrations in the Elements and Strategies sections are stock photographs, © Jupiter Images; such photographs are reproduced under license to the author/designer and used in accordance with the terms of that licensing agreement.

Printed in Singapore

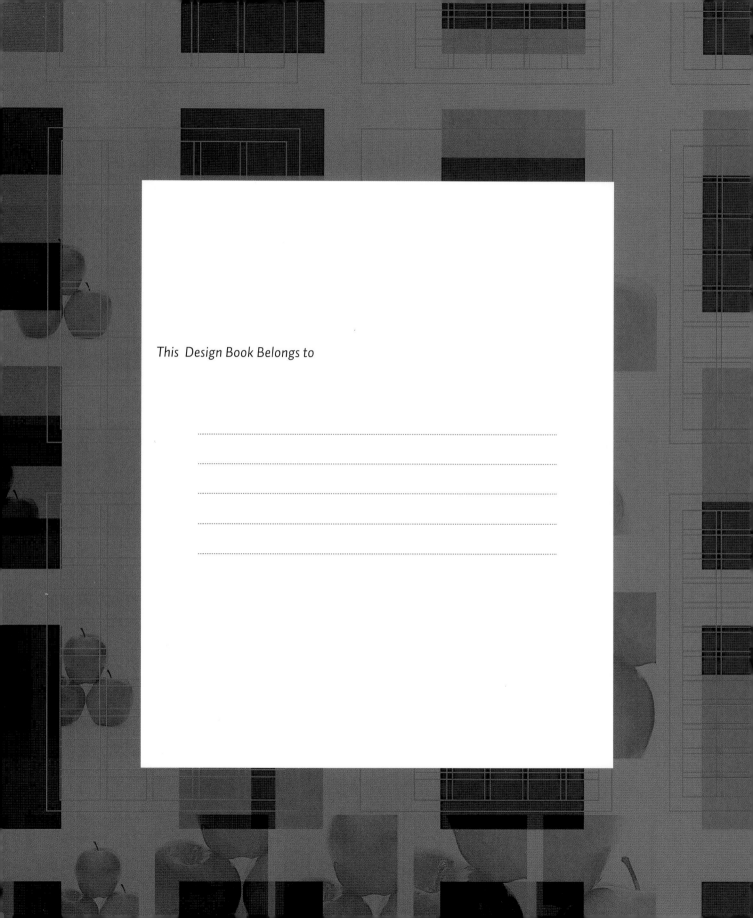

This Design Book Belongs to

....

....

....

....

....

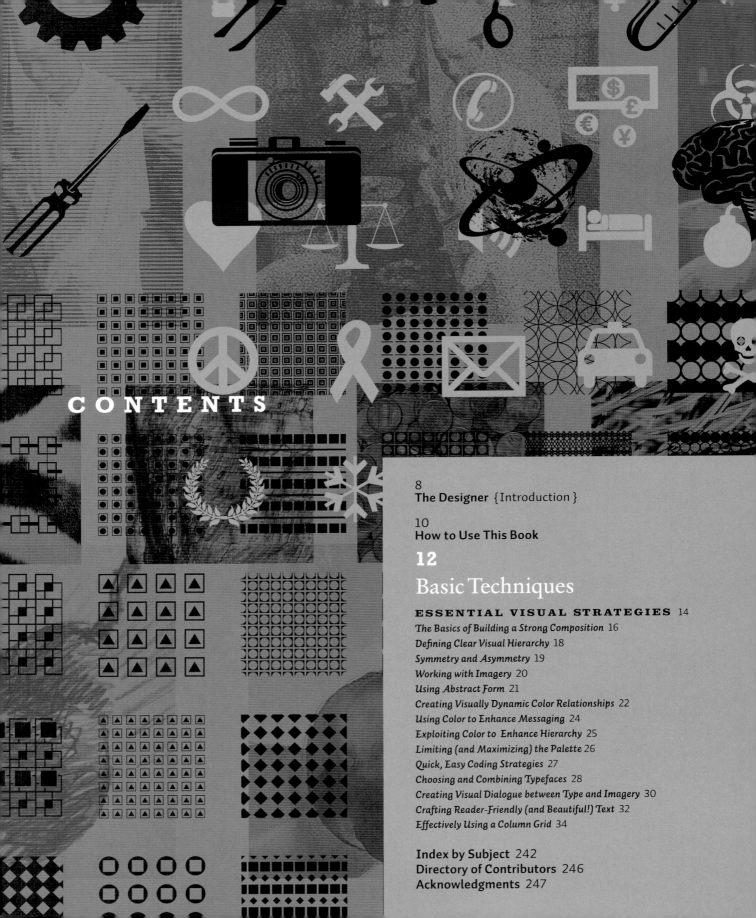

CONTENTS

Introduction

THE DESIGNER

AT THE
READY

I have often compared graphic designers and the work they do—composing visual stimuli and organizing it into clear and dynamic structures—to architects, chefs, and musical conductors. Each confronts an empty space, charged with the task of producing a memorable, meaningful, and hopefully enjoyable experience. To do so, each peruses his or her catalog of content, styles, methods, and details to envision an end result that will speak to his or her audience with depth, drawing on the history of his or her particular craft and interpreting it with distinction.

What is it, after all, that a designer does that is so different from the work of these other creative professionals?

A designer gives form to ideas by inventing images through painting and drawing, choosing and manipulating photography, selecting colors, formatting type and all these other elements into various configurations, spaces, rhythms, layers—much the way an architect shapes a building, a chef conjures a new dish, or a conductor orchestrates a performance. Testing conventions of page structure, type style, and pictorial options, the designer arrives at a vision for conceptualizing the content he or she must convey—and proceeds, through iterative experimentation, with the precise drawing techniques, color palettes, sharper or softer serif typefaces, textural fields or blocks of pattern, the larger or smaller instance of a photograph, to arrive at a design that delivers its message clearly, forcefully, and memorably.

And, like his or her creative counterparts, the designer must have a firm grasp not only of the historical framework and conventions in which he or she is working, but also of the myriad options on hand for transcending mere formula to create something that is entirely new.

Accomplishing a virtuoso performance means being ready—having the right tools on hand and knowing the possibilities they offer.

A good chef knows the flavor and texture of every ingredient; a conductor is intimately familiar with the tonality of each instrument and how it affects the others. Likewise, a good designer is aware not only of all the different ways of visualizing an idea but also how each combines to deliver their message, and which combinations will best create experiences that are ideally suited for the specific needs of the client and the intended audience.

For whatever reason, be it an entrenched routine, an outright creative block, or the pressure of a tight deadline, designers sometimes find themselves at a loss for how to proceed: Photo or icon? Violet or gray? Oldstyle or slab serif? To ensure readiness and spark ideas on the fly, this book offers designers an at-a-glance resource of essential options for spurring the imagination and getting the job done—with style, originality, appropriate meaning, and aesthetic delight for client and audience alike.

How to Use This Book

The majority of this book catalogs a varied collection of graphical elements to which a graphic designer can turn in developing unique, engaging visual solutions on behalf of his or her clients—a breadth of compositional devices that can be used as is, or combined as needed for more intriguing results. This section, "Graphic Elements," presents fifty-seven categories of such elements, divided into four distinct groups: "Pictorial Staples" (icons, abstract languages, textures, and patterns); "Chromatic Concepts" (formal and conceptual color palettes); "Typographic Stylings" (typeface combinations, form manipulations, editorial configurations, and ornamental devices); and "Layout Strategies" (methods for dividing pages, cropping, and grid structures).

Each category fills two pages and has been assigned a number; within those pages, the individual elements are also numbered. The category number, plus the individual element number, create a reference code for that particular combination. For example, the pictorial category *Textures: Representational* is numbered **10**. The last element in that category (in the lower-right corner) is numbered **072**, so that element's reference code is **10072**.

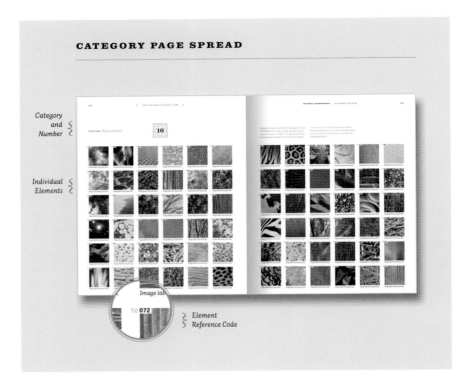

CATEGORY PAGE SPREAD

Category and Number

Individual Elements

Image tab

10 **072**

Element Reference Code

Once a designer has established the elements to be mixed, he or she must then be able to consider what possibilities exist for these combinations in practical application—and how different elements may combine to create appropriate communications. In the second major section, "Project Strategies," the elements are used in hypothetical layouts for a range of project types—design strategies formulated to illustrate specific compositional and conceptual goals. Each project strategy begins with a *Project Communication Brief*—a design brief that outlines the project's conceptual and visual communication goals to provide readers a context for the approaches being demonstrated. Translation of the English language typography that appears in the design solutions is also provided in this introduction. All of the elements used are listed by their reference codes and a brief *Visual Profile* describes how those elements interact, both visually and with regard to the meanings they evoke. Furthermore, the effect of substituting one or more elements in the same strategy is shown as a series of variations, so designers may understand both the visual and the evocative results of mixing different elements in similar kinds of layouts. Scattered among the strategy pages are real-world examples of related projects—prepared by some of the world's top designers.

While the catalog of elements is comprehensive, and the strategies offer broad approaches that will help a designer start conceptualizing a project, it's important to note that no formula is offered here, only a mindset—an excursion into some of the limitless possibilities of bringing image, type, and layout together. It will always be the designer's task to determine not just which elements go together, but also what modifications an element will need to work best. It's the idea of using an archetypal icon, rather than a photograph, embodied in that element; what the icon shows, and its specific drawing quality, are other questions to be pondered.

Similarly, the strategies present methodologies, rather than set procedures, for using the graphic elements—just as cooking recipes do for the chef. A good cook knows that *Chicken Milanese* is a recipe for a breaded cutlet in a white wine and butter sauce; but the thickness of the cutlet, the amount of flour and egg, the proportion of wine to butter, and the duration of cooking are all variables the cook is free to change to accomplish his or her own vision of the dish. So, too, graphic designers must look beyond the hard-and-fast strategy presentation to determine which aspects of the strategy are most appropriate, which need modification for his or her particular purposes, and which must be discarded or combined with other strategy concepts to resolve the project in the most compelling and satisfying manner.

PROJECT STRATEGY OPENING PAGE SPREAD

Each recipe is accompanied by a **Project Communication Brief** *that describes the reasoning behind ingredient selection and layout decisions.*

Elements used in a given recipe are listed by their reference codes, categorized by section, and supplemented by their respective page numbers.

BASIC TECHNIQUES

Essential Visual Strategies

NEARLY ALL DESIGN problems share some fundamental aspects: Typefaces will need to be selected or photographs arranged in an interesting way across a layout. Regardless of specific concerns that may need to be addressed in a particular project, there are general strategies most designers will use as foundations for more complex visual concepts, or to ensure common notions of quality (e.g., that a layout is dynamic) are met in the final presentation.

In this preliminary section, you'll find a sampling of such essential visual techniques: developing rich color palettes; reliably mixing typefaces for contrast and style; using abstract forms to support other imagery and customize visual experiences; achieving dynamic picture placement within a column grid; and many more. Consider these strategies as building blocks—as you add each component to your repertoire, you're one step closer to becoming the most confident, assured designer in your studio.

GUI COMPUTER
It's the studio workhorse. When comparison shopping, realize that there are few roses among the thorns—choose the best you can afford.

DESIGNER'S GOUACHE
Rich, opaque finish in both color and black and white; for the old-school virtuoso.

SABLE BRUSHES
There's nothing like Kolinsky hair for precise handling. Two sizes— No. 4 and No. 6—are sufficient, but have three of each size on hand: one for black, one for white, and one for color.

Basic Equipment, Tools, and Supplies

Being able to conceptualize and compose seamlessly, while efficiently working among various media, to explore different ideas means having all the tools you need—and the best ones for the job—on hand at all times. Here are the items no well-appointed studio can do without.

SPOT- AND PROCESS-COLOR SWATCH BOOKS
Don't trust the computer screen for color: See the real thing. They're an expensive, but ultimately indispensable, investment.

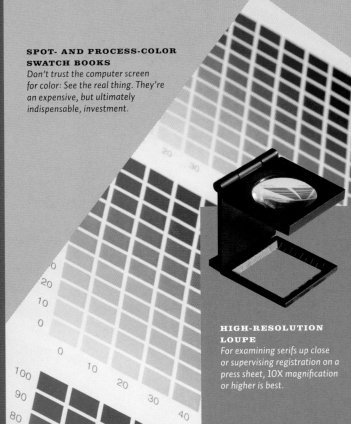

HIGH-RESOLUTION LOUPE
For examining serifs up close or supervising registration on a press sheet, 10X magnification or higher is best.

WHITE AND KNEADED ERASERS
White is for serious erasing from tough stocks. The kneaded version is best for delicate papers, or for slight tonal adjustments.

CUTTING MAT
Self-healing is best, to prevent making grooves that will misdirect your blade in the future.

STEEL STRAIGHTEDGE AND TRIANGLE
Avoid aluminum for these tools—knife blades shred aluminum and, after a short while, a true edge is no longer a given. The triangle, archaic as it may seem, helps ensure 90° angles.

STUDIO KNIFE
Get a good knife with a textured gripping surface, and an array of interchangeable blades. Replace the blade every 6 to 8 cuts to keep the slicing sharp and clean.

LUCITE BRAYER
Unlike a rubber brayer, whose porous surface may stain or encourage peel-up, this rolls hard and fast, and cleans up spotlessly.

PRECISION RULERS
The master designer measures in 1/64" (0.396 mm) increments, and it's even better when the measuring device is transparent and flexible

BONE FOLDER
At some point, you'll need to make mock-ups to show clients. This is what you'll use to fold pages and covers.

The Basics of Building a Strong Composition

Seeing Form and Space
The first step in composing a dynamic layout is being able to decipher what, exactly, a visual element really is—to understand the visual element in the simplest way possible. A silhouetted image of a teapot, for instance, is really a dot: radial, enclosed, curvilinear; a spoon, seen on edge, is a line. As far as composition is concerned, the meaning or content of a visual form is unimportant; its true identity is what determines how it will behave when juxtaposed with other forms.

FORM IDENTITY CONVERSION TABLE

DOT *The fundamental building block of visual form: a fixed point. Simultaneously radiates and contracts.*

LINE *A dot in motion. Describes direction, separates elements, defines spaces; may be solid or broken.*

PLANE *A dot large enough for its outer contour to become important; also referred to as* **shape***. Geometric forms are mathematical and often angular, while organic forms are irregular, soft, or "natural" in appearance.*

SURFACE ACTIVITY *Also called* **texture** *or* **pattern***, which are themselves distinct: texture [A] is irregular, random, or organic; a pattern [B] is repetitive and/or geometric—hence, artificial or invented.*

A   B

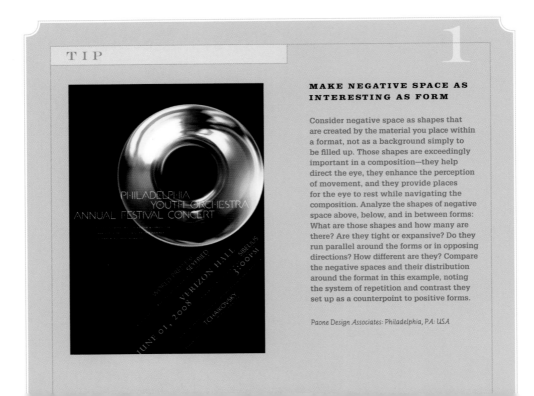

TIP 1

MAKE NEGATIVE SPACE AS INTERESTING AS FORM

Consider negative space as shapes that are created by the material you place within a format, not as a background simply to be filled up. Those shapes are exceedingly important in a composition—they help direct the eye, they enhance the perception of movement, and they provide places for the eye to rest while navigating the composition. Analyze the shapes of negative space above, below, and in between forms: What are those shapes and how many are there? Are they tight or expansive? Do they run parallel around the forms or in opposing directions? How different are they? Compare the negative spaces and their distribution around the format in this example, noting the system of repetition and contrast they set up as a counterpoint to positive forms.

Paone Design Associates: Philadelphia, PA: USA

Scale, Contrast, and Organization

After identifying the essential forms being considered, the next step is to look at how they're going to behave when they're mixed together. Form, or figure, is considered a positive element, or the ingredients of the layout; while space, or ground, is considered the negative, or opposite, of form—it's the pot the ingredients are being mixed in, or the plate on which they'll be arranged and served. Because page or screen space is intrinsically flat, as are the forms within them, viewers are predisposed to taking them for granted (much the way bored gourmands do with oatmeal).

To ensure a rich, engaging optical experience, the designer must compose form in space in such a way that the viewer perceives not only that the forms are interacting three dimensionally, but also that there is a kind of harmonic rhythm among all the layout's aspects. This harmonic rhythm is often called *tension*—it's a perceived vibrancy or liveliness that one experiences in layouts where all the parts are relating to each other. But as the term itself implies, tension isn't only about formal and spatial relationships being the same. Just as must be in a successful culinary creation, some elements must oppose each other in some way, or create contrast, in order to appreciate each of the parts more clearly. A strong composition consists of visual relationships that support and restate each other, as well as some that conflict with the expectations that those mutually supportive relationships create.

Every successful composition organizes a variety of compositional characteristics, held in a state of tension, to impart a sense of resolution. This property of a composition is called its *gestalt*, meaning "totality"; the viewer senses an underlying logic that unifies individual relationships into a whole. Individual relationships among forms and, therefore, the gestalt, will change each time a single element is altered; be aware of these changes as the design process leads you from rough iterations through the eventual solution.

While forms of the same size appear flat, making forms different sizes creates the perception of three-dimensional space: Larger forms appear closer, and smaller forms appear farther away.

Play unique properties or proportions against each other by bringing them into close proximity: angle against curve, line against mass, vertical against horizontal.

Creating repetitions of, or variations on, a particular kind of form or spatial area invites the eye to compare and re-examine its understanding of a visual idea.

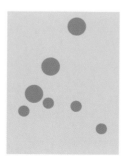

Position elements so that there is a sense of movement and, ideally, a recognizable rhythm.Organize the elements across an invisible superstructure, such as a triangle, curve, or grid.

Create clear, purposeful relationships that appear intentional: If you mean for two elements to align or to appear the same size, make sure these attributes are unquestionable.

Defining Clear Visual Hierarchy

Strong composition depends not only on the compositional states of the various elements, but also on how those states contribute to the viewer being able to navigate, or understand, the content, and in what order the content should be "read" (whether in terms of type or purely pictorial content). Defining this order, or *hierarchy*, and controlling the sequence in which viewers will perceive and assimilate each level of information is an unavoidable process in every design project, no matter how straightforward it is.

In coming to determine the most important element (whether pictorial or typographic), the designer most often relies on common sense by answering the simple question: What do I need to look at first? Beyond simply establishing this entry point into a sequence, the designer must also ensure that elements don't compete with each other. This often means making some formal attributes—such as relative sizes, densities, or spatial intervals—subtler or more nuanced, while exaggerating others so that the viewer can process the material more efficiently without sacrificing vitality and tension.

General Methods for Ordering Material

Focusing attention on one form within a composition most often results from two primary strategies: differentiating that element from all others (by means of exaggerated scale, density, or color distinction), and/or arranging surrounding elements so that the orientation of their angles, curves, or interstitial spaces directs the eye toward it. With the first strategy, viewers tend to perceive a special emphasis on a form or space that separates itself in some way from the gestalt of the composition: While all other forms share similar relationships, the most important form has unique attributes. To create a more complex hierarchy using this approach—establishing decreasing levels of importance in a sequence of elements—the unique attribute applied to the top element may be applied in diminishing degrees to each subsequent form.

Under the second general strategy, known as *continuity*, the relative proximity of surrounding forms creates an emphasis on the primary form and then directs the eye to a secondary location. Designers may use each strategy individually or in tandem.

HIERARCHICAL STRATEGIES

DIFFERENTIATION

Scale	*Weight or Density*	*Alignment*	*Direction*	*Rhythm*	*Proximity*	*Identity or Proportion*	*Orientation*

CONTINUITY

Rotational Alignment	*Axial Alignment*	*Spatial Progression: Interval*	*Spatial Progression: Scale/Depth*	*Structural Focus*	*Triangulation*	*Spiraling*	*Stepping*

Symmetry and Asymmetry

Two basic kinds of gestalt logic govern composition in every layout: symmetry and asymmetry. Symmetry is a compositional state in which the arrangement of forms responds to the central axis of the format (either the vertical or the horizontal axis); forms also may be oriented relative to their individual central axes. Symmetrical arrangements create a "mirroring" effect—spaces or contours on either side of the orga-nizational axis are the same. Asymmetry is an opposing logic: The arrangement of every form defies relationship with any central axis or among the forms themselves. The result is a collection of spatial proportions that are inherently different from each other.

Visual and Metaphorical Differences in Compositional Logic

Symmetry and asymmetry produce very different visual experiences in a viewer. The similarity of spaces or shapes in a symmetrical configuration is very direct and efficient, but can be too simple or static, causing viewers to hastily gloss over information. Asymmetrical arrangements provoke rigorous involvement—they require continual assessment of differences in space, stimulating the eye to greater movement. From the standpoint of communication, asymmetry improves the ability to differentiate, catalog, and recall content because the viewer's investigation of spatial difference becomes tied to the ordering, or cognition, of the content itself.

On another level, symmetry and asymmetry come with cultural and conceptual baggage. Prior to the early twentieth century, all design was ordered symmetrically. As a result, symmetrical, or centered, layouts tend to be perceived as traditional or historical; because design prior to the Industrial Revolution was primarily created by religious, governmental, and academic institutions, symmetrical layouts also are generally perceived as formal, careful, decorative, or institutional. Choosing the best gestalt logic for a given project depends on which association will be most appropriate for the target audience—compositional logic itself is a message to be conveyed.

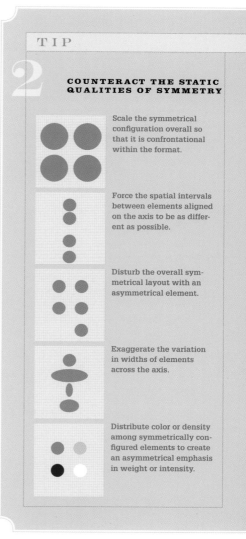

TIP

2

COUNTERACT THE STATIC QUALITIES OF SYMMETRY

Scale the symmetrical configuration overall so that it is confrontational within the format.

Force the spatial intervals between elements aligned on the axis to be as different as possible.

Disturb the overall symmetrical layout with an asymmetrical element.

Exaggerate the variation in widths of elements across the axis.

Distribute color or density among symmetrically configured elements to create an asymmetrical emphasis in weight or intensity.

COMPARING ATTRIBUTES

SYMMETRY	ASYMMETRY
Static	Dynamic
Quiet	Loud
Formal	Casual
Studied	Spontaneous
Historical	Contemporary
Conservative	Innovative
Decorative	Essential
Solid	Fragmented
Simple	Complex

Working with Imagery

Every pictorial element falls on a continuum between the literal, or representational, and the abstract. The method of making the pictorial element is referred to as its *mode*, and the degree of stylization and, therefore, interpretation, imposed by the designer is defined as *mediation*. A photograph of a figure and a stylized, geometric drawing of a figure are both representational—but if the photograph is lit dramatically and the figure's position highly contrived (in contrast to the neutral presentation of the drawing), the photograph may be considered more mediated than the drawing. Still, photographic images tend to be perceived as "real," or "believable," simply because they depict an empirical experience. Illustrative images, even if extremely naturalistic, will always be perceived as inventions and, therefore, less credible than photos. Choose the degree of abstraction, the image mode, and mediate it according to the conceptual and informational necessities of the project.

Mixing Image Treatments

As with all compositional strategies, creating contrast among visual elements is key—and this is no less true for imagery. Along with overall compositional contrast (achieved through scale, spacing, and positioning changes), combining different image modes is effective in creating tension and liveliness in a layout. It's important, however, that while the different image modes being combined contrast each other decisively, they also share some visual qualities so as to clearly relate.

All three images depict the same subject, an apple, but using different modes. In this example, the "pure" photograph is the least mediated; while the two illustrative images are inherently more mediated than the photograph, the paper collage is more mediated than the charcoal drawing.

Although the semantic content of the images is the same (seeing any of them establishes the same factual knowledge), the mode of representation has consequences for our perception of meaning that may be associated with the image. The photograph's clarity alludes to the apple's freshness and organicism; the charcoal drawing skews its allusion toward the act of creation, and may be read with a somber overlay; the collage of cut paper in primary colors suggests a childlike, or educational, metaphor.

TIP 3

Whenever Possible, Customize Photography

1 Colorize, tone, or ghost the image to reduce the sense of realism.

2 Crop subjects in an unconventional, dramatic way.

3 Combine photographs—or parts of several—in unusual configurations.

4 Introduce a texture, pattern, or abstract visual language into the photographic space.

5 Silhouette objects or figures to remove them from their expected, natural environments.

6 Present photographs in unconventional shapes, instead of rectangles.

Sharpened, stylized plant images drive the identity for a design studio, above. Grow Creative: Portland, OR: United States

Important elements in the book cover, right, are colorized in the production process. DesignLiga: Munich, Germany

*Combining different kinds of images adds interest and contrast to the overall visual language of a project.
(top) People Design: Grand Rapids, MI: USA
(bottom) Stein Øvre: Oslo: Norway*

Using Abstract Form

All pictorial form carries meaning—and that includes abstraction, or form that doesn't represent anything we actually experience in real life. However, abstract form has the potential to convey stronger, more direct, and more universally understood messages, because it is a distilled representation of something that is real, so it can transcend cultural and linguistic barriers. Abstract images are also more open to interpretation, involving the audience and helping them to make deeper, richer connections; for this reason, abstraction can easily take on the role of symbol or metaphor more fluidly than representational images. Finally, the uniqueness and simplicity of abstraction deliver a powerfully memorable experience, building recall and equity in designed messages.

The power of abstraction to communicate universally— and to evoke greater interpretation or association beyond simple depiction— is demonstrated in this comparison of two simple, elemental geometric forms.

Organic · Totality · Continuum · Biology · Water · Planet · Cell · Cycle · Endless · Unity · Fluidity

Logic · Mathematics · Artificial · Order · Intellectual · Finite · Rational · Architectural · Partitioned · Solid

TIP

4

How to Develop Abstract Form That Communicates

1 Distill the essential idea of a message as an emotion: What is the feeling to be communicated, in one word? What kinds of forms feel that way?

2 Consider the idea as an action word: What should the form appear to be doing? What kinds of forms will appear to perform that action?

3 Translate the visual structure of an elemental force or a kind of place or object into its basic geometry: What kinds of shapes—dots, lines, curves, and so on— make up that thing's physical structure? How many marks or shapes are needed to recognize what it is?

Creating Visually Dynamic Color Relationships

Understanding how to use color effectively depends first on understanding its visual attributes—how colors are identified, how they can be varied, and the optical effects they have on each other in juxtaposition. Every color has a core identity, or hue; a color is first generally recognized as blue or green or orange. Any hue, however, may be intense or dull (degrees of saturation); it may also be dark or light (degrees of value); and it may be perceived as cool or warm (degrees of temperature).

Palettes Based on Chromatic Interaction
The first direction a designer may pursue in developing a color palette for a project is that of optical interaction. Creating a rich palette depends on combining colors that can be clearly distinguished from each other, but that also share some unifying optical relationships. Because of the strong opposition of complements, palettes based on this relationship tend to be the most optically dynamic—that is, cells in the eye are stimulated more aggressively, and the brain is provoked into greater activity as a result. Analogous colors, by their very similarity, create more complex, but less varied, palettes.

Using such a basic relationship as a starting point guarantees a viewer's clear perception of a color idea; the designer may opt to maintain that simplicity, using the hues of that relationship in purer form, or introduce complexity—adjusting the value or intensity differences between the base colors, or adding colors that support and expand the relationship between the base colors.

Color identity is often mapped on a color wheel, a diagrammatic model developed by British artist and scientist Albert Munsell. The relative positions of the hues around the wheel help describe their relationships to each other.

Hues that are adjacent are made of similar wavelengths, and are referred to as being **analogous.**

Hues that lie opposite each other are made up of wavelengths that stimulate opposing cells in the eye and optically negate each other; these pairs are called **complements.**

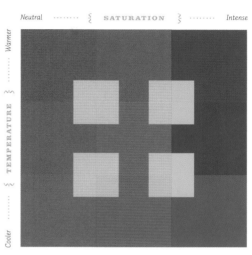

Neutral ⋯⋯ § **SATURATION** § ⋯⋯ Intense

TEMPERATURE — Warmer ⋯ Cooler

This matrix helps visualize the complexity resulting from variations in saturation, temperature, and value that are possible for a single hue—in this case, violet. Swatches increase in saturation left to right while progressing from warm at the top to cool at the bottom—all at the same relatively dark value. Smaller, light-value swatches of each variant are positioned in the corners for comparison across their respective boundaries.

Hues positioned at 120° to each other (in a triangular relationship) are called **triads,** or **split complements.**

Color identity is relative—the perception of hue, saturation, value, and temperature of a color changes depending on the colors around it and how much of each is present. This effect, called **simultaneous contrast,** is demonstrated by the change in apparent color of the central swatch as it appears in different contexts.

The process of defining a palette can begin very simply: choosing two complementary colors, for example, because their interaction is so strong.

Adjusting the relative values of the complements creates greater contrast without disturbing the clarity of the relationship.

Seeking a richer experience, the designer may shift the temperature of the complements, maintaining the relationship but skewing it slightly.

Altering the intensities of one or both introduces yet greater complexity.

The addition of a neutral version of one of the complements expands the palette; a second version of the neutral, lighter

in value, introduces greater variation.

To this already complex mix, the designer lastly adds the analog of one of the base complements, adjusting its

value and intensity to correspond more closely to one of the neutrals.

Using Color to Enhance Messaging

Selecting Color for Meaningful Effect

Color, of course, can also mean something. Very often, that meaning is tied to associations we make between colors and objects or environments—water is blue, vegetation is green, and so on. But colors also evoke intangible feelings, whether by association or by the biological effects resulting from their perception. Red, for example, connotes hunger and violence (because of the color of blood), but provokes arousal and even anger, because it takes more energy to process red lightwaves—resulting in increased metabolic activity. Further, colors carry cultural or social meanings, related to their use in religious ceremonies or iconography, or in heraldry, in flags, or historically in clothing or art. For Westerners, violet and gold signify nobility; among Hindus, white signifies death. Select colors wisely with regard to specific cultural and psychological associations to ensure the messages they carry are appropriate.

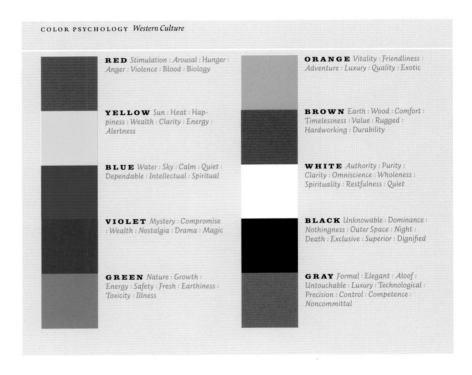

COLOR PSYCHOLOGY *Western Culture*

RED *Stimulation : Arousal : Hunger : Anger : Violence : Blood : Biology*

YELLOW *Sun : Heat : Happiness : Wealth : Clarity : Energy : Alertness*

BLUE *Water : Sky : Calm : Quiet : Dependable : Intellectual : Spiritual*

VIOLET *Mystery : Compromise : Wealth : Nostalgia : Drama : Magic*

GREEN *Nature : Growth : Energy : Safety : Fresh : Earthiness : Toxicity : Illness*

ORANGE *Vitality : Friendliness : Adventure : Luxury : Quality : Exotic*

BROWN *Earth : Wood : Comfort : Timelessness : Value : Rugged : Hardworking : Durability*

WHITE *Authority : Purity : Clarity : Omniscience : Wholeness : Spirituality : Restfulness : Quiet*

BLACK *Unknowable : Dominance : Nothingness : Outer Space : Night : Death : Exclusive : Superior : Dignified*

GRAY *Formal : Elegant : Aloof : Untouchable : Luxury : Technological : Precision : Control : Competence : Noncommittal*

Be careful when assigning unusual coloration to images of people or food. While the hue shift toward the warm end of the spectrum (left) may convey fun or vitality, a shift toward yellow or green (right) conveys a sense of illness or toxicity.

Exploiting Color to Enhance Hierarchy

Our optical system (the eyes and brain) allows us to perceive colors as occupying different spatial depths. Red appears stationary at a middle distance; yellow appears to advance toward us; blue appears to recede. In general, cool colors appear to recede, while warm colors advance.

Consider the spatial property of color carefully with regard to hierarchy, whether visual or typographic. Clearly, form elements colored in red, orange, and yellow are likely to capture attention easily because they will appear to advance toward the viewer; in a field of neutrals, a more saturated color will draw attention. But the degree of value contrast between elements, or between elements and background—tends to trump temperature or saturation with respect to establishing hierarchy. A very light element will appear to advance forward of any element whose value is relatively dark when both are situated on an even darker background—no matter how cool or warm, dull or saturated, any of the hues involved may be, and no matter how small the light element is. Conversely, a very dark element situated within a light field will advance forward of any other form that is also of light value.

A

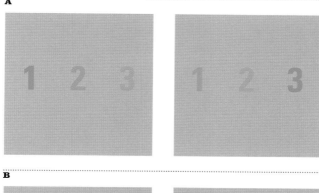

Note how simple it is to alter the sequence in which the numbers are read by changing the temperature relationships [A], saturation relationships [B], or value relationships [C] among them, relative to the background.

B

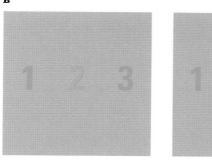

C

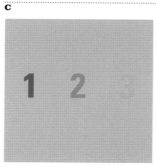

Limiting (and Maximizing) the Palette

Designers very often make the mistake of using too many colors, especially in process-color projects—simply because they can. While full-color imagery is always dynamic and engaging, too many hues being present dilutes the color experience. Even when all colors are possible, limiting the palette creates a more focused, and therefore, more memorable color experience. This is especially important to consider in branded communications, where the color story of the client—first established by the color(s) of its logo—must always reinforce its identity, building recognition and recall of the brand. Working with only two or three colors can be challenging, but also extremely rewarding.

A

B

C

D

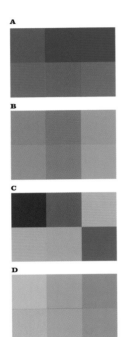

If the lightness and darkness, dullness and brilliance, coolness and warmth of every color all are allowed to change, the specificity of the color idea is radically diminished—the viewer can't tell what the color idea may be. But if the hues are relatively analogous in temperature and are all of the same value—with shifts only in saturation—the constraint in variables allows the viewer to more clearly understand the color idea by focusing their attention on the variable that does change. Palette A: Analogous hue, value, and saturation / Palette B: Analogous temperature, value, and saturation / Palette C: Analogous hue, temperature, and saturation / Palette D: Analogous temperature and value only.

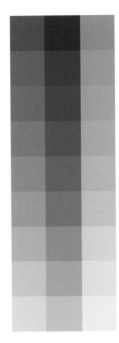

In a spot-color job, the trick is to build in as much flexibility for combining the two or three ink colors as possible. Printing a job with two complements as counterparts, for example, is an intuitive first possibility. The complements need not be exact, that is, as with blue and orange; skewing the relationship can create more interesting combinations that retain the complements' inherent contrast: a blue-violet and orange, for example. Because most printing inks are translucent, a designer has the option of surprinting just two inks, as solids or tints, on top of each other to create a vast array of interrelated tones.

Quick, Easy Coding Strategies

Color is very effective for coding—using different colors to identify parts of a system, sections in publications, or counterparts in a line of products. When using color this way, the designer's first concern must be what the needs of the audience might be in terms of understanding how the coding relates the parts to each other. If the project is a packaging system, for instance, are all the products being packaged remarkably different or does each represent a grade or level? Is there one family of products, or are there several related lines, each with its own subproducts? The answers to questions such as these will help determine the complexity that the color coding must address and, therefore, how much variation in hue (or combinations of hues) will be useful to the audience. Although each component within a coded system must be clearly distinguishable, the colors used to distinguish them must bear some relation to support an understanding that the components are a family. Carefully controlling the aspects of hue, value, saturation, and relationships created with accent or secondary colors becomes critical.

To distinguish components by grade or level, select a single hue and, for each grade, change the saturation or value, or both.

For components that are more closely related and equivalent to each other in their quality or grade, choose a single base hue and create analogous counterparts for the components by shifting the temperature. As an alternative, choose a single unifying hue and then combine it with secondary hues that communicate each component's difference, but still under some limitation (all still analogous, or of the same value).

To code a system of three or more components that are remarkably different from each other, choose very different hues—but create a sense of family by constraining their values and intensities.

In a system of multiple families, try to first establish a limited palette to distinguish each family—perhaps hues that are analogous—clearly projecting the fundamental relationship between the families as parts of a greater whole. One might also choose a highly differentiated hue for each family, such as those in a triad, or sets of complements, and then unify the families with a single hue. The components within each family could be coded as grades (using the value or intensity of the family color) or themselves differentiated through subtle analogous relationships.

Choosing and Combining Typefaces

Many designers are baffled by the prospect of selecting a typeface for a project—where to begin? A text's intended use is the best starting point for narrowing down the many options: Is it for display or extended reading? For display, the imagelike quality of the face, and its personality, are of utmost concern. If it's continuous reading, eschew dramatically styled faces in favor of simplicity. Next, consider the subject or ideas to be communicated in the project. If the text is formal, for example, perhaps a serif is appropriate; but if the subject is technology, a sharply cut sans serif may be better. The feeling the typeface's texture generates—tight, dark, open, light, romantic, organic, fresh, fluid, chunky, and so on—should reflect both the subject itself and the tone of the language used. Designers must be familiar with the stylistic classes of type and be able to analyze and compare the internal attributes of various styles.

TIME-TESTED TYPEFACE FLAVORS *A Go-To List to Get You Started*

AB
Archaic Capitals *Roman* Titles, headlines, subheads, callouts. *Formal, dramatic, authoritarian, dramatic, elegant, classical, cultured*

AaB
Blackletter *Germanic* Titles, initials, very short callouts. *Medieval, sinister, formal, aggressive, Old-World, superstitious, dangerous, magical, exotic, punk*

Aab
Gothic Oldstyle Serif *German, Dutch* Titles, headlines, decks, short to mid-length texts, subheads, callouts, captions. *Austere, authoritarian, formal, quirky, elegant*

AaB
Humanist (Rounded) Oldstyle *French, Italian* Titles, headlines, decks, extensive texts, subheads, callouts, captions. *Formal, soft, classical, academic, elegant, poetic, organic, friendly, fluid*

AaB
Transitional Serif *English* Titles, headlines, decks, extensive texts, subheads, callouts, captions. *Formal, academic, refined, sharp, delicate, elegant, poetic, cultured, prestigious, well-bred*

AaB
Neoclassical (Modern) Serif *French, Italian* Titles, headlines, decks, shorter texts, subheads, callouts, captions. *Precise, vibrant, sharp, elegant, mechanical, strong, progressive, scientific, corporate*

AaB
Slab Serif *American* Titles, headlines, subheads, callouts, initials. *Strong, heavy, promotional, industrial, mechanical, chunky, informal, aggressive, loud, dark*

AaB
Art Nouveau Types *French, Austrian, English* Titles, subheads, short callouts, initials. *Fanciful, elegant, organic, informal, fluid, artistic, exotic, handcrafted*

AaB
Grotesk Sans Serif *English, German, Belgian, Dutch* Titles, headlines, decks, short to mid-length texts, subheads, callouts, captions. *Strong, authoritarian, stiff, industrial, scientific, mechanical, journalistic*

AaB
Geometric Sans Serif *German, English* Titles, headlines, decks, extensive texts, subheads, callouts, captions. *Sharp, vibrant, rhythmic, industrial, mechanical, avant-garde, scientific, mathematical, informal, aggressive, elegant, strong*

AaB
Transitional Sans Serif *Swiss* Titles, headlines, decks, extensive texts, subheads, callouts, captions. *Neutral, international, minimal, cold, authoritarian, accessible, precise, corporate, progressive, calculated, scientific, aloof, direct, clean*

AaB
Humanistic Sans Serif *Dutch, German, Swiss* Titles, headlines, decks, extensive texts, subheads, callouts, captions. *International, accessible, friendly, corporate, progressive, inclusive, honest*

AaB
Serif/Sans Hybrids *German* Titles, headlines, decks, extensive texts, subheads, callouts, captions. *Multicultural, inclusive, corporate, respect for history, inventive, competent, academic, sharp, elegant*

AaB
Florid Scripts *Dutch, French* Titles, headlines, decks, callouts. *Formal, romantic, elegant, feminine, exotic, magical, fluid, organic, poetic, fanciful, idiosyncratic*

AaB
Italic/Script Hybrids *English, French, Italian, German* Titles, headlines, decks, subheads, callouts. *Formal, romantic, elegant, stately, rhythmic, steady, academic*

UNIVERS TYPE FAMILY *Selected Variants*

Typeface Combinations

More daunting still is contemplating how to pair type styles—or, worse yet, combine three or four. Conventional wisdom suggests first that designers limit themselves to two type families and, if possible, to only two specific weights or styles in each. The point of this constraint focuses solely on making it easier for a reader to recognize and catalog different treatments among editorial components such as heads, decks, subheads, captions, and so on; the more styles applied, the easier it is to lose one's way. From an aesthetic standpoint, a bit of restraint makes the visual language that much clearer. But by all means, if fifteen faces are needed, use them—but choose wisely. The essential issue in combining faces is that of visual texture relative to function (function, here, also including supporting metaphor or enriching visual language overall). Each of the typefaces added to the mix must be different enough to bring some noticeable change to the page, and it must fulfill some function. There are myriad possibilities with which to approach combinations.

The Single Family Theory
Choosing a type family with enough variants in weight, width, and posture ensures great flexibility in typographic texture while respecting a certain level of restraint.

For Modernists, this option is the best expression of the "do less with more" tenet of their cooking philosophy. The classic face that demonstrates this technique most admirably is Univers. Each

variant offers a different cadence, rhythm, value, and mass that not only offers rich visual experience, but also will address the most complex typesetting demands.

The classic serif/sans serif combination is often the first combination strategy that designers will turn to when looking for something a little more flavorful. Conventionally, a serif makes up the text and a sans serif is used for subheads, callouts, or large titling elements; but feel free to reverse this relationship.

Select counterparts with enough stylistic contrast, but be aware of their similarities—overall width; tightness or shape of curves; degree of contrast among strokes; heights of joints; shapes of similar elements, such as the leg on the uppercase R; angle at which the terminals are cut; angle of axis in the curved forms; and so on.

Mixing within a single style is usually not a good idea, unless the textural difference is unmistakable. Combining two transitional serifs in text, for instance—or even a Venetian oldstyle and a transitional—is indecisive. Combining the small caps of the Venetian with the transitional text—that's another story altogether.

On a functional level, sometimes the bold weight of a serif, relative to its Roman counterpart, isn't quite bold enough to be easily distinguished, as in this example. It's perfectly acceptable to substitute an alternative bold face, as long as the substitute is credibly similar in detail and structure.

Riffing off a single idea can create interesting combinations. For instance, finding a variety of slab-serif faces that all vary in weight, contrast, and width could be very dynamic, yet clearly unified by overall style.

Combinations established for the purpose of exaggerating abstract visual form can be very dynamic. In this combination, linearity and dotlike mass play off each other for exaggerated contrast.

Creating Visual Dialogue between Type and Imagery

Getting type to interact with imagery poses a serious problem that must always be overcome, no matter how simple the layout. The first step in doing so is to recognize this basic fact: Just like images, type is made up of lights and darks, linear motion and volume, contours, open and closed space, mass, and texture. Consider type not only the equal of image with respect to layout—but an element that completes the image. If type can be removed from a layout and the remaining image composition still appears strong, type and image aren't talking to each other. There are as many strategies for getting type and image to meld with each other as there are ways of mixing vegetables and herbs in soup; the trick is always to establish not only some balance and similarity among the elements, but also a certain degree of contrast.

A

B

C

D

E

F

G

Type can respond to scale, directional movement, and tonal variation. Among these studies type relates to the image by virtue of: [A] similarity in general shape and structure; [B] repetition of linear movement; [C] alternation of weight; [D] restating of proportional division; [E] mimicry of depth and perspective; [F] angle alignments; [G] response to light and dark value arrangement.

Translate Macro-Level Image and Type Treatments into Text Detailing

STIM *Visual Communication*
Brooklyn, NY: USA

Don't leave small-sized running text, captions, and editorial elements such as folios and runners off the plate when you serve up the dramatic headline/picture collage. Instead, look for ways to bring the ideas that occur in the big picture down into how you style the little stuff. The splicing and layered transparency of this poster's image gives rise to unusual spatial breaks and details within smaller text elements.

Type appears to change spatial relationships when placed on, in, or next to an image—it either becomes part of the image or acts as a "bridge" between image and external space.

Crafting Reader-Friendly (and Beautiful!) Text

Making a comfortable, easily read text that is pleasant to look at is much like developing reliable pastry dough. The amount of water, flour, egg, and milk and the working temperature all need to work together or the dough will be too tough, too flaky, and so on. Similarly, a good text setting is one in which a constellation of variables achieves a harmonic balance.

Text that is legible in size, encourages sequential reading, shows decisive (and consistent) rags and spacing, clearly separates paragraphs, and exhibits a minimum of hyphens, widows, and orphans—this often becomes the foundation of a strong layout.

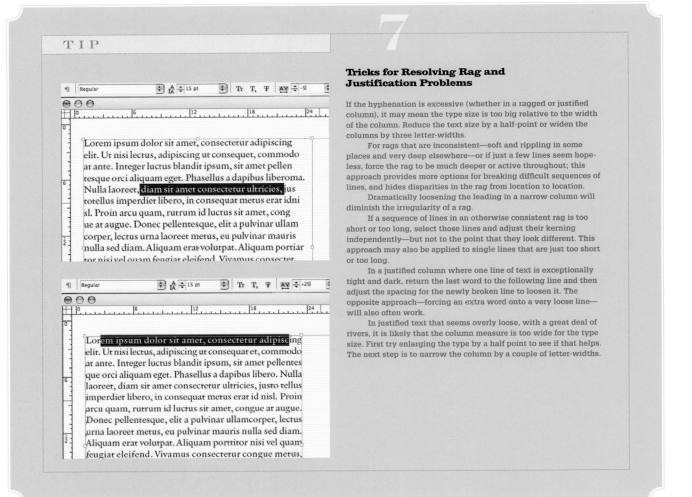

T I P 7

Tricks for Resolving Rag and Justification Problems

If the hyphenation is excessive (whether in a ragged or justified column), it may mean the type size is too big relative to the width of the column. Reduce the text size by a half-point or widen the columns by three letter-widths.

For rags that are inconsistent—soft and rippling in some places and very deep elsewhere—or if just a few lines seem hopeless, force the rag to be much deeper or active throughout; this approach provides more options for breaking difficult sequences of lines, and hides disparities in the rag from location to location.

Dramatically loosening the leading in a narrow column will diminish the irregularity of a rag.

If a sequence of lines in an otherwise consistent rag is too short or too long, select those lines and adjust their kerning independently—but not to the point that they look different. This approach may also be applied to single lines that are just too short or too long.

In a justified column where one line of text is exceptionally tight and dark, return the last word to the following line and then adjust the spacing for the newly broken line to loosen it. The opposite approach—forcing an extra word onto a very loose line—will also often work.

In justified text that seems overly loose, with a great deal of rivers, it is likely that the column measure is too wide for the type size. First try enlarging the type by a half point to see if that helps. The next step is to narrow the column by a couple of letter-widths.

1

Lorem ipsum dolor sit amet consectitur adipscing elit summa duis autem velure quod meri

Lorem ipsum dolor sit amet consectitur adipscing elit summa duis autem velure quod meri

Most often, the first step is to pick a typeface and establish a comfortable size. Because most people will read a newspaper without complaint, this can be a good barometer for choosing type size. If the type looks like 9-point Times (top) or 10-point Garamond Oldstyle (bottom) regardless of the actual face or size, chances are most readers will find it legible.

2

Lorem ipsum dolor sit amet consectitur adipscing elitas summa duis autem velure quod meri uismod. Indeo summa erat, nunc et semper, fiat equame gloriosa interfectus est

Lorem ipsum dolor sit amet consectitur adipscing elitas summa duis autem velure quod meri uismod. Indeo sum erat, nunc et semper, fiat equame gloriosa interfectus est

Strive to get fifty-five to seventy-five characters on a single line before a return. Determining text width on this average number of characters (in English) results in the most consistent overall appearance—meaning the rag will be very consistent and there will be very few hyphens. If setting justified, the result is much more consistent word spacing without rivers, and limited hyphenation.

Counting characters is fine, but grabbing the right-hand anchor point in a text box and slowly pulling it left and right to see how the text within the box reflows is a quick, on-the-fly method. At certain widths, the rag (or spacing) will suddenly snap into a state of near perfection—this state is an optimal width for that text.

3

ipsum: velut   ipsum; velut

ipsum : velut   **ipsum ; velut**

velure! delicit   velure? delicit

velure! delicit   **velure? delicit**

Colons and semicolons need additional space preceding them and less space following them. Exclamation points and question marks often benefit from being separated from their sentences by an extra bit of space. A full word space is too much, as is half a word space; but +20 to +40 tracking is usually sufficient.

4

duis autem vegure nunc et semper interfectus

The leading (measured from baseline to baseline) should be about 120 percent of the point size. This usually means that for 10-point text, the leading should be 12; for 12-point text, the leading should be 14; and so on. A rule of thumb: The leading can be tighter or looser, but it should always appear bigger than the space between words. Leading needs to be loosened if the ascenders and descenders in the chosen typeface are exceptionally long; if the x-height is large; if the text width is greater than seventy-five characters; or if the text width is narrower than fifty characters.

5

Lorem ipsum dolor sit amet consectit adipscer elit summa duis autem velure quod meri uismor ind eosum erat, nunc et semper, quam gloriosa invectus est. Quae coelis interfectus in deo fiat eternam, duis autem velure et consequat carborundu est.

A paragraph rag should be made by hand. Aim for a consistent short/long/short rhythm from the top of the column to the bottom. The most comfortable depth for rags is between one-fifth and one-seventh the width of the text. Ideally, there are no hyphens, but if they are necessary, one every ten to fifteen lines is ideal (and never two in a row).

6

Don't allow the last line of a paragraph to begin the top of a column. This "orphan" is especially distracting if there is a space separating the paragraph that follows, and is really irritating if it occurs at the very beginning of the left-hand page. Run the text back so that the new page starts a paragraph, or space out the preceding text so that the paragraph continues with at least three lines after the page break.

7

-er   -al
-ed   -il
-ly   -es
-ing   -or

Avoid breaking words across lines (hyphenating) so that short or incomplete stubs, such as those shown above, begin the line following. Make sure there are at least four letters in the word ending the line before the break.

8

Lorem ipsum dolor sit amet con sectitur adipscing elit summa duis autem.

Lorem ipsum dolor sit amet con sectitur adipscing elit summa duis autem velure fiat.

Never allow a single word, or **widow***, to end a paragraph. If* **widows** *constantly appear in the rough setting of a body of text, the column width should be adjusted. Ideally, the last line of a paragraph should be more than half the paragraph's width, but three words (no matter their length) are acceptable.*

9

When possible, avoid hard returns between paragraphs that are aligning (or nearly aligning) between adjacent columns. As the horizontal negative channels created by the returns approach each other, not only do they become distracting but also they tend to redirect the eye across the columns and break reading sequence.

10

In justified setting, the relative lightness and darkness of the lines, as well as spacing between words, should remain consistent. When lines are extremely dark (having too many characters) or light (having too few), or if there is a significant occurrence of rivers (wide gaps between words), adjust the tracking, the line breaks, and the column width as needed.

Effectively Using a Column Grid

Most any three-, four-, six-, or eight-column grids will usually work well; it's the way in which columns of text interact with negative space—and with each other—that truly determines how a grid is articulated. The spaces above and below columns play an active part in giving the columns a rhythm as they relate to each other across pages and spreads. Every approach has a dramatic impact on the overall rhythm of the pages within a publication, ranging from austere and geometric to wildly organic in feeling—all the while ordered by the underlying grid. Changing the column logic from section to section provides yet another method of differ-entiating informational areas.

Column Logic and Baseline Alignment

When columns begin to separate vertically, shifting up and down past one another—or dropping to different depths while adhering to a single hangline above—consider the relationship between lines of text across the gutter separating the columns. In a grouping of columns set justified, with no line breaks (or a hard return of the same leading) between paragraphs, the baselines between columns will align. Any other situation, and the baselines between columns will not align.

In hanging columns, text will align between columns until a paragraph change. Because the depth of the hanging columns changes, this might feel appropriate. A problem will occur in a page spread set with columns justifying top and bottom, however, if the paragraph space introduces an uneven line: The lines of text at the foot margin will be noticeably off.

UNDERSTANDING THE OPTIONS

A Columns of text may justify to the head and foot margins, broken by the introduction of images into the text field and by the insertion of callouts. This approach creates a very dense page and emphasizes the image proportions over the shaping of the text, which becomes a neutral field.

B Text columns may justify to specific flowlines or module depths, creating a very rigidly geometric shift up and down across the page.

C Columns may hang or grow from margin or flowline, ragging in depth at the opposite end. This option provides a strong, unifying constant that is counterbalanced by the organic change in depth.

D Columns of the same depth can stagger up and down, either responding to flowlines and rows, or at random. The consistency of the column depths plays counterpoint to the irregularity of the vertical motion across the spread.

E The most organic approach is one in which the columns change depth as well as stagger up and down. The effect is extremely rhythmic, with text pushing and pulling fluidly against the consistency of the head and foot margins.

Positioning Images Dynamically

Given the regularity of proportions inherent in using a grid, the potential for image placement to feel a bit static or regular can be a problem designers need to overcome to produce dynamic layouts. It's very important to remember that a grid allows the designer to size and position an image any way he or she wants, as long as the image corresponds to the columns (and rows, if the grid is modular). Showing as much variation in arrangement as possible helps the reader see the grid in different ways, reinforcing its presence, while keeping him or her from getting bored. One way to ensure dynamic image placement on a grid—on a single page, across a spread, or from spread to spread—is to establish a formula for size, proportion, and position calculated to vary the composition as methodically as possible. This method, called *bounce*, usually results in dynamic layout changes from spread to spread.

Relating Full-Bleed Images to the Structure

Large images that bleed the margins offer strong counterpoint to small images and text-only pages; but even though the image fills the entire page, it doesn't mean it can ignore the grid underneath. To the contrary, such images must be scaled and positioned within the frame of the page so that some geometric element within aligns with the column or row and helps articulate it.

T I P

How to Size and Position Silhouetted Images on a Column Grid

8

Regardless of where the text may fall around the image, position it so that major vertical or horizontal stresses align with column edges; alternatively, size the image so that the proportions of internal elements correspond to the proportions of columns or rows.

Allow the silhouetted image to move freely—even sliding it "behind" an area of solid text. Or wrap the text around the image. If the image is positioned between columns, make sure one part of it extends past the enclosing portions of the text; this will prevent it from appearing "boxed in."

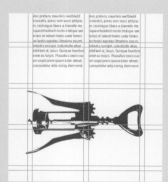

When aligning a silhouetted image to a text column, enlarge the image so that its contours expand beyond the guides that establish the column, especially if it's a circular or organic form; otherwise, the image will appear too small to visually correspond to the width of the column.

Step-by-Step

Creating Rhythmic Image Arrangements, or "Bounce," on a Grid Structure

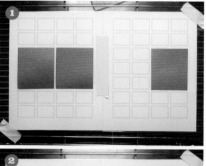

Begin with three images of the same size. Working with odd numbers of elements tends to throw off regularity off a bit. Place the images in the layout, aligned by their heights and distributed across the spread according to the columns.

Move the first image up and the second image down, creating triangular movement—the most basic kind of bounce. The top and bottom edges of the image boxes may align or not.

Change the proportions of two images: Substitute a narrow vertical for one, and a relatively deep horizontal for the other. Adjusting the images' relative sizes and proximity increases their three-dimensional play.

Once a basic bounce layout is set for a spread, use the same image elements on the next spread—but swap their positions high/low and left/right. The viewer will recognize the proportions and sizes, and appreciate the new experience. Another simple change is to group all the images in one area, perhaps low on the first spread... and on the subsequent spread, move them all high.

Gr

Mie

BEATUS LUXAT
Duis autemer
semperi nunc

Gr

Mie

Beatus luxat
Duis autemer
semperi nunc

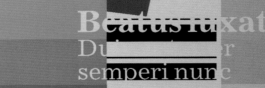

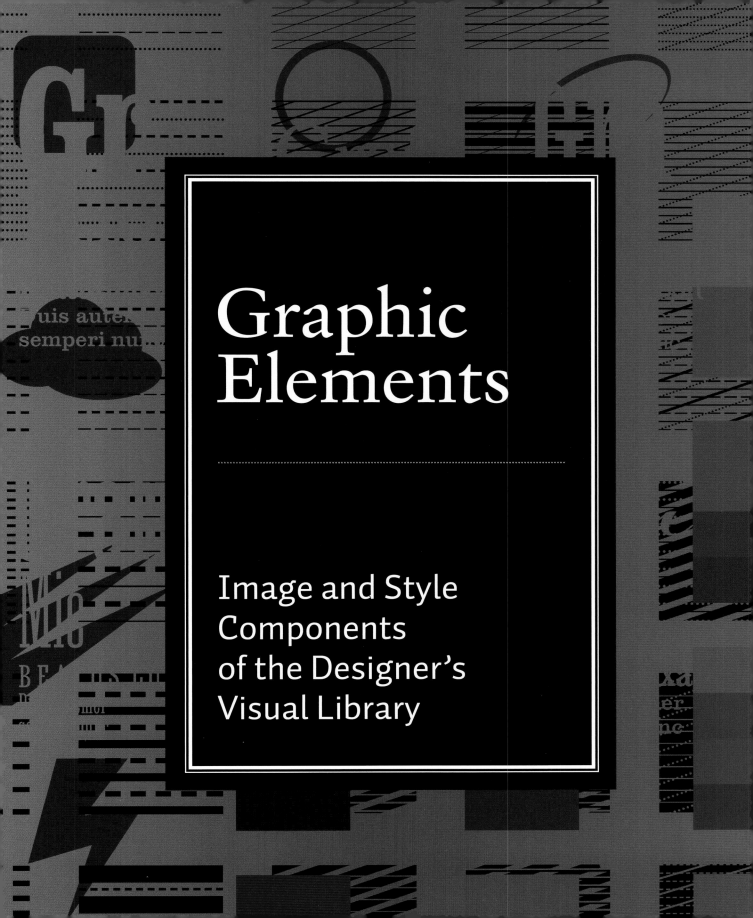

Graphic Elements

Image and Style Components of the Designer's Visual Library

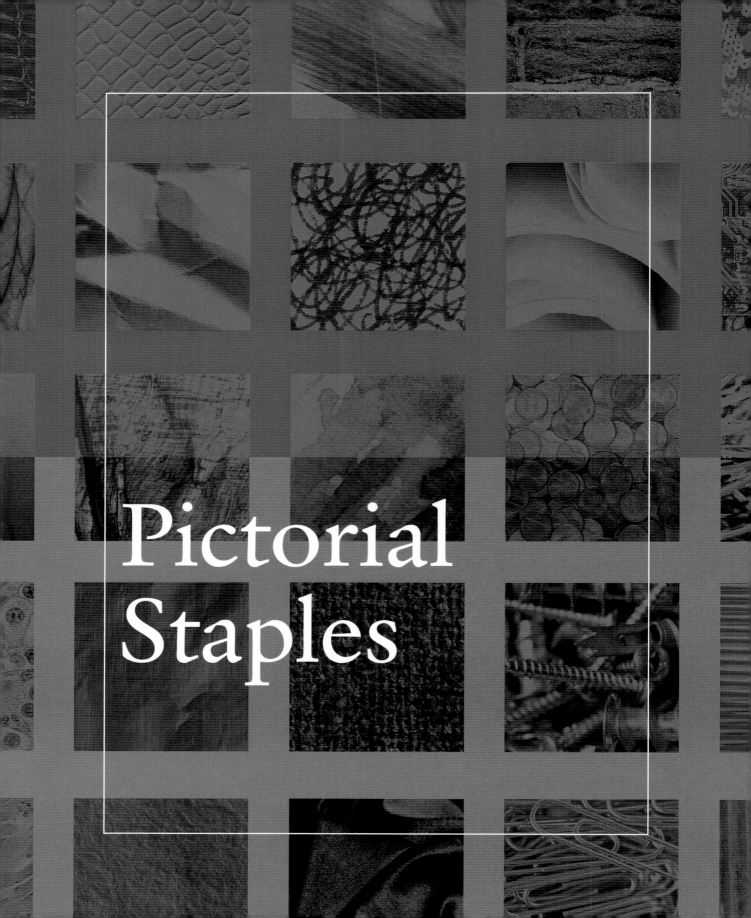

Pictorial Staples

IMAGERY IS, PERHAPS, the heart of visual communication. Although text usually supports designed messages, symbols, icons, photographs, and illustrations speak to audiences with the greatest impact. Photography offers depth and credibility that commands an audience's attention on first glance, while illustration customizes communication and adds a human element. For quick hits of information, or where a harder-edged, contemporary feel is needed, try icons and abstract graphic languages.

Texture and pattern add detail and depth to the simplest of layouts. Many of the individual components in this section may be easily altered (e.g., enlarging the scale of a pattern to create larger graphic elements, or housing an icon within a shape) or combined for greater visual variety. The designer who is well versed in the distinct qualities of the pictorial resources at his or her fingertips can experiment with their use to create dynamic and inventive visual communications.

FUNDAMENTAL FORMS *Basic Shapes and Behaviors* **01**

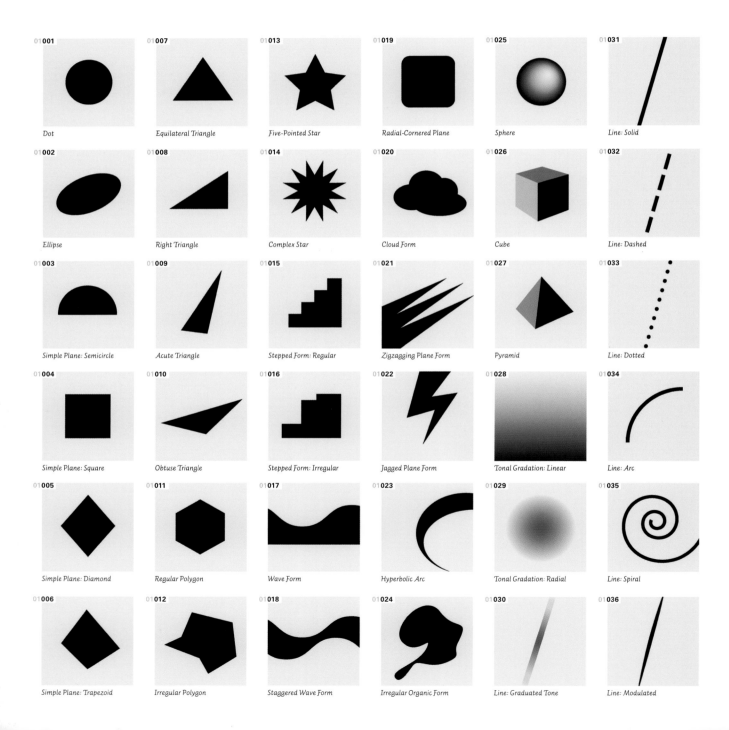

01001 Dot	**01007** Equilateral Triangle	**01013** Five-Pointed Star	**01019** Radial-Cornered Plane	**01025** Sphere	**01031** Line: Solid
01002 Ellipse	**01008** Right Triangle	**01014** Complex Star	**01020** Cloud Form	**01026** Cube	**01032** Line: Dashed
01003 Simple Plane: Semicircle	**01009** Acute Triangle	**01015** Stepped Form: Regular	**01021** Zigzagging Plane Form	**01027** Pyramid	**01033** Line: Dotted
01004 Simple Plane: Square	**01010** Obtuse Triangle	**01016** Stepped Form: Irregular	**01022** Jagged Plane Form	**01028** Tonal Gradation: Linear	**01034** Line: Arc
01005 Simple Plane: Diamond	**01011** Regular Polygon	**01017** Wave Form	**01023** Hyperbolic Arc	**01029** Tonal Gradation: Radial	**01035** Line: Spiral
01006 Simple Plane: Trapezoid	**01012** Irregular Polygon	**01018** Staggered Wave Form	**01024** Irregular Organic Form	**01030** Line: Graduated Tone	**01036** Line: Modulated

The simplest visual elements—circular, planar, linear, solid, and graded—that make up the basis of all other compositional forms are outlined here. Their seeming simplicity belies their tremendous graphic power, whether used alone or in combination, as building blocks for patterns, or as backdrops for type and image. Identifying and understanding the most basic forms is the design chef's first step toward mastering all others.

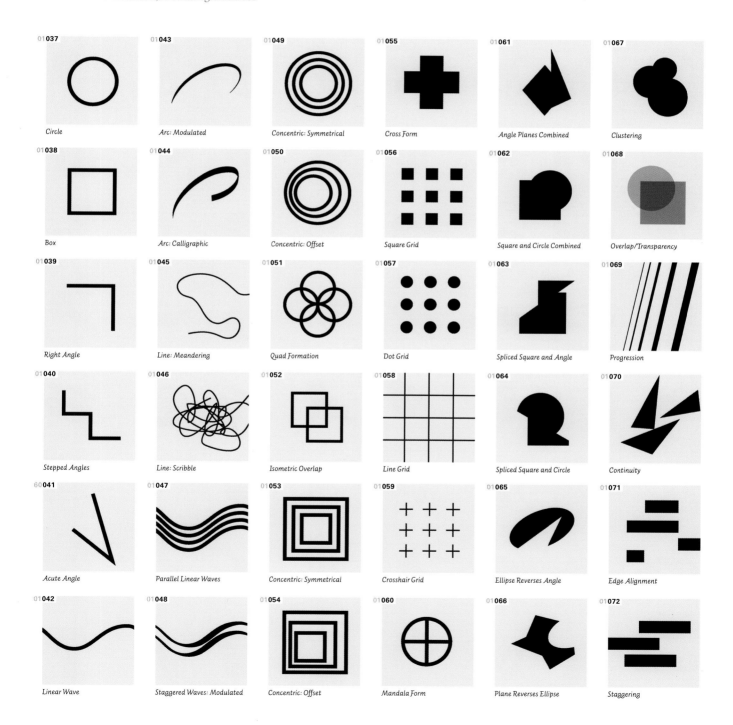

01037 Circle

01043 Arc: Modulated

01049 Concentric: Symmetrical

01055 Cross Form

01061 Angle Planes Combined

01067 Clustering

01038 Box

01044 Arc: Calligraphic

01050 Concentric: Offset

01056 Square Grid

01062 Square and Circle Combined

01068 Overlap/Transparency

01039 Right Angle

01045 Line: Meandering

01051 Quad Formation

01057 Dot Grid

01063 Spliced Square and Angle

01069 Progression

01040 Stepped Angles

01046 Line: Scribble

01052 Isometric Overlap

01058 Line Grid

01064 Spliced Square and Circle

01070 Continuity

01041 Acute Angle

01047 Parallel Linear Waves

01053 Concentric: Symmetrical

01059 Crosshair Grid

01065 Ellipse Reverses Angle

01071 Edge Alignment

01042 Linear Wave

01048 Staggered Waves: Modulated

01054 Concentric: Offset

01060 Mandala Form

01066 Plane Reverses Ellipse

01072 Staggering

ICONIC IMAGES *Naturalistic*

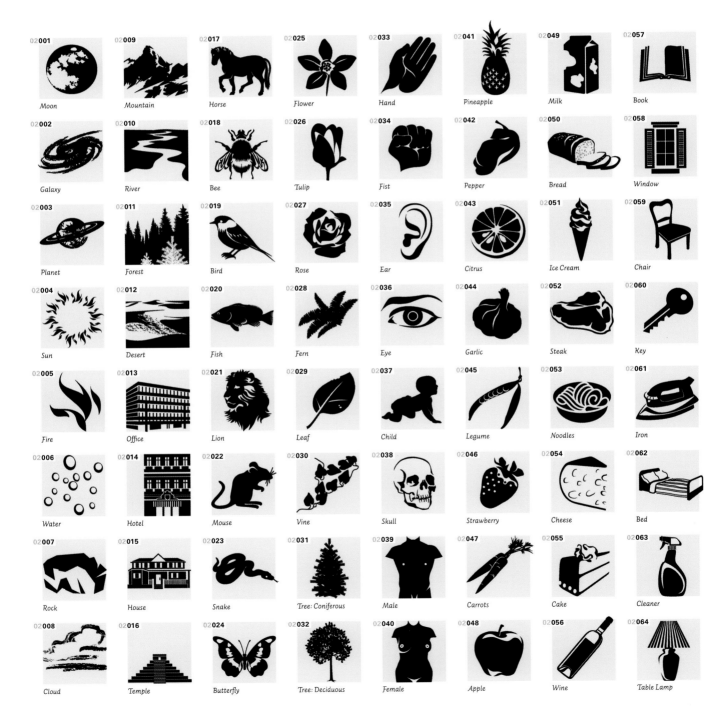

02001 Moon	**02009** Mountain	**02017** Horse	**02025** Flower	**02033** Hand	**02041** Pineapple	**02049** Milk	**02057** Book
02002 Galaxy	**02010** River	**02018** Bee	**02026** Tulip	**02034** Fist	**02042** Pepper	**02050** Bread	**02058** Window
02003 Planet	**02011** Forest	**02019** Bird	**02027** Rose	**02035** Ear	**02043** Citrus	**02051** Ice Cream	**02059** Chair
02004 Sun	**02012** Desert	**02020** Fish	**02028** Fern	**02036** Eye	**02044** Garlic	**02052** Steak	**02060** Key
02005 Fire	**02013** Office	**02021** Lion	**02029** Leaf	**02037** Child	**02045** Legume	**02053** Noodles	**02061** Iron
02006 Water	**02014** Hotel	**02022** Mouse	**02030** Vine	**02038** Skull	**02046** Strawberry	**02054** Cheese	**02062** Bed
02007 Rock	**02015** House	**02023** Snake	**02031** Tree: Coniferous	**02039** Male	**02047** Carrots	**02055** Cake	**02063** Cleaner
02008 Cloud	**02016** Temple	**02024** Butterfly	**02032** Tree: Deciduous	**02040** Female	**02048** Apple	**02056** Wine	**02064** Table Lamp

Simple and clean, icons offer immediate recognizability and concrete messages in a distilled, illustrative form. Use them alone or housed in graphic shapes, as small notational elements, or as large-scale primary illustrations.

The simplicity of their form allows them to accept texture and participate actively in a collage with other imagery.

02065 Blender	02073 Comb	02081 Wrench	02089 Clock	02097 Computer	02105 Microscope	02113 Pill	02121 Bicycle
02066 Kettle	02074 Umbrella	02082 Hammer	02090 Compass: Directional	02098 Telephone	02106 Cell	02114 Syringe	02122 Auto
02067 Whisk	02075 Needle+Thread	02083 Saw	02091 Compass	02099 Stapler	02107 Satellite	02115 Crutch	02123 Airplane
02068 Pot	02076 Wallet	02084 Gear	02092 Tweezers	02100 Scissors	02108 Test Tube	02116 Monitor	02124 Rocket
02069 Oven MItt	02077 Hair Dryer	02085 Screwdriver	02093 Camera	02101 Pen	02109 Brain	02117 Thermometer	02125 Boat
02070 Spatula	02078 Perfume	02086 Axe	02094 Army Knife	02102 Filing Cabinet	02110 Atom	02118 Scalpel	02126 Train
02071 Toaster	02079 Wristwatch	02087 Nut and Bolt	02095 Weight Scale	02103 Desk	02111 Beaker	02119 Stethoscope	02127 Bus
02072 Measures	02080 Toothbrush	02088 Drill	02096 Magnifying Glass	02104 Calculator	02112 Telescope	02120 Bandage	02128 Truck

ICONIC IMAGES *Stylized Languages*

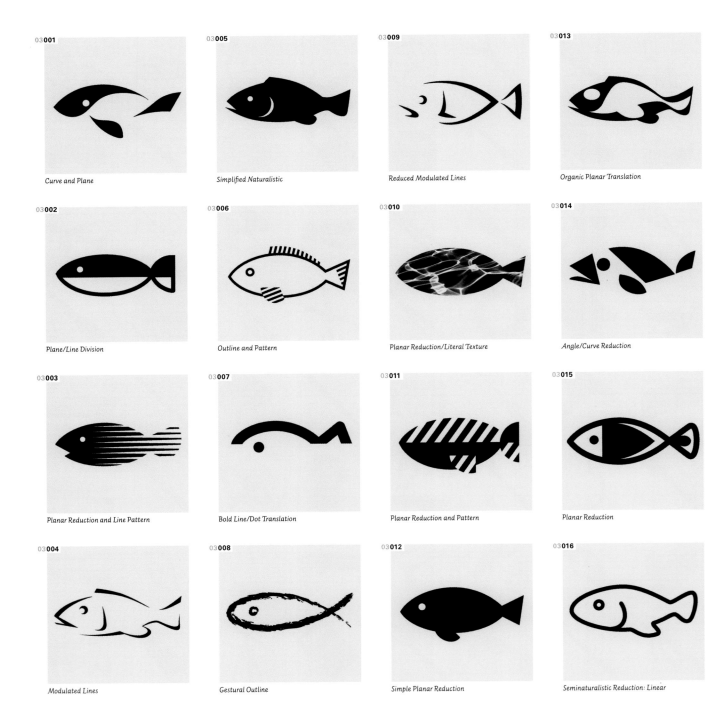

03 001
Curve and Plane

03 002
Plane/Line Division

03 003
Planar Reduction and Line Pattern

03 004
Modulated Lines

03 005
Simplified Naturalistic

03 006
Outline and Pattern

03 007
Bold Line/Dot Translation

03 008
Gestural Outline

03 009
Reduced Modulated Lines

03 010
Planar Reduction/Literal Texture

03 011
Planar Reduction and Pattern

03 012
Simple Planar Reduction

03 013
Organic Planar Translation

03 014
Angle/Curve Reduction

03 015
Planar Reduction

03 016
Seminaturalistic Reduction: Linear

Working from a naturalistic form as a base, designers may opt for more stylized icons for a bolder, more abstract, or metaphorical quality, supported by the clarity offered by the underlying concrete depiction. Shown here are a number of varied approaches to stylizing an icon, based on the fish form in the previous category.

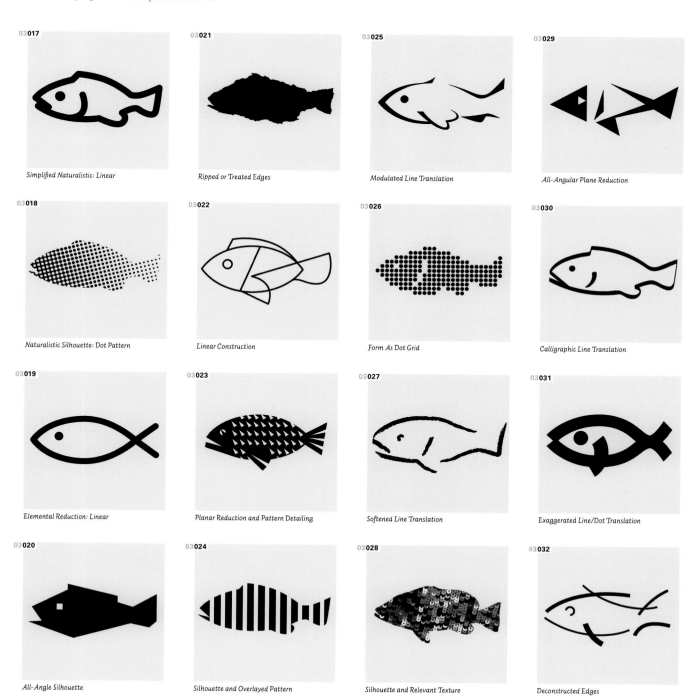

03**017**

Simplified Naturalistic: Linear

03**021**

Ripped or Treated Edges

03**025**

Modulated Line Translation

03**029**

All-Angular Plane Reduction

03**018**

Naturalistic Silhouette: Dot Pattern

03**022**

Linear Construction

03**026**

Form As Dot Grid

03**030**

Calligraphic Line Translation

03**019**

Elemental Reduction: Linear

03**023**

Planar Reduction and Pattern Detailing

03**027**

Softened Line Translation

03**031**

Exaggerated Line/Dot Translation

03**020**

All-Angle Silhouette

03**024**

Silhouette and Overlayed Pattern

03**028**

Silhouette and Relevant Texture

03**032**

Deconstructed Edges

PHOTOGRAPHY *Color and Toning Treatments*

04

CMYK: Full Color

CMYK: Even Ghosting

CMYK: Ghosting: Supersaturated

CMYK: Full Density: Desaturated

CMYK: Color Balance Shift: Cyan

CMYK: Overall Hue Shift: Warm

CMYK: Low Contrast: Supersaturated

CMYK: Solid Color Overprint

BW Halftone

BW Halftone: Even Ghosting: Unchanged Contrast

BW Halftone: Ghosting: High Contrast

BW Halftone: Ghosting: Low Contrast

BW Halftone: High Contrast

BW Halftone: Low Contrast: Midtone

BW Halftone: High Contrast: Midtone

BW Halftone: Solid Color Overprint

The simplicity of altering the color or tonality of photographs belies its potential to achieve visual interest. Varying contrast levels and ink mixture can offer a variety of distinctive results, especially for budget-conscious one- or two-color projects. Tonal treatments can also help enhance communication by changing the perceived feeling of images.

04**017**

Color Halftone

04**021**

Duotone: Black plus Warm Gray

04**025**

Duotone: Black plus Color: Black Dominant

04**029**

Duotone: Two Colors

04**018**

Color Halftone: Reversed from Background: Light

04**022**

Duotone: Black plus Warm Gray: Even Ghosting

04**026**

Duotone: Black plus Color: Color Dominant

04**030**

Duotone: Two Colors: Color 1 Dominant

04**019**

Color Halftone: Reversed from Background: Vibrant

04**023**

Duotone: Black plus Color

04**027**

Duotone: Black plus Color: Color Midtone Range Exaggerated

04**031**

Duotone: Two Colors: Color 2 Dominant

04**020**

Color Halftone: Overprint Solid Color

04**024**

Duotone: Black plus Color: Even Ghosting

04**028**

Duotone: Black plus Color: Black Dominant in Shadows/Color Ghosted

04**032**

Duotone: Two Colors: Selective Highlight and Midtone Application

PHOTOGRAPHY *Texture and Filter Treatments*

05

CMYK: Coarse Dot Screen

BW: Coarse Dot Screen

CMYK: Coarse Line Screen

BW: Coarse Line Screen

BW: Pixel Dither

CMYK: Linear Mezzotint

BW: Reticulation Pattern

CMYK: Noise Texture

Color Painting over CMYK Image

Color Painting over BW Image

Color Painting over Mezzotint Image

Color Painting over Coarse Dot Screen

Posterization: BW: One Level

Posterization: BW: Four Levels

Posterization: CMYK: Eight Levels

BW: Xerography

More dramatic, even, than tonal change, is the possibility of introducing texture within a photographic image—whether digitally or through conventional means. Textural alterations lend tactility, may evoke symbolism and metaphor, or help relate photographs to illustrative elements through similar visual vocabulary.

05 **017**

Linear Pattern Overlay: Opaque

05 **021**

Typographic Overlay: Opaque

05 **025**

Digital Pointillization

05 **029**

Digital Diffusion

05 **018**

Linear Pattern Overlay: Transparent

05 **022**

Typographic Overlay: Transparent: Color Blended

05 **026**

Digital Solarization

05 **030**

Digital Blurring

05 **019**

Ornamental Pattern Overlay: Transparent

05 **023**

Photographic Texture Overlay: Ghosted

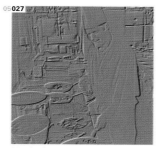

05 **027**

Digital Embossing

05 **031**

Digital Mosaic Pixellation

05 **020**

Ornamental Pattern Overlay: Transparent: Color Blended

05 **024**

Photographic Texture Overlay: Color Blended

05 **028**

Digital Edge Enhancement

05 **032**

Digital Fragmenting

PHOTOGRAPHY *Form Manipulations*

06

06001
Selective Toning

06002
Selective Blurring

06003
Selective Filtering Treatment

06004
Selective Resizing

06005
Silhouetted: Tight Contour

06006
Silhouetted: Simplified Contour: Angular

06007
Silhouetted: Simplified Contour: Curvilinear

06008
Silhouetted: Ripped Contour

06009
Masking: Secondary Image

06010
Masking: Large-Scale Pattern: Angular

06011
Masking: Large-Scale Pattern: Grid

06012
Masking: Large-Scale Texture

06013
Cutting and Separation: Part-Relative

06014
Cutting and Separation: Arbitrary

06015
Recomposition: Integral

06016
Recomposition: Additive

Presented here are a variety of options for affecting the physical form of photographic content: selective alterations of internal components; silhouetting; deconstructing and reordering parts; and splicing and combining multiple images. Together with other toning or texturing techniques, these approaches provide further possibilities for evolving photography into unique visual languages.

06**017**

Component Distortion

06**018**

Overall Distortion

06**019**

Perspective

06**020**

Spherizing

06**021**

Vignetted or Feathered Edge

06**022**

Alternate Frame Shape: Angular

06**023**

Alternate Frame Shape: Curvilinear

06**024**

Alternate Frame Shape: Organic

06**025**

Splicing: Staggered

06**026**

Splicing: Alternation with Secondary Image

06**027**

Splicing: Alternation with Image Inverse

06**028**

Splicing: Alternation with Rotated Splices

06**029**

Image Repeated: Offset: Overlaid

06**030**

Image Repeated: Offset: Rotated: Overlaid

06**031**

Overlay: Secondary Image

06**032**

Overlay: Secondary Image: Spliced

ILLUSTRATION *Styles and Media*

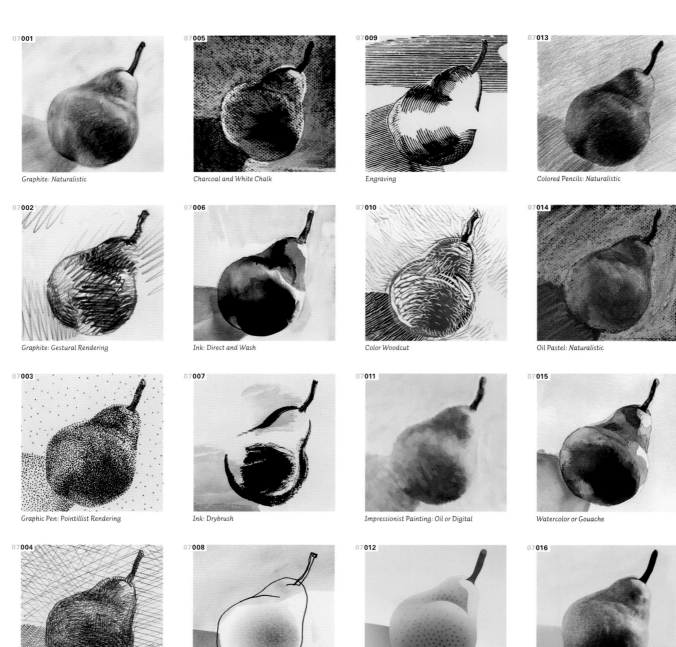

07**001** Graphite: Naturalistic

07**002** Graphite: Gestural Rendering

07**003** Graphic Pen: Pointillist Rendering

07**004** Ballpoint Pen: Crosshatch

07**005** Charcoal and White Chalk

07**006** Ink: Direct and Wash

07**007** Ink: Drybrush

07**008** Etching with Aquatint

07**009** Engraving

07**010** Color Woodcut

07**011** Impressionist Painting: Oil or Digital

07**012** Idealized Vector Drawing

07**013** Colored Pencils: Naturalistic

07**014** Oil Pastel: Naturalistic

07**015** Watercolor or Gouache

07**016** Aribrushed Photorealism

Illustration frees designers from real-world constraints of depiction inherent in photography. In this sampling: conventional styles created with paint, collage, and printmaking, as well as graphic vector-based approaches and digital montage. The left-hand page presents naturalistic approaches; on the right-hand page, interpretive styles are shown. Whether handmade or digital, drawing and painting techniques impart a human touch and a sense of invention.

07**017**

Icon Clustering

07**021**

Interpretive Doodling

07**025**

Aggressive Contour and Line

07**029**
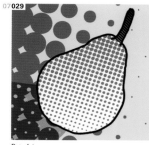
Pop Art

07**018**
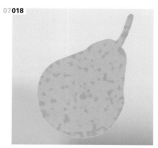
Texture and Gradation Fill

07**022**

Vector Symbol Kitsch

07**026**

Silhouette and Pattern

07**030**
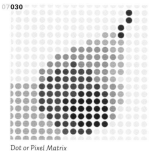
Dot or Pixel Matrix

07**019**

Decorative Cuteness

07**023**

Playful Painted-Pattern Cutouts

07**027**
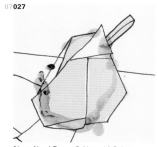
Linear Hand-Drawn Cubism with Paint

07**031**

Vector Cartoon Environment

07**020**
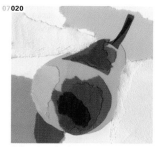
Collage: Ripped and Cut Paper

07**024**
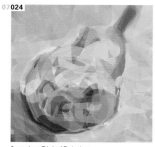
Luminous Digital Painting

07**028**
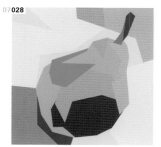
Color-Field Brutalism

07**032**
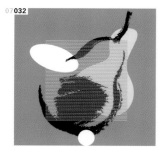
Retro Mixed-Media Collage

ABSTRACT LANGUAGES *Geometric*

08

08**001**

Urban

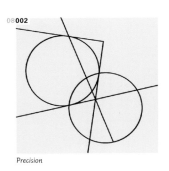

08**002**

Precision

08**003**

Conflict

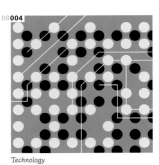

08**004**

Technology

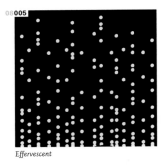

08**005**

Effervescent

08**006**

Traffic or Momentum

08**007**

Rage

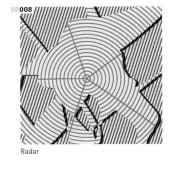

08**008**

Radar

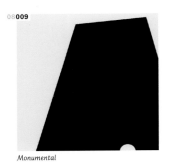

08**009**

Monumental

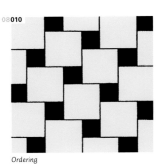

08**010**

Ordering

08**011**

Unity

08**012**

Fractal

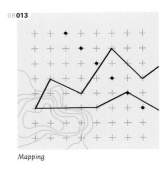

08**013**

Mapping

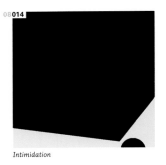

08**014**

Intimidation

08**015**

Internal Mechanisms

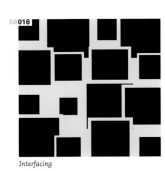

08**016**

Interfacing

The power of abstraction to communicate, as well as to create unique, custom design statements, is demonstrated in this collection of geometric shapes and environments. Use these languages—evoking architecture, industry, science, and other concepts suggested by pure geometry—as backgrounds, components for collage, or stand-alone images. Cropping, scale changes, positive/negative reversal, and repetition may introduce variation for branding systems or to build more complex forms.

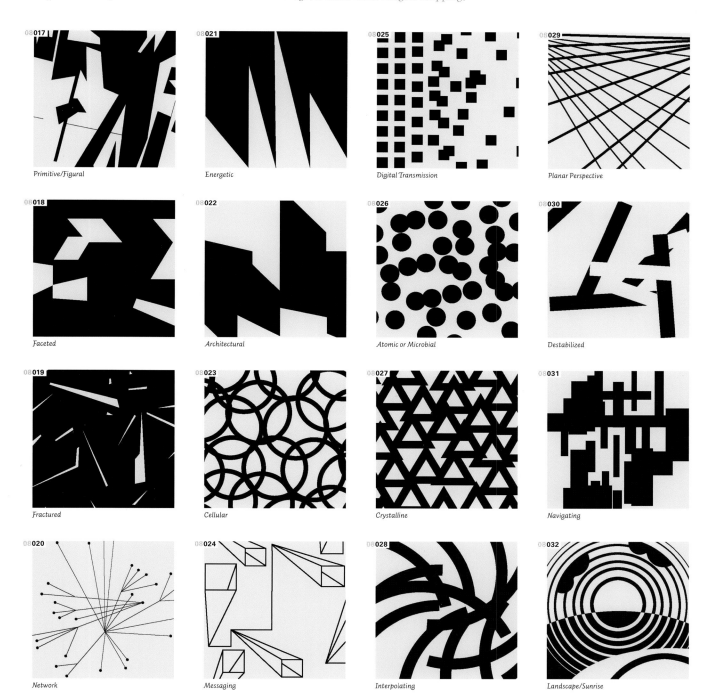

08**017**
Primitive/Figural

08**021**
Energetic

08**025**
Digital Transmission

08**029**
Planar Perspective

08**018**
Faceted

08**022**
Architectural

08**026**
Atomic or Microbial

08**030**
Destabilized

08**019**
Fractured

08**023**
Cellular

08**027**
Crystalline

08**031**
Navigating

08**020**
Network

08**024**
Messaging

08**028**
Interpolating

08**032**
Landscape/Sunrise

ABSTRACT LANGUAGES *Organic*

09**001**
Replicating

09**005**
Unfocused

09**009**
Rhythmic

09**013**
Evolution

09**002**
Deliberate

09**006**
Accidental

09**010**
Forest

09**014**
Sensuous

09**003**
Weathered

09**007**
Woven

09**011**
Wind

09**015**
Landscape

09**004**
Graffiti

09**008**
Primitive

09**012**
Obscuring

09**016**
Elemental

These abstract languages, in their softness, irregularity, and curvilinear qualities, reference the endless diversity of natural form. Use them as backgrounds or housing for photography, in combination with geometric abstraction or icons, as inspiration for logos, or as support for typographic configurations—for messages as far-ranging as the environment, emotions, life sciences, and poetic metaphor.

09**017**
Nebulous

09**021**
Reproduction

09**025**
Formulating

09**029**
Layered

09**018**
Intuitive

09**022**
Robust

09**026**
Activity

09**030**
Roiling

09**019**
Dissolution

09**023**
Biological

09**027**
Topographical

09**031**
Contemplative

09**020**
Stormy

09**024**
Oppositional

09**028**
Rugged

09**032**
Building

TEXTURES *Representational*

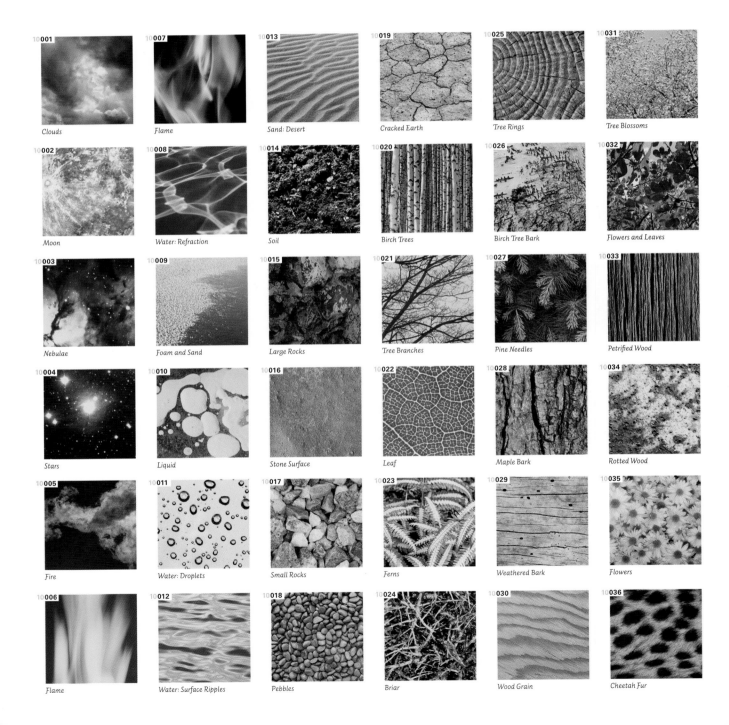

10|001 Clouds	**10|007** Flame	**10|013** Sand: Desert	**10|019** Cracked Earth	**10|025** Tree Rings	**10|031** Tree Blossoms
10|002 Moon	**10|008** Water: Refraction	**10|014** Soil	**10|020** Birch Trees	**10|026** Birch Tree Bark	**10|032** Flowers and Leaves
10|003 Nebulae	**10|009** Foam and Sand	**10|015** Large Rocks	**10|021** Tree Branches	**10|027** Pine Needles	**10|033** Petrified Wood
10|004 Stars	**10|010** Liquid	**10|016** Stone Surface	**10|022** Leaf	**10|028** Maple Bark	**10|034** Rotted Wood
10|005 Fire	**10|011** Water: Droplets	**10|017** Small Rocks	**10|023** Ferns	**10|029** Weathered Bark	**10|035** Flowers
10|006 Flame	**10|012** Water: Surface Ripples	**10|018** Pebbles	**10|024** Briar	**10|030** Wood Grain	**10|036** Cheetah Fur

As page backgrounds, fills for graphical forms, or overlays for image or type, textures whose sources a viewer is able to recognize present a concrete, grounded reference that can speed communication. These textures are drawn from archetypal sources, such as the elements, materials in the environment, animals, and manmade objects.

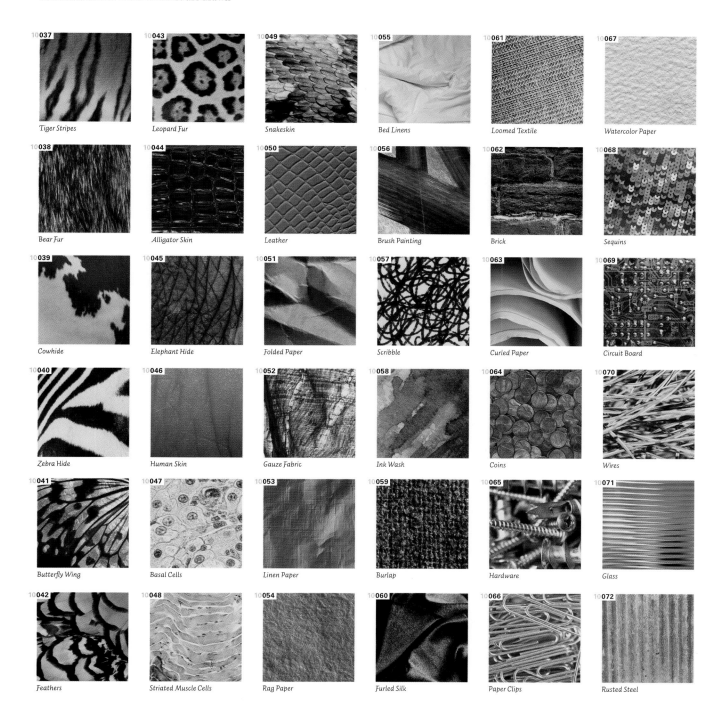

10037 Tiger Stripes	10043 Leopard Fur	10049 Snakeskin	10055 Bed Linens	10061 Loomed Textile	10067 Watercolor Paper
10038 Bear Fur	10044 Alligator Skin	10050 Leather	10056 Brush Painting	10062 Brick	10068 Sequins
10039 Cowhide	10045 Elephant Hide	10051 Folded Paper	10057 Scribble	10063 Curled Paper	10069 Circuit Board
10040 Zebra Hide	10046 Human Skin	10052 Gauze Fabric	10058 Ink Wash	10064 Coins	10070 Wires
10041 Butterfly Wing	10047 Basal Cells	10053 Linen Paper	10059 Burlap	10065 Hardware	10071 Glass
10042 Feathers	10048 Striated Muscle Cells	10054 Rag Paper	10060 Furled Silk	10066 Paper Clips	10072 Rusted Steel

TEXTURES *Abstract*

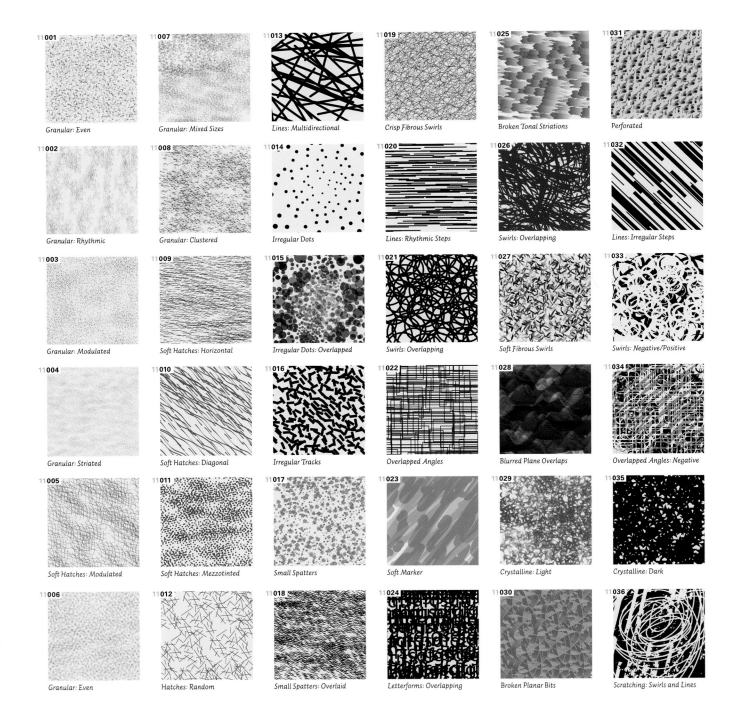

11 001 Granular: Even

11 002 Granular: Rhythmic

11 003 Granular: Modulated

11 004 Granular: Striated

11 005 Soft Hatches: Modulated

11 006 Granular: Even

11 007 Granular: Mixed Sizes

11 008 Granular: Clustered

11 009 Soft Hatches: Horizontal

11 010 Soft Hatches: Diagonal

11 011 Soft Hatches: Mezzotinted

11 012 Hatches: Random

11 013 Lines: Multidirectional

11 014 Irregular Dots

11 015 Irregular Dots: Overlapped

11 016 Irregular Tracks

11 017 Small Spatters

11 018 Small Spatters: Overlaid

11 019 Crisp Fibrous Swirls

11 020 Lines: Rhythmic Steps

11 021 Swirls: Overlapping

11 022 Overlapped Angles

11 023 Soft Marker

11 024 Letterforms: Overlapping

11 025 Broken Tonal Striations

11 026 Swirls: Overlapping

11 027 Soft Fibrous Swirls

11 028 Blurred Plane Overlaps

11 029 Crystalline: Light

11 030 Broken Planar Bits

11 031 Perforated

11 032 Lines: Irregular Steps

11 033 Swirls: Negative/Positive

11 034 Overlapped Angles: Negative

11 035 Crystalline: Dark

11 036 Scratching: Swirls and Lines

The textures in this category are simply that—randomized, abstract surface activity without the limitations imposed by recognizability. As such, their use as overlays, fills, or backgrounds offers room for interpretation or suggests real-world associations on a more conceptual level. Use them on their own, combine them with representational textures, or use them to enrich photographs, icons, and illustrations.

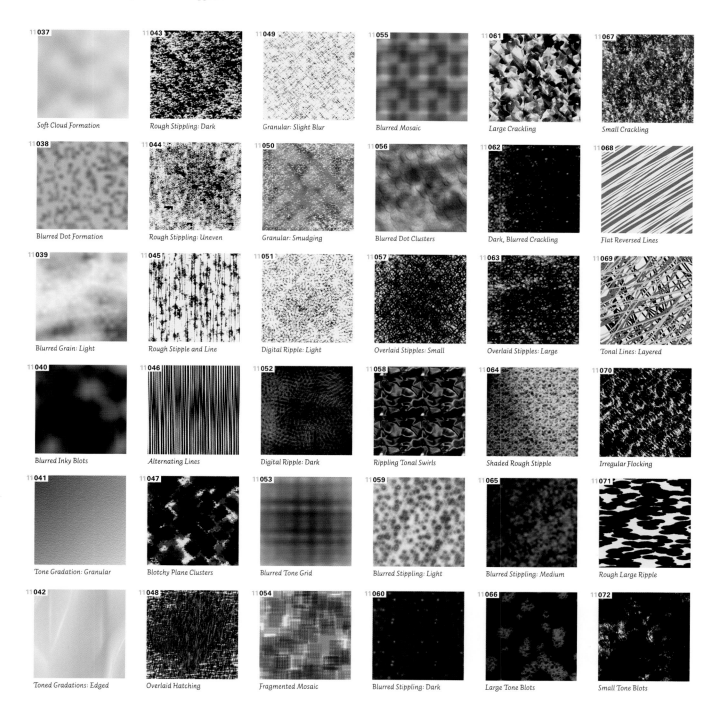

11 037 Soft Cloud Formation	11 043 Rough Stippling: Dark	11 049 Granular: Slight Blur	11 055 Blurred Mosaic	11 061 Large Crackling	11 067 Small Crackling
11 038 Blurred Dot Formation	11 044 Rough Stippling: Uneven	11 050 Granular: Smudging	11 056 Blurred Dot Clusters	11 062 Dark, Blurred Crackling	11 068 Flat Reversed Lines
11 039 Blurred Grain: Light	11 045 Rough Stipple and Line	11 051 Digital Ripple: Light	11 057 Overlaid Stipples: Small	11 063 Overlaid Stipples: Large	11 069 Tonal Lines: Layered
11 040 Blurred Inky Blots	11 046 Alternating Lines	11 052 Digital Ripple: Dark	11 058 Rippling Tonal Swirls	11 064 Shaded Rough Stipple	11 070 Irregular Flocking
11 041 Tone Gradation: Granular	11 047 Blotchy Plane Clusters	11 053 Blurred Tone Grid	11 059 Blurred Stippling: Light	11 065 Blurred Stippling: Medium	11 071 Rough Large Ripple
11 042 Toned Gradations: Edged	11 048 Overlaid Hatching	11 054 Fragmented Mosaic	11 060 Blurred Stippling: Dark	11 066 Large Tone Blots	11 072 Small Tone Blots

PATTERNS *Concrete: Photographic*

12**001** Mesh	12**007** Rolled Towels	12**013** Crates	12**019** Struts and Wires	12**025** Tire Tread	12**031** Glass and Steel Facade
12**002** Mixing Board	12**008** Circuit Board	12**014** Lace	12**020** Metal Cables	12**026** Ornamental Ironwork	12**032** Plaid Fabric
12**003** Palladian Windows	12**009** Corrugated Cardboard	12**015** Baling Wire	12**021** Steel Plating	12**027** Mailbox Doors	12**033** Ribbed Stone
12**004** Dot Screen	12**010** Stacked Pots	12**016** Noodles	12**022** Metal Grate	12**028** Cheese Grater	12**034** Woven Rope
12**005** Office Windows	12**011** Bamboo	12**017** Bricks	12**023** Basket Weave	12**029** Doily	12**035** Plant Stem
12**006** Cedar Shakes	12**012** Glazed Tiles	12**018** Wood	12**024** Cement Blocks	12**030** Strawberry Seeds	12**036** Computer Keyboard

Repeating structures of representational and semiconcrete forms can provide backdrops for layouts or packaging, fills for abstract shapes, or foundations for complex collages where the element of recognition helps add depth to simpler, more concise images. Explore combinations of these pattern elements to create rich, illustrative tapestries.

12037	12043	12049	12055	12061	12067
Pasta	Aluminum Cans	Small Tiles	Thread Spools	Tweed Weave	Diamond Plate Steel
12038	12044	12050	12056	12062	12068
Circuit Board	Fabric Beading	Ball Bearings	Roofing Surface	Iron Fencing	Clay Roof Tiles
12039	12045	12051	12057	12063	12069
Peacock Feathers	Corn Kernels	Piano Keys	Loomed Fabric	Circular Basketweave	Studded Steel Plate
12040	12046	12052	12058	12064	12070
Foam Packing	Ornamental Grate	Fish Scales	Striped Cloth	Office Windows	Manhole Cover
12041	12047	12053	12059	12065	12071
Honeycomb	Plant Leaves	Pineapple Rind	Perspective Tiles	Stacked Kiwifruit	Embossed Ornamentation
12042	12048	12054	12060	12066	12072
Woven Wire Sheathing	Diamond Plate Steel	Crochet	Ornamental Screen	Wood Flooring	Duct Grate

PATTERNS *Ornamental*

13

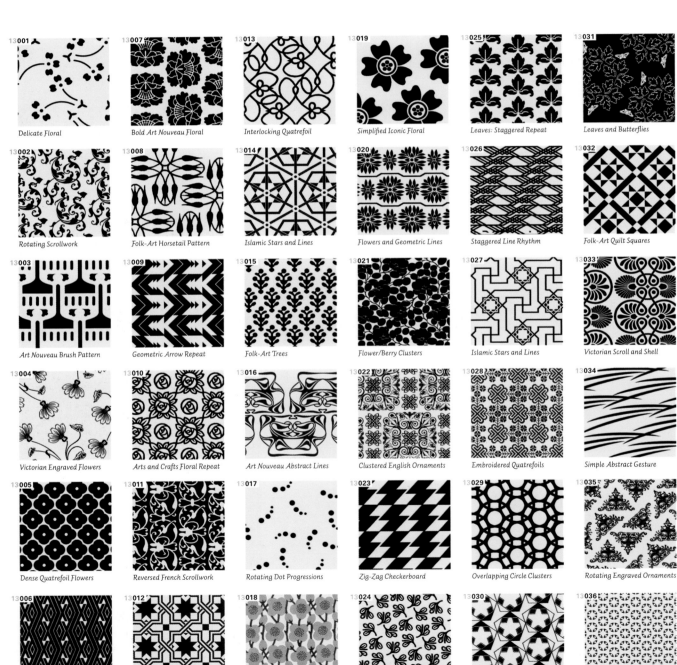

13001 Delicate Floral

13007 Bold Art Nouveau Floral

13013 Interlocking Quatrefoil

13019 Simplified Iconic Floral

13025 Leaves: Staggered Repeat

13031 Leaves and Butterflies

13002 Rotating Scrollwork

13008 Folk-Art Horsetail Pattern

13014 Islamic Stars and Lines

13020 Flowers and Geometric Lines

13026 Staggered Line Rhythm

13032 Folk-Art Quilt Squares

13003 Art Nouveau Brush Pattern

13009 Geometric Arrow Repeat

13015 Folk-Art Trees

13021 Flower/Berry Clusters

13027 Islamic Stars and Lines

13033 Victorian Scroll and Shell

13004 Victorian Engraved Flowers

13010 Arts and Crafts Floral Repeat

13016 Art Nouveau Abstract Lines

13022 Clustered English Ornaments

13028 Embroidered Quatrefoils

13034 Simple Abstract Gesture

13005 Dense Quatrefoil Flowers

13011 Reversed French Scrollwork

13017 Rotating Dot Progressions

13023 Zig-Zag Checkerboard

13029 Overlapping Circle Clusters

13035 Rotating Engraved Ornaments

13006 Native American Weave

13012 Islamic Stars and Lines

13018 Two-Tone Flowers/Branches

13024 Rotating Bud Clusters

13030 Art Deco Pentagram

13036 Dense Circle/Triangle Repeat

These decorative patterns run the gamut from Old-World inspirations in architectural engravings and textiles to stripped-down, modern, yet still intricate, interwoven rhythms of geometry. Overlaying related patterns, enlarging and reducing their scales, rotating them in different locations—as well as using them to interact with photography and illustration—provides limitless possibilities.

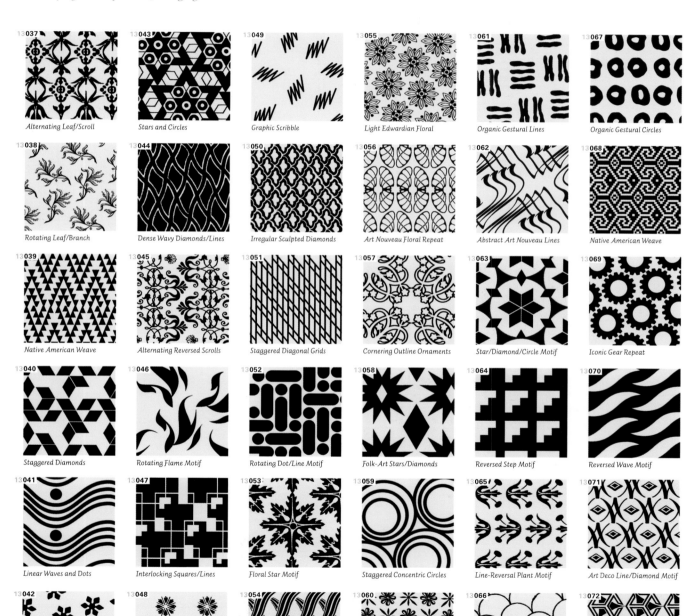

13037 *Alternating Leaf/Scroll*	13043 *Stars and Circles*	13049 *Graphic Scribble*	13055 *Light Edwardian Floral*	13061 *Organic Gestural Lines*	13067 *Organic Gestural Circles*
13038 *Rotating Leaf/Branch*	13044 *Dense Wavy Diamonds/Lines*	13050 *Irregular Sculpted Diamonds*	13056 *Art Nouveau Floral Repeat*	13062 *Abstract Art Nouveau Lines*	13068 *Native American Weave*
13039 *Native American Weave*	13045 *Alternating Reversed Scrolls*	13051 *Staggered Diagonal Grids*	13057 *Cornering Outline Ornaments*	13063 *Star/Diamond/Circle Motif*	13069 *Iconic Gear Repeat*
13040 *Staggered Diamonds*	13046 *Rotating Flame Motif*	13052 *Rotating Dot/Line Motif*	13058 *Folk-Art Stars/Diamonds*	13064 *Reversed Step Motif*	13070 *Reversed Wave Motif*
13041 *Linear Waves and Dots*	13047 *Interlocking Squares/Lines*	13053 *Floral Star Motif*	13059 *Staggered Concentric Circles*	13065 *Line-Reversal Plant Motif*	13071 *Art Deco Line/Diamond Motif*
13042 *Folk-Art Star Flowers*	13048 *Neoclassical Ornament Repeat*	13054 *Art Deco Wave Chevrons*	13060 *Alternating Flowers/Stars*	13066 *Fish Scale Motif*	13072 *Art Deco Cube/Arrow Motif*

PATTERNS *Geometric: Lines*

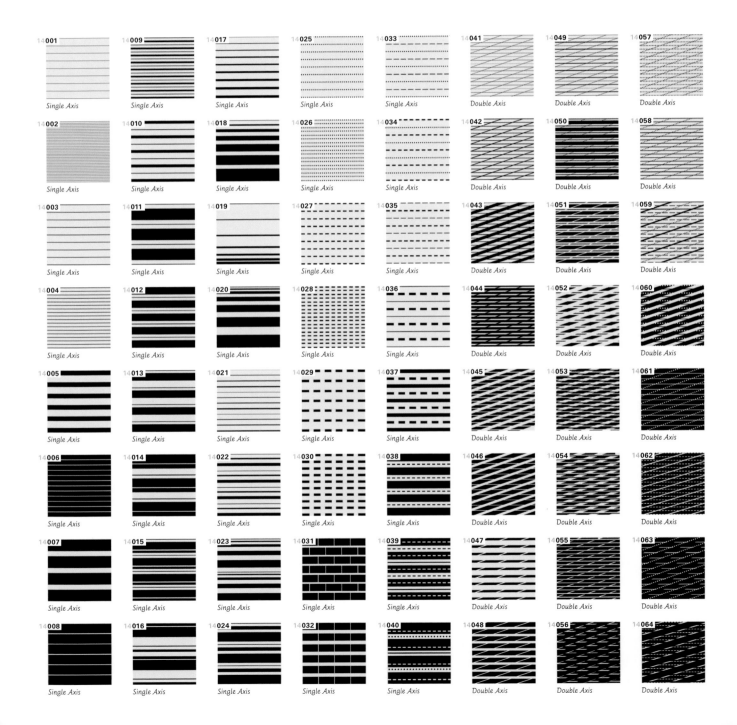

14**001**	14**009**	14**017**	14**025**	14**033**	14**041**	14**049**	14**057**
Single Axis	Single Axis	Single Axis	Single Axis	Single Axis	Double Axis	Double Axis	Double Axis
14**002**	14**010**	14**018**	14**026**	14**034**	14**042**	14**050**	14**058**
Single Axis	Single Axis	Single Axis	Single Axis	Single Axis	Double Axis	Double Axis	Double Axis
14**003**	14**011**	14**019**	14**027**	14**035**	14**043**	14**051**	14**059**
Single Axis	Single Axis	Single Axis	Single Axis	Single Axis	Double Axis	Double Axis	Double Axis
14**004**	14**012**	14**020**	14**028**	14**036**	14**044**	14**052**	14**060**
Single Axis	Single Axis	Single Axis	Single Axis	Single Axis	Double Axis	Double Axis	Double Axis
14**005**	14**013**	14**021**	14**029**	14**037**	14**045**	14**053**	14**061**
Single Axis	Single Axis	Single Axis	Single Axis	Single Axis	Double Axis	Double Axis	Double Axis
14**006**	14**014**	14**022**	14**030**	14**038**	14**046**	14**054**	14**062**
Single Axis	Single Axis	Single Axis	Single Axis	Single Axis	Double Axis	Double Axis	Double Axis
14**007**	14**015**	14**023**	14**031**	14**039**	14**047**	14**055**	14**063**
Single Axis	Single Axis	Single Axis	Single Axis	Single Axis	Double Axis	Double Axis	Double Axis
14**008**	14**016**	14**024**	14**032**	14**040**	14**048**	14**056**	14**064**
Single Axis	Single Axis	Single Axis	Single Axis	Single Axis	Double Axis	Double Axis	Double Axis

Patterns such as those shown here create directional movement and optical rhythm. Enlarging the scale of a pattern, relative to the format in which it is used, increases the number of options—as do rotating it, changing the tonality or color of its line elements, and so on.

14**065**	14**073**	14**081**	14**089**	14**097**	14**105**	14**113**	14**121**
Triple Axis	Triple Axis	Triple Axis	Triple Axis	Stepped	Stepped	Stepped	Stepped
14**066**	14**074**	14**082**	14**090**	14**098**	14**106**	14**114**	14**122**
Triple Axis	Triple Axis	Triple Axis	Triple Axis	Stepped	Stepped	Stepped	Stepped
14**067**	14**075**	14**083**	14**091**	14**099**	14**107**	14**115**	14**123**
Triple Axis	Triple Axis	Triple Axis	Triple Axis	Stepped	Stepped	Stepped	Stepped
14**068**	14**076**	14**084**	14**092**	14**100**	14**108**	14**116**	14**124**
Triple Axis	Triple Axis	Triple Axis	Triple Axis	Stepped	Stepped	Stepped	Stepped
14**069**	14**077**	14**085**	14**093**	14**101**	14**109**	14**117**	14**125**
Triple Axis	Triple Axis	Triple Axis	Triple Axis	Stepped	Stepped	Stepped	Stepped
14**070**	14**078**	14**086**	14**094**	14**102**	14**110**	14**118**	14**126**
Triple Axis	Triple Axis	Triple Axis	Triple Axis	Stepped	Stepped	Stepped	Stepped
14**071**	14**079**	14**087**	14**095**	14**103**	14**111**	14**119**	14**127**
Triple Axis	Triple Axis	Triple Axis	Triple Axis	Stepped	Stepped	Stepped	Stepped
14**072**	14**080**	14**088**	14**096**	14**104**	14**112**	14**120**	14**128**
Triple Axis	Triple Axis	Triple Axis	Triple Axis	Stepped	Stepped	Stepped	Stepped

PATTERNS *Geometric: Curves*

15

15001 Concentric 15009 Concentric 15017 Concentric 15025 Concentric 15033 Concentric 15041 Doubled 15049 Tripled 15057 Offset

15002 Concentric 15010 Concentric 15018 Concentric 15026 Concentric 15034 Concentric 15042 Doubled 15050 Tripled 15058 Offset

15003 Concentric 15011 Concentric 15019 Concentric 15027 Concentric 15035 Concentric 15043 Doubled 15051 Tripled 15059 Offset

15004 Concentric 15012 Concentric 15020 Concentric 15028 Concentric 15036 Concentric 15044 Doubled 15052 Tripled 15060 Offset

15005 Concentric 15013 Concentric 15021 Concentric 15029 Concentric 15037 Concentric 15045 Doubled 15053 Tripled 15061 Offset

15006 Concentric 15014 Concentric 15022 Concentric 15030 Concentric 15038 Concentric 15046 Doubled 15054 Tripled 15062 Offset

15007 Concentric 15015 Concentric 15023 Concentric 15031 Concentric 15039 Concentric 15047 Doubled 15055 Tripled 15063 Offset

15008 Concentric 15016 Concentric 15024 Concentric 15032 Concentric 15040 Concentric 15048 Doubled 15056 Tripled 15064 Offset

The pure directionality and vibration of linear patterns is made more complex when the line elements are curved or waved, as in the selection provided here. At extremely large scales, these structures can be used not only to activate surface area but also to create exceptionally three-dimensional environments or direct the eye from one element to another. At very small scales, they make very active fills within shapes or within other enlarged pattern elements.

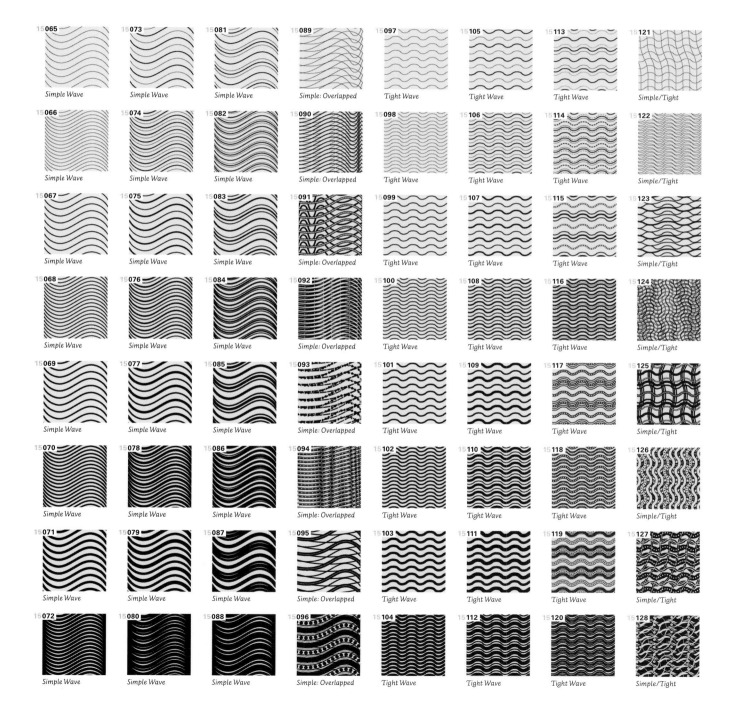

15 065	15 073	15 081	15 089	15 097	15 105	15 113	15 121
Simple Wave	Simple Wave	Simple Wave	Simple: Overlapped	Tight Wave	Tight Wave	Tight Wave	Simple/Tight
15 066	15 074	15 082	15 090	15 098	15 106	15 114	15 122
Simple Wave	Simple Wave	Simple Wave	Simple: Overlapped	Tight Wave	Tight Wave	Tight Wave	Simple/Tight
15 067	15 075	15 083	15 091	15 099	15 107	15 115	15 123
Simple Wave	Simple Wave	Simple Wave	Simple: Overlapped	Tight Wave	Tight Wave	Tight Wave	Simple/Tight
15 068	15 076	15 084	15 092	15 100	15 108	15 116	15 124
Simple Wave	Simple Wave	Simple Wave	Simple: Overlapped	Tight Wave	Tight Wave	Tight Wave	Simple/Tight
15 069	15 077	15 085	15 093	15 101	15 109	15 117	15 125
Simple Wave	Simple Wave	Simple Wave	Simple: Overlapped	Tight Wave	Tight Wave	Tight Wave	Simple/Tight
15 070	15 078	15 086	15 094	15 102	15 110	15 118	15 126
Simple Wave	Simple Wave	Simple Wave	Simple: Overlapped	Tight Wave	Tight Wave	Tight Wave	Simple/Tight
15 071	15 079	15 087	15 095	15 103	15 111	15 119	15 127
Simple Wave	Simple Wave	Simple Wave	Simple: Overlapped	Tight Wave	Tight Wave	Tight Wave	Simple/Tight
15 072	15 080	15 088	15 096	15 104	15 112	15 120	15 128
Simple Wave	Simple Wave	Simple Wave	Simple: Overlapped	Tight Wave	Tight Wave	Tight Wave	Simple/Tight

PATTERNS *Geometric: Grids*

16

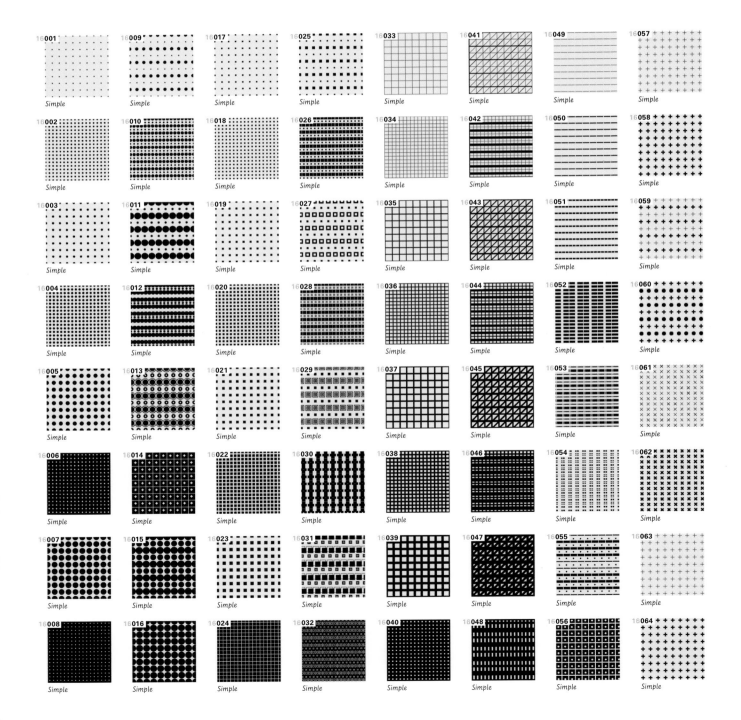

16**001** Simple	16**009** Simple	16**017** Simple	16**025** Simple	16**033** Simple	16**041** Simple	16**049** Simple	16**057** Simple
16**002** Simple	16**010** Simple	16**018** Simple	16**026** Simple	16**034** Simple	16**042** Simple	16**050** Simple	16**058** Simple
16**003** Simple	16**011** Simple	16**019** Simple	16**027** Simple	16**035** Simple	16**043** Simple	16**051** Simple	16**059** Simple
16**004** Simple	16**012** Simple	16**020** Simple	16**028** Simple	16**036** Simple	16**044** Simple	16**052** Simple	16**060** Simple
16**005** Simple	16**013** Simple	16**021** Simple	16**029** Simple	16**037** Simple	16**045** Simple	16**053** Simple	16**061** Simple
16**006** Simple	16**014** Simple	16**022** Simple	16**030** Simple	16**038** Simple	16**046** Simple	16**054** Simple	16**062** Simple
16**007** Simple	16**015** Simple	16**023** Simple	16**031** Simple	16**039** Simple	16**047** Simple	16**055** Simple	16**063** Simple
16**008** Simple	16**016** Simple	16**024** Simple	16**032** Simple	16**040** Simple	16**048** Simple	16**056** Simple	16**064** Simple

The patterns shown here are all based on modular, square-based repeating structures—whether the pattern components are square themselves, linear, or dotlike in shape. From simple checker patterns to intricate configurations of several base components, these patterns are systematic, architectonic, and three-dimensional.

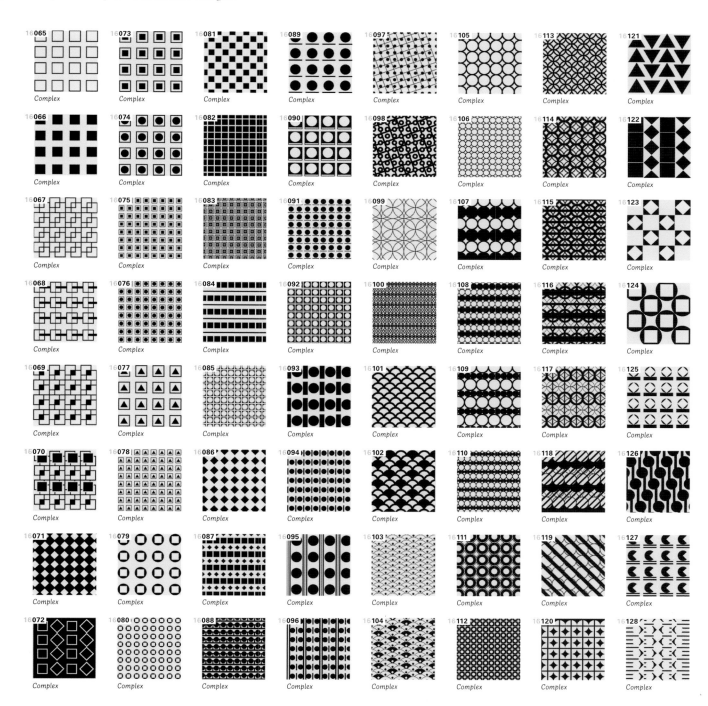

065 Complex · 073 Complex · 081 Complex · 089 Complex · 097 Complex · 105 Complex · 113 Complex · 121 Complex

066 Complex · 074 Complex · 082 Complex · 090 Complex · 098 Complex · 106 Complex · 114 Complex · 122 Complex

067 Complex · 075 Complex · 083 Complex · 091 Complex · 099 Complex · 107 Complex · 115 Complex · 123 Complex

068 Complex · 076 Complex · 084 Complex · 092 Complex · 100 Complex · 108 Complex · 116 Complex · 124 Complex

069 Complex · 077 Complex · 085 Complex · 093 Complex · 101 Complex · 109 Complex · 117 Complex · 125 Complex

070 Complex · 078 Complex · 086 Complex · 094 Complex · 102 Complex · 110 Complex · 118 Complex · 126 Complex

071 Complex · 079 Complex · 087 Complex · 095 Complex · 103 Complex · 111 Complex · 119 Complex · 127 Complex

072 Complex · 080 Complex · 088 Complex · 096 Complex · 104 Complex · 112 Complex · 120 Complex · 128 Complex

BORDERS *Page and Object Edge Forms*

17

17001

Linear Pattern

17002

Linear Pattern

17003

Linear Pattern

17004

Linear Pattern

17005

Linear Pattern

17006

Linear Pattern

17007

Linear Pattern

17008

Linear Pattern

17009

Linear Pattern

17010

Linear Pattern

17011

Linear Pattern

17012

Linear Pattern

17013

Gridded Pattern

17014

Gridded Pattern

17015

Gridded Pattern

17016

Gridded Pattern

17017

Gridded Pattern

17018

Gridded Pattern

17019

Gridded Pattern

17020

Waved Line Screen

17021

Gridded Pattern

17022

Gridded Pattern

17023

Gridded Pattern

17024

Gridded Pattern

17025

Rough Rip: Shallow or Deep

17026

Brush Stroke

17027

Charcoal Stroke

17028

Torn Spiral Paper

17029

Torn Ring-Bound Paper

17030

Engraved Page Curl

17031

Stitching

17032

Fibrous Edge

17033

Photographic Paper Edge: Deckled or Crumpled

17034

Watercolor Edge: Wet Bleed

17035

Wire Binding: Spine/Interior

17036

Wire Binding: Spine/Edge View

Use these edging devices—striped bands, rips, brush strokes, double lines, and so on—to enclose images, surround typographic elements, alter the edges of abstract graphic forms, or border page edges. Carefully cropped, they are also useful as shapes unto themselves, or as containers for icons, patterns, page numbers, or titling elements.

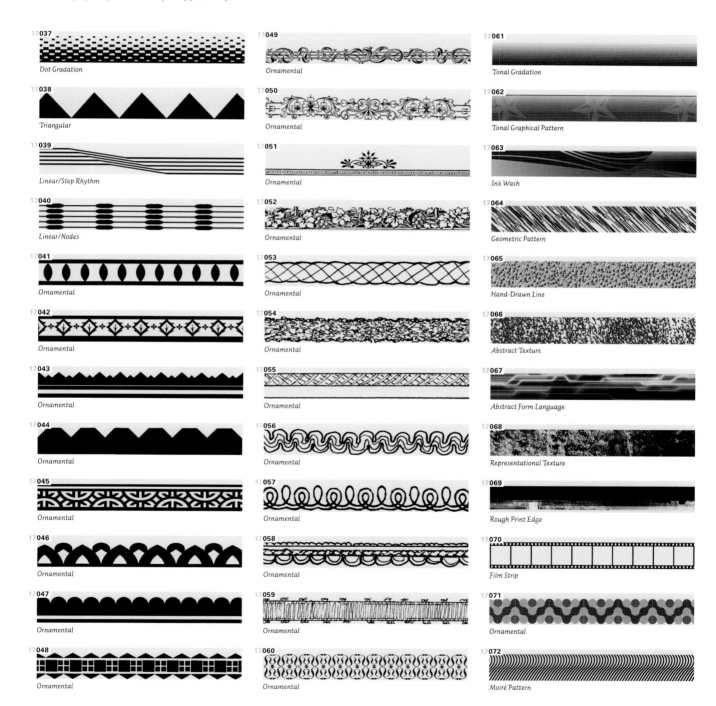

17**037**
Dot Gradation

17**038**
Triangular

17**039**
Linear/Step Rhythm

17**040**
Linear/Nodes

17**041**
Ornamental

17**042**
Ornamental

17**043**
Ornamental

17**044**
Ornamental

17**045**
Ornamental

17**046**
Ornamental

17**047**
Ornamental

17**048**
Ornamental

17**049**
Ornamental

17**050**
Ornamental

17**051**
Ornamental

17**052**
Ornamental

17**053**
Ornamental

17**054**
Ornamental

17**055**
Ornamental

17**056**
Ornamental

17**057**
Ornamental

17**058**
Ornamental

17**059**
Ornamental

17**060**
Ornamental

17**061**
Tonal Gradation

17**062**
Tonal Graphical Pattern

17**063**
Ink Wash

17**064**
Geometric Pattern

17**065**
Hand-Drawn Line

17**066**
Abstract Texture

17**067**
Abstract Form Language

17**068**
Representational Texture

17**069**
Rough Print Edge

17**070**
Film Strip

17**071**
Ornamental

17**072**
Moiré Pattern

SYMBOLS AND SIGNS *Visual Metaphors*

18

18001
Ying-Yang: Equilibrium/Buddhism

18002
Upper Cross: Christianity

18003
Icthus: Christianity

18004
Islam

18005
Zodiac

18006
Om: Hinduism

18007
Six-Pointed Star: Judaism

18008
Lotus: Buddism/Hinduism

18009
Peace/Hope: Christianity

18010
Maltese Cross: Treasure/Piracy

18011
Inspiration/Creativity

18012
Infinity

18013
Love/Intimacy

18014
Peace/Activism

18015
Laurel Wreath: Victory/Imperialism

18016
Imagination/Private Thoughts

18017
Industry

18018
Justice

18019
Remembrance/Unity

18020
Snowflake: Winter/General Seasons

18021
Speech/Dialogue

18022
Communication/Public Telephone

18023
Sound/Directive

18024
Mail

18025
Fast-Forward

In addition to using literal images for direct representation, a designer may opt for symbolic forms, or for representational images that have acquired metaphorical meaning.

Shown here is but a small sampling of commonly understood symbols that can add humor or unexpected conceptual overlay.

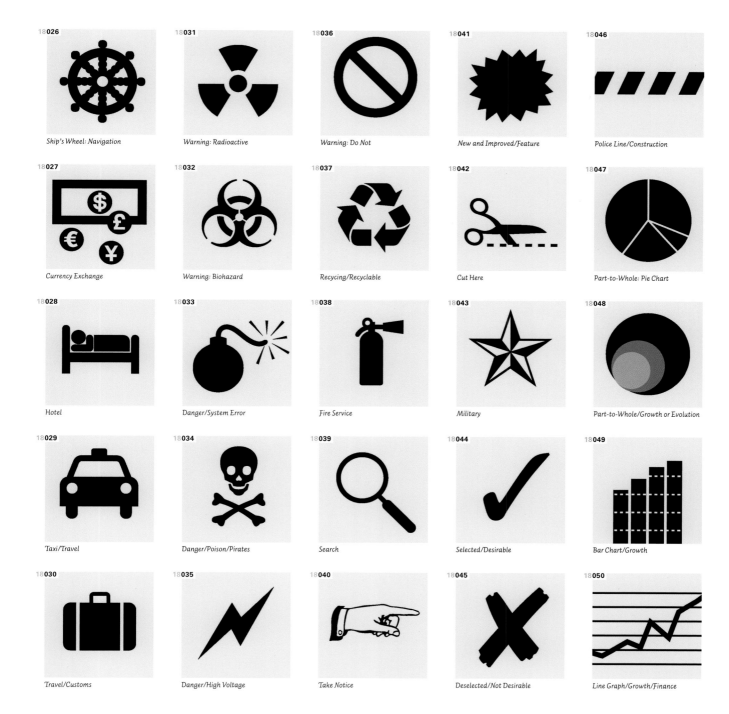

18026 Ship's Wheel: Navigation

18031 Warning: Radioactive

18036 Warning: Do Not

18041 New and Improved/Feature

18046 Police Line/Construction

18027 Currency Exchange

18032 Warning: Biohazard

18037 Recycling/Recyclable

18042 Cut Here

18047 Part-to-Whole: Pie Chart

18028 Hotel

18033 Danger/System Error

18038 Fire Service

18043 Military

18048 Part-to-Whole/Growth or Evolution

18029 Taxi/Travel

18034 Danger/Poison/Pirates

18039 Search

18044 Selected/Desirable

18049 Bar Chart/Growth

18030 Travel/Customs

18035 Danger/High Voltage

18040 Take Notice

18045 Deselected/Not Desirable

18050 Line Graph/Growth/Finance

Chromatic Concepts

WHILE THE PERCEPTION OF COLOR may be highly subjective, there is no denying its power to stimulate and influence us. Even the most seasoned designers, however, are often at a loss when selecting colors, especially when the budget is tight and printing is at a premium. The first few categories here offer purely formal options for two- and three-color palettes—sets of colors chosen as partners because their optical interactions are especially dynamic. Two-color palettes are excellent starting points for branding or identity programs—if a given project already comes with a corporate color or two, one of the simple palettes here may be used for support. Even when full-color printing is an option, limiting one's color palette to two or three colors will create a stronger impression. Audiences' emotional and cultural expectations play important roles in developing color for products and services, as well as for projects of a metaphorical nature. Colors based on time periods, moods, age groups, and concepts as diverse as health care and telecommunications, men's grooming, and forestry are distilled here into palettes that you can build on to create complex color systems in any project.

TWO-COLOR PALETTES *Formal*

19001

C 0
M 20
Y 100
K 0

C 22
M 25
Y 0
K 0

Complements

19002

C 0
M 43
Y 100
K 0

C 35
M 23
Y 0
K 0

Complements

19003

C 3
M 58
Y 100
K 0

C 47
M 22
Y 0
K 0

Complements

19004

C 0
M 78
Y 100
K 0

C 67
M 11
Y 0
K 0

Complements

19005

C 6
M 85
Y 100
K 1

C 100
M 16
Y 31
K 0

Complements

19006

C 13
M 100
Y 89
K 4

C 100
M 15
Y 60
K 2

Complements

19007

C 25
M 23
Y 54
K 0

C 28
M 27
Y 12
K 0

Complements

19008

C 23
M 34
Y 64
K 0

C 35
M 25
Y 13
K 0

Complements

19009

C 21
M 38
Y 58
K 1

C 41
M 25
Y 15
K 0

Complements

19010

C 24
M 49
Y 55
K 2

C 45
M 25
Y 25
K 0

Complements

19011

C 24
M 58
Y 58
K 4

C 56
M 25
Y 31
K 1

Complements

19012

C 28
M 70
Y 48
K 7

C 56
M 33
Y 42
K 4

Complements

19013

C 14
M 100
Y 42
K 0

C 98
M 9
Y 100
K 0

Complements

19014

C 32
M 96
Y 0
K 0

C 42
M 25
Y 100
K 3

Complements

19015

C 55
M 89
Y 0
K 0

C 27
M 18
Y 100
K 2

Complements

19016

C 71
M 83
Y 0
K 0

C 7
M 26
Y 88
K 0

Complements

19017

C 70
M 70
Y 0
K 0

C 15
M 55
Y 100
K 2

Complements

19018

C 100
M 88
Y 12
K 6

C 23
M 84
Y 100
K 15

Complements

19019

C 31
M 71
Y 31
K 2

C 59
M 35
Y 51
K 7

Complements

19020

C 43
M 67
Y 23
K 2

C 41
M 30
Y 62
K 3

Complements

19021

C 53
M 66
Y 24
K 4

C 20
M 16
Y 53
K 0

Complements

19022

C 60
M 62
Y 21
K 2

C 28
M 32
Y 54
K 0

Complements

19023

C 60
M 56
Y 18
K 1

C 25
M 34
Y 45
K 0

Complements

19024

C 78
M 61
Y 31
K 10

C 36
M 45
Y 51
K 5

Complements

19025

C 100
M 45
Y 16
K 1

C 5
M 64
Y 100
K 0

Complements

19026

C 100
M 45
Y 36
K 12

C 35
M 84
Y 100
K 0

Complements

19027

C 100
M 35
Y 48
K 12

C 25
M 86
Y 98
K 1

Complements

19028

C 100
M 11
Y 82
K 1

C 15
M 94
Y 93
K 2

Complements

19029

C 70
M 11
Y 100
K 1

C 10
M 92
Y 4
K 0

Complements

19030

C 35
M 11
Y 100
K 0

C 13
M 58
Y 0
K 0

Complements

19031

C 64
M 38
Y 20
K 12

C 21
M 33
Y 43
K 0

Complements

19032

C 70
M 43
Y 42
K 10

C 27
M 56
Y 57
K 6

Complements

19033

C 65
M 44
Y 47
K 13

C 35
M 52
Y 48
K 6

Complements

19034

C 60
M 37
Y 59
K 8

C 31
M 53
Y 44
K 0

Complements

19035

C 52
M 29
Y 55
K 4

C 24
M 47
Y 15
K 0

Complements

19036

C 31
M 18
Y 56
K 0

C 18
M 31
Y 10
K 0

Complements

A simple, yet rich, chromatic relationship between two colors can be the foundation for a strong color language, whether used literally by printing in two spot-ink colors or limiting oneself in a process-color project. The colors in each pair may be tinted or overprinted to produce color families. The values of all the swatches are dark enough to be used for type, as well as imagery.

TWO-COLOR PALETTES *One Color + Neutral*

20001 C 0 M 20 Y 100 K 0 / C 36 M 35 Y 38 K 1 — Warm Neutral	**20007** C 25 M 23 Y 54 K 0 / C 36 M 35 Y 38 K 1 — Warm Neutral	**20013** C 14 M 100 Y 42 K 1 / C 36 M 35 Y 38 K 1 — Warm Neutral
20019 C 36 M 67 Y 35 K 2 / C 36 M 35 Y 38 K 1 — Warm Neutral	**20025** C 100 M 45 Y 16 K 1 / C 36 M 35 Y 38 K 1 — Warm Neutral	**20031** C 60 M 39 Y 24 K 12 / C 36 M 35 Y 38 K 1 — Warm Neutral
20002 C 0 M 43 Y 100 K 0 / C 36 M 35 Y 38 K 1 — Warm Neutral	**20008** C 23 M 34 Y 64 K 1 / C 36 M 35 Y 38 K 1 — Warm Neutral	**20014** C 32 M 96 Y 0 K 0 / C 36 M 35 Y 38 K 1 — Warm Neutral
20020 C 44 M 63 Y 29 K 2 / C 36 M 35 Y 38 K 1 — Warm Neutral	**20026** C 100 M 45 Y 36 K 12 / C 36 M 35 Y 38 K 1 — Warm Neutral	**20032** C 67 M 45 Y 44 K 10 / C 36 M 35 Y 38 K 1 — Warm Neutral
20003 C 3 M 58 Y 100 K 0 / C 36 M 35 Y 38 K 1 — Warm Neutral	**20009** C 21 M 38 Y 58 K 1 / C 36 M 35 Y 38 K 1 — Warm Neutral	**20015** C 55 M 89 Y 0 K 0 / C 36 M 35 Y 38 K 1 — Warm Neutral
20021 C 52 M 62 Y 29 K 4 / C 36 M 35 Y 38 K 1 — Warm Neutral	**20027** C 100 M 35 Y 48 K 12 / C 36 M 35 Y 38 K 1 — Warm Neutral	**20033** C 64 M 45 Y 49 K 13 / C 36 M 35 Y 38 K 1 — Warm Neutral
20004 C 0 M 78 Y 100 K 0 / C 36 M 35 Y 38 K 1 — Warm Neutral	**20010** C 24 M 49 Y 55 K 2 / C 36 M 35 Y 38 K 1 — Warm Neutral	**20016** C 71 M 83 Y 0 K 0 / C 36 M 35 Y 38 K 2 — Warm Neutral
20022 C 57 M 58 Y 26 K 3 / C 36 M 35 Y 38 K 1 — Warm Neutral	**20028** C 100 M 11 Y 82 K 1 / C 36 M 35 Y 38 K 1 — Warm Neutral	**20034** C 58 M 39 Y 57 K 8 / C 36 M 35 Y 38 K 1 — Warm Neutral
20005 C 6 M 85 Y 100 K 0 / C 36 M 35 Y 38 K 2 — Warm Neutral	**20011** C 24 M 58 Y 58 K 4 / C 36 M 35 Y 38 K 1 — Warm Neutral	**20017** C 70 M 70 Y 0 K 0 / C 36 M 35 Y 38 K 1 — Warm Neutral
20023 C 56 M 53 Y 24 K 1 / C 36 M 35 Y 38 K 1 — Warm Neutral	**20029** C 70 M 11 Y 100 K 0 / C 36 M 35 Y 38 K 1 — Warm Neutral	**20035** C 51 M 31 Y 53 K 4 / C 36 M 35 Y 38 K 1 — Warm Neutral
20006 C 13 M 100 Y 89 K 4 / C 36 M 35 Y 38 K 1 — Warm Neutral	**20012** C 28 M 70 Y 48 K 7 / C 36 M 35 Y 38 K 1 — Warm Neutral	**20018** C 100 M 88 Y 12 K 6 / C 36 M 35 Y 38 K 1 — Warm Neutral
20024 C 73 M 60 Y 36 K 10 / C 36 M 35 Y 38 K 1 — Warm Neutral	**20030** C 35 M 11 Y 100 K 0 / C 36 M 35 Y 38 K 1 — Warm Neutral	**20036** C 32 M 21 Y 53 K 0 / C 36 M 35 Y 38 K 1 — Warm Neutral

For a bold and very specific color impression, combine a saturated color with a neutral color—instead of with black, which can deaden the chromatic intensity of other colors with which it is juxtaposed. Each of the vibrant colors is shown twice: on the left page paired with a warm neutral gray, and on the right page paired with a cool neutral gray, to show the effect of temperature difference.

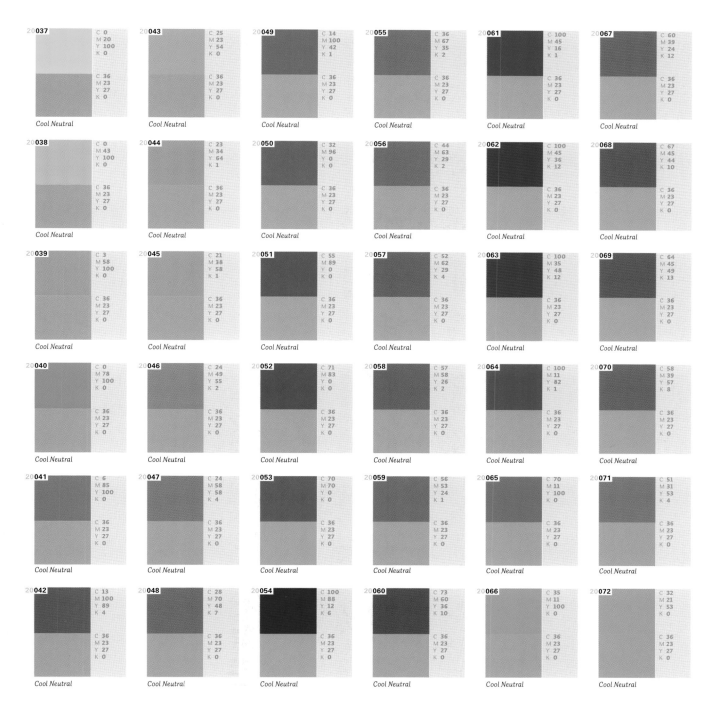

20 **037**	20 **043**	20 **049**	20 **055**	20 **061**	20 **067**
C 0 / M 20 / Y 100 / K 0 — C 36 / M 23 / Y 27 / K 0	C 25 / M 23 / Y 54 / K 0 — C 36 / M 23 / Y 27 / K 0	C 14 / M 100 / Y 42 / K 1 — C 36 / M 23 / Y 27 / K 0	C 36 / M 67 / Y 35 / K 2 — C 36 / M 23 / Y 27 / K 0	C 100 / M 45 / Y 16 / K 1 — C 36 / M 23 / Y 27 / K 0	C 60 / M 39 / Y 24 / K 12 — C 36 / M 23 / Y 27 / K 0
Cool Neutral	*Cool Neutral*	*Cool Neutral*	*Cool Neutral*	*Cool Neutral*	*Cool Neutral*

20 **038**	20 **044**	20 **050**	20 **056**	20 **062**	20 **068**
C 0 / M 43 / Y 100 / K 0 — C 36 / M 23 / Y 27 / K 0	C 23 / M 34 / Y 64 / K 1 — C 36 / M 23 / Y 27 / K 0	C 32 / M 96 / Y 0 / K 0 — C 36 / M 23 / Y 27 / K 0	C 44 / M 63 / Y 29 / K 2 — C 36 / M 23 / Y 27 / K 0	C 100 / M 45 / Y 36 / K 12 — C 36 / M 23 / Y 27 / K 0	C 67 / M 45 / Y 44 / K 10 — C 36 / M 23 / Y 27 / K 0
Cool Neutral	*Cool Neutral*	*Cool Neutral*	*Cool Neutral*	*Cool Neutral*	*Cool Neutral*

20 **039**	20 **045**	20 **051**	20 **057**	20 **063**	20 **069**
C 3 / M 58 / Y 100 / K 0 — C 36 / M 23 / Y 27 / K 0	C 21 / M 38 / Y 58 / K 1 — C 36 / M 23 / Y 27 / K 0	C 55 / M 89 / Y 0 / K 0 — C 36 / M 23 / Y 27 / K 0	C 52 / M 62 / Y 29 / K 4 — C 36 / M 23 / Y 27 / K 0	C 100 / M 35 / Y 48 / K 12 — C 36 / M 23 / Y 27 / K 0	C 64 / M 45 / Y 49 / K 13 — C 36 / M 23 / Y 27 / K 0
Cool Neutral	*Cool Neutral*	*Cool Neutral*	*Cool Neutral*	*Cool Neutral*	*Cool Neutral*

20 **040**	20 **046**	20 **052**	20 **058**	20 **064**	20 **070**
C 0 / M 78 / Y 100 / K 0 — C 36 / M 23 / Y 27 / K 0	C 24 / M 49 / Y 55 / K 2 — C 36 / M 23 / Y 27 / K 0	C 71 / M 83 / Y 0 / K 0 — C 36 / M 23 / Y 27 / K 0	C 57 / M 58 / Y 26 / K 2 — C 36 / M 23 / Y 27 / K 0	C 100 / M 11 / Y 82 / K 1 — C 36 / M 23 / Y 27 / K 0	C 58 / M 39 / Y 57 / K 8 — C 36 / M 23 / Y 27 / K 0
Cool Neutral	*Cool Neutral*	*Cool Neutral*	*Cool Neutral*	*Cool Neutral*	*Cool Neutral*

20 **041**	20 **047**	20 **053**	20 **059**	20 **065**	20 **071**
C 6 / M 85 / Y 100 / K 0 — C 36 / M 23 / Y 27 / K 0	C 24 / M 58 / Y 58 / K 4 — C 36 / M 23 / Y 27 / K 0	C 70 / M 70 / Y 0 / K 0 — C 36 / M 23 / Y 27 / K 0	C 56 / M 53 / Y 24 / K 1 — C 36 / M 23 / Y 27 / K 0	C 70 / M 11 / Y 100 / K 0 — C 36 / M 23 / Y 27 / K 0	C 51 / M 31 / Y 53 / K 4 — C 36 / M 23 / Y 27 / K 0
Cool Neutral	*Cool Neutral*	*Cool Neutral*	*Cool Neutral*	*Cool Neutral*	*Cool Neutral*

20 **042**	20 **048**	20 **054**	20 **060**	20 **066**	20 **072**
C 13 / M 100 / Y 89 / K 4 — C 36 / M 23 / Y 27 / K 0	C 28 / M 70 / Y 48 / K 7 — C 36 / M 23 / Y 27 / K 0	C 100 / M 88 / Y 12 / K 6 — C 36 / M 23 / Y 27 / K 0	C 73 / M 60 / Y 36 / K 10 — C 36 / M 23 / Y 27 / K 0	C 35 / M 11 / Y 100 / K 0 — C 36 / M 23 / Y 27 / K 0	C 32 / M 21 / Y 53 / K 0 — C 36 / M 23 / Y 27 / K 0
Cool Neutral	*Cool Neutral*	*Cool Neutral*	*Cool Neutral*	*Cool Neutral*	*Cool Neutral*

THREE-COLOR PALETTES *Formal*

21

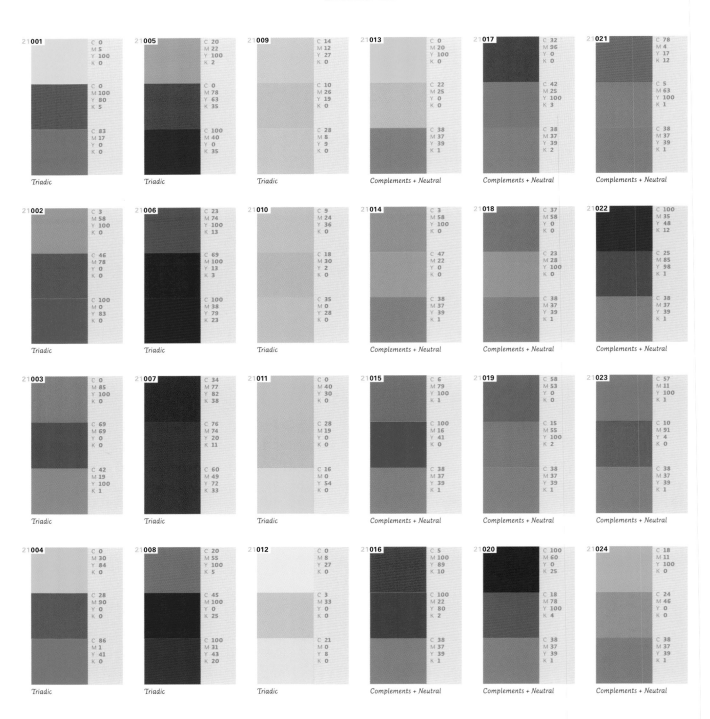

21001
C 0 / M 5 / Y 100 / K 0
C 0 / M 100 / Y 80 / K 5
C 83 / M 17 / Y 0 / K 0
Triadic

21005
C 20 / M 22 / Y 100 / K 2
C 0 / M 78 / Y 63 / K 35
C 100 / M 40 / Y 0 / K 35
Triadic

21009
C 14 / M 12 / Y 27 / K 0
C 10 / M 26 / Y 19 / K 0
C 28 / M 8 / Y 9 / K 0
Triadic

21013
C 0 / M 20 / Y 100 / K 0
C 22 / M 25 / Y 0 / K 0
C 38 / M 37 / Y 39 / K 1
Complements + Neutral

21017
C 32 / M 96 / Y 0 / K 0
C 42 / M 25 / Y 100 / K 3
C 38 / M 37 / Y 39 / K 2
Complements + Neutral

21021
C 78 / M 4 / Y 17 / K 12
C 5 / M 63 / Y 100 / K 1
C 38 / M 37 / Y 39 / K 1
Complements + Neutral

21002
C 3 / M 58 / Y 100 / K 0
C 46 / M 78 / Y 0 / K 0
C 100 / M 0 / Y 83 / K 0
Triadic

21006
C 23 / M 74 / Y 100 / K 13
C 69 / M 100 / Y 13 / K 3
C 100 / M 38 / Y 79 / K 23
Triadic

21010
C 9 / M 24 / Y 36 / K 0
C 18 / M 30 / Y 2 / K 0
C 35 / M 0 / Y 28 / K 0
Triadic

21014
C 3 / M 58 / Y 100 / K 0
C 47 / M 22 / Y 0 / K 0
C 38 / M 37 / Y 39 / K 1
Complements + Neutral

21018
C 37 / M 58 / Y 0 / K 0
C 23 / M 28 / Y 100 / K 0
C 38 / M 37 / Y 39 / K 1
Complements + Neutral

21022
C 100 / M 35 / Y 48 / K 12
C 25 / M 85 / Y 98 / K 1
C 38 / M 37 / Y 39 / K 1
Complements + Neutral

21003
C 0 / M 85 / Y 100 / K 0
C 69 / M 69 / Y 0 / K 0
C 42 / M 19 / Y 100 / K 1
Triadic

21007
C 34 / M 77 / Y 82 / K 38
C 76 / M 74 / Y 20 / K 11
C 60 / M 49 / Y 72 / K 33
Triadic

21011
C 0 / M 40 / Y 30 / K 0
C 28 / M 19 / Y 0 / K 0
C 16 / M 0 / Y 54 / K 0
Triadic

21015
C 6 / M 79 / Y 100 / K 1
C 100 / M 16 / Y 41 / K 0
C 38 / M 37 / Y 39 / K 1
Complements + Neutral

21019
C 58 / M 53 / Y 0 / K 0
C 15 / M 55 / Y 100 / K 2
C 38 / M 37 / Y 39 / K 1
Complements + Neutral

21023
C 57 / M 11 / Y 100 / K 1
C 10 / M 91 / Y 4 / K 0
C 38 / M 37 / Y 39 / K 1
Complements + Neutral

21004
C 0 / M 30 / Y 84 / K 0
C 28 / M 90 / Y 0 / K 0
C 86 / M 1 / Y 41 / K 0
Triadic

21008
C 20 / M 55 / Y 100 / K 5
C 45 / M 100 / Y 0 / K 25
C 100 / M 31 / Y 43 / K 20
Triadic

21012
C 0 / M 8 / Y 27 / K 0
C 3 / M 33 / Y 0 / K 0
C 21 / M 0 / Y 8 / K 0
Triadic

21016
C 5 / M 100 / Y 89 / K 10
C 100 / M 22 / Y 80 / K 2
C 38 / M 37 / Y 39 / K 1
Complements + Neutral

21020
C 100 / M 60 / Y 0 / K 25
C 18 / M 78 / Y 100 / K 4
C 38 / M 37 / Y 39 / K 1
Complements + Neutral

21024
C 18 / M 11 / Y 100 / K 0
C 24 / M 46 / Y 0 / K 0
C 38 / M 37 / Y 39 / K 1
Complements + Neutral

The palettes shown here offer complex optical relationships. The triads—or split complements—can be individually tinted to soften their optical activity, and even combined in overprinting to produce exotic secondary colors and neutrals. Two complements, paired with a warm neutral, also present dynamic interaction. The analogous sets, in contrast, provide a more in-depth experience of one color feeling; use them as shown, or as a backdrop for a contrasting complement.

21025
C 1 M 13 Y 100 K 0
C 3 M 58 Y 100 K 0
C 11 M 85 Y 97 K 2
Analogous

21029
C 23 M 38 Y 100 K 2
C 22 M 67 Y 100 K 9
C 31 M 92 Y 82 K 39
Analogous

21033
C 1 M 13 Y 100 K 0
C 3 M 58 Y 100 K 0
C 49 M 70 Y 0 K 0
Analogous + Complement

21037
C 84 M 56 Y 0 K 0
C 100 M 36 Y 25 K 2
C 18 M 80 Y 100 K 7
Analogous + Complement

21041
C 0 M 13 Y 100 K 0
C 3 M 58 Y 100 K 0
C 38 M 37 Y 39 K 1
Analogous + Neutral

21045
C 84 M 56 Y 0 K 0
C 100 M 36 Y 25 K 2
C 38 M 37 Y 39 K 1
Analogous + Neutral

21026
C 0 M 75 Y 90 K 13
C 36 M 100 Y 7 K 5
C 69 M 100 Y 9 K 1
Analogous

21030
C 26 M 85 Y 96 K 21
C 56 M 96 Y 32 K 16
C 84 M 100 Y 16 K 9
Analogous

21034
C 0 M 75 Y 90 K 13
C 36 M 100 Y 7 K 5
C 97 M 9 Y 100 K 1
Analogous + Complement

21038
C 100 M 36 Y 25 K 1
C 100 M 11 Y 82 K 1
C 12 M 61 Y 100 K 1
Analogous + Complement

21042
C 0 M 75 Y 90 K 13
C 36 M 100 Y 7 K 5
C 38 M 37 Y 39 K 1
Analogous + Neutral

21046
C 100 M 36 Y 25 K 2
C 100 M 11 Y 82 K 1
C 38 M 37 Y 39 K 1
Analogous + Neutral

21027
C 84 M 100 Y 26 K 3
C 77 M 82 Y 2 K 0
C 84 M 56 Y 0 K 0
Analogous

21031
C 36 M 56 Y 0 K 0
C 58 M 55 Y 0 K 0
C 33 M 16 Y 1 K 0
Analogous

21035
C 36 M 11 Y 7 K 5
C 69 M 100 Y 9 K 1
C 23 M 38 Y 100 K 2
Analogous + Complement

21039
C 100 M 11 Y 82 K 1
C 50 M 27 Y 100 K 6
C 23 M 100 Y 66 K 13
Analogous + Complement

21043
C 36 M 100 Y 7 K 5
C 69 M 100 Y 9 K 1
C 38 M 37 Y 39 K 1
Analogous + Neutral

21047
C 100 M 11 Y 82 K 1
C 50 M 27 Y 100 K 6
C 38 M 37 Y 39 K 1
Analogous + Neutral

21028
C 100 M 31 Y 24 K 1
C 100 M 11 Y 82 K 1
C 42 M 19 Y 100 K 1
Analogous

21032
C 46 M 11 Y 18 K 0
C 28 M 0 Y 59 K 0
C 11 M 4 Y 58 K 0
Analogous

21036
C 77 M 82 Y 2 K 0
C 84 M 56 Y 0 K 0
C 24 M 67 Y 94 K 0
Analogous + Complement

21040
C 29 M 9 Y 86 K 6
C 5 M 27 Y 80 K 1
C 10 M 43 Y 0 K 0
Analogous + Complement

21044
C 77 M 82 Y 2 K 0
C 84 M 56 Y 0 K 0
C 38 M 37 Y 39 K 1
Analogous + Neutral

21048
C 29 M 9 Y 86 K 6
C 5 M 27 Y 80 K 1
C 38 M 37 Y 39 K 1
Analogous + Neutral

THREE-COLOR PALETTES *Monochrome*

22

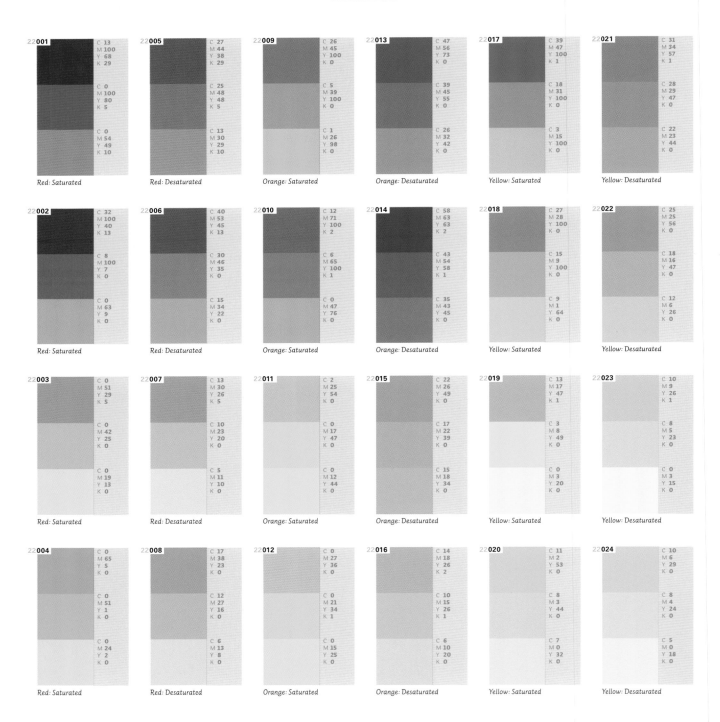

22001
C 13 / M 100 / Y 68 / K 29
C 0 / M 100 / Y 80 / K 5
C 0 / M 54 / Y 49 / K 10
Red: Saturated

22005
C 27 / M 44 / Y 38 / K 29
C 25 / M 48 / Y 48 / K 5
C 13 / M 26 / Y 29 / K 10
Red: Desaturated

22009
C 26 / M 45 / Y 100 / K 0
C 5 / M 39 / Y 100 / K 0
C 1 / M 26 / Y 98 / K 0
Orange: Saturated

22013
C 47 / M 56 / Y 73 / K 0
C 39 / M 45 / Y 55 / K 0
C 26 / M 32 / Y 42 / K 0
Orange: Desaturated

22017
C 39 / M 47 / Y 100 / K 1
C 18 / M 31 / Y 100 / K 0
C 3 / M 15 / Y 100 / K 0
Yellow: Saturated

22021
C 31 / M 34 / Y 57 / K 1
C 28 / M 29 / Y 47 / K 0
C 22 / M 23 / Y 44 / K 0
Yellow: Desaturated

22002
C 32 / M 100 / Y 40 / K 13
C 8 / M 100 / Y 7 / K 0
C 0 / M 63 / Y 9 / K 0
Red: Saturated

22006
C 40 / M 53 / Y 45 / K 13
C 30 / M 46 / Y 35 / K 0
C 15 / M 34 / Y 22 / K 0
Red: Desaturated

22010
C 12 / M 71 / Y 100 / K 2
C 6 / M 65 / Y 100 / K 1
C 0 / M 47 / Y 76 / K 0
Orange: Saturated

22014
C 58 / M 63 / Y 63 / K 2
C 43 / M 54 / Y 58 / K 1
C 35 / M 43 / Y 45 / K 0
Orange: Desaturated

22018
C 27 / M 28 / Y 100 / K 0
C 15 / M 9 / Y 100 / K 0
C 9 / M 1 / Y 64 / K 0
Yellow: Saturated

22022
C 25 / M 25 / Y 56 / K 0
C 18 / M 16 / Y 47 / K 0
C 12 / M 6 / Y 26 / K 0
Yellow: Desaturated

22003
C 0 / M 51 / Y 29 / K 5
C 0 / M 42 / Y 25 / K 0
C 0 / M 19 / Y 13 / K 0
Red: Saturated

22007
C 13 / M 30 / Y 26 / K 5
C 10 / M 23 / Y 20 / K 0
C 5 / M 11 / Y 10 / K 0
Red: Desaturated

22011
C 2 / M 25 / Y 54 / K 0
C 0 / M 17 / Y 47 / K 0
C 0 / M 12 / Y 44 / K 0
Orange: Saturated

22015
C 22 / M 26 / Y 49 / K 0
C 17 / M 22 / Y 39 / K 0
C 15 / M 18 / Y 34 / K 0
Orange: Desaturated

22019
C 13 / M 17 / Y 47 / K 1
C 3 / M 8 / Y 49 / K 0
C 0 / M 3 / Y 20 / K 0
Yellow: Saturated

22023
C 10 / M 9 / Y 26 / K 1
C 8 / M 5 / Y 23 / K 0
C 0 / M 3 / Y 15 / K 0
Yellow: Desaturated

22004
C 0 / M 65 / Y 5 / K 0
C 0 / M 51 / Y 1 / K 0
C 0 / M 24 / Y 2 / K 0
Red: Saturated

22008
C 17 / M 38 / Y 23 / K 0
C 12 / M 27 / Y 16 / K 0
C 6 / M 13 / Y 8 / K 0
Red: Desaturated

22012
C 0 / M 27 / Y 36 / K 0
C 0 / M 21 / Y 34 / K 1
C 0 / M 15 / Y 25 / K 0
Orange: Saturated

22016
C 14 / M 18 / Y 26 / K 2
C 10 / M 15 / Y 26 / K 1
C 6 / M 10 / Y 20 / K 0
Orange: Desaturated

22020
C 11 / M 2 / Y 53 / K 0
C 8 / M 3 / Y 44 / K 0
C 7 / M 0 / Y 32 / K 0
Yellow: Saturated

22024
C 10 / M 6 / Y 29 / K 0
C 8 / M 4 / Y 24 / K 0
C 5 / M 0 / Y 18 / K 0
Yellow: Desaturated

The three components of each of these palettes are all of the same base hue, with variation expressed in terms of temperature, saturation, and value changes. The selections on the left page are warm tonalities; the ones on the right are cool combinations. These restrained combinations are rich for use alone, in combination, or as the base upon which other two- or three-color palettes can interact.

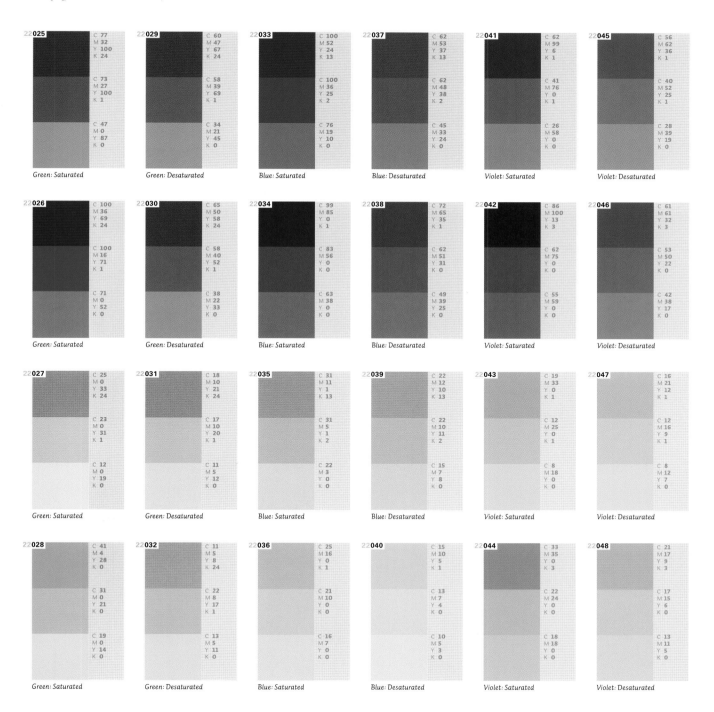

22**025**
C 77 M 32 Y 100 K 24
C 73 M 27 Y 100 K 1
C 47 M 0 Y 87 K 0
Green: Saturated

22**029**
C 60 M 47 Y 67 K 24
C 58 M 39 Y 69 K 1
C 34 M 21 Y 45 K 0
Green: Desaturated

22**033**
C 100 M 52 Y 24 K 13
C 100 M 36 Y 25 K 2
C 76 M 19 Y 10 K 0
Blue: Saturated

22**037**
C 62 M 53 Y 37 K 13
C 62 M 48 Y 38 K 2
C 45 M 33 Y 24 K 0
Blue: Desaturated

22**041**
C 62 M 99 Y 6 K 1
C 41 M 76 Y 0 K 1
C 26 M 58 Y 0 K 0
Violet: Saturated

22**045**
C 56 M 62 Y 36 K 1
C 40 M 52 Y 25 K 1
C 28 M 39 Y 19 K 0
Violet: Desaturated

22**026**
C 100 M 36 Y 69 K 24
C 100 M 16 Y 71 K 1
C 71 M 0 Y 52 K 0
Green: Saturated

22**030**
C 65 M 50 Y 58 K 24
C 58 M 40 Y 52 K 1
C 38 M 22 Y 33 K 0
Green: Desaturated

22**034**
C 99 M 85 Y 0 K 1
C 83 M 56 Y 0 K 0
C 63 M 38 Y 0 K 0
Blue: Saturated

22**038**
C 72 M 65 Y 35 K 1
C 62 M 51 Y 31 K 0
C 49 M 39 Y 25 K 0
Blue: Desaturated

22**042**
C 86 M 100 Y 13 K 3
C 62 M 75 Y 0 K 0
C 55 M 59 Y 0 K 0
Violet: Saturated

22**046**
C 61 M 61 Y 32 K 3
C 53 M 50 Y 22 K 0
C 42 M 38 Y 17 K 0
Violet: Desaturated

22**027**
C 25 M 0 Y 33 K 24
C 23 M 0 Y 31 K 1
C 12 M 0 Y 19 K 0
Green: Saturated

22**031**
C 18 M 10 Y 21 K 24
C 17 M 10 Y 20 K 1
C 11 M 5 Y 12 K 0
Green: Desaturated

22**035**
C 31 M 11 Y 1 K 13
C 31 M 5 Y 1 K 2
C 22 M 3 Y 0 K 0
Blue: Saturated

22**039**
C 22 M 12 Y 10 K 13
C 22 M 10 Y 11 K 2
C 15 M 7 Y 8 K 0
Blue: Desaturated

22**043**
C 19 M 33 Y 0 K 1
C 12 M 25 Y 0 K 1
C 8 M 18 Y 0 K 0
Violet: Saturated

22**047**
C 16 M 21 Y 12 K 1
C 12 M 16 Y 9 K 1
C 8 M 12 Y 7 K 0
Violet: Desaturated

22**028**
C 41 M 4 Y 28 K 0
C 31 M 0 Y 21 K 0
C 19 M 0 Y 14 K 0
Green: Saturated

22**032**
C 11 M 5 Y 8 K 24
C 22 M 8 Y 17 K 1
C 13 M 5 Y 11 K 0
Green: Desaturated

22**036**
C 25 M 16 Y 0 K 1
C 21 M 10 Y 0 K 0
C 16 M 7 Y 0 K 0
Blue: Saturated

22**040**
C 15 M 10 Y 5 K 1
C 13 M 7 Y 4 K 0
C 10 M 5 Y 3 K 0
Blue: Desaturated

22**044**
C 33 M 35 Y 0 K 3
C 22 M 24 Y 0 K 0
C 18 M 18 Y 0 K 0
Violet: Saturated

22**048**
C 21 M 17 Y 9 K 3
C 17 M 15 Y 6 K 0
C 13 M 11 Y 5 K 0
Violet: Desaturated

COLOR SYSTEMS *One Variable*

23

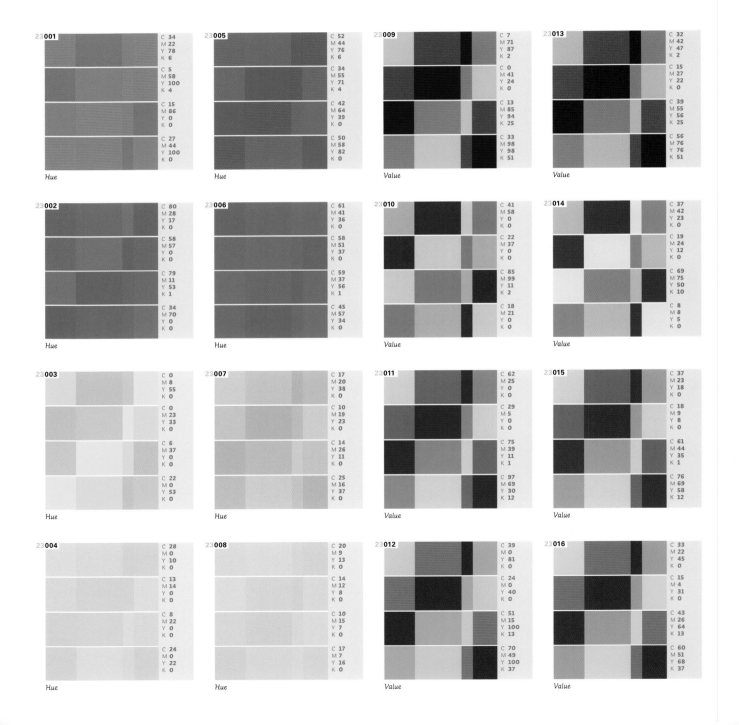

23001

C	34
M	22
Y	78
K	6

C	5
M	58
Y	100
K	4

C	15
M	86
Y	0
K	0

C	27
M	44
Y	100
K	0

Hue

23002

C	80
M	28
Y	17
K	0

C	58
M	57
Y	0
K	0

C	79
M	11
Y	53
K	1

C	34
M	70
Y	0
K	0

Hue

23003

C	0
M	8
Y	55
K	0

C	0
M	23
Y	33
K	0

C	6
M	37
Y	0
K	0

C	22
M	0
Y	53
K	0

Hue

23004

C	28
M	9
Y	10
K	0

C	13
M	14
Y	0
K	0

C	8
M	22
Y	0
K	0

C	24
M	0
Y	22
K	0

Hue

23005

C	52
M	44
Y	76
K	6

C	34
M	55
Y	71
K	4

C	42
M	64
Y	39
K	0

C	50
M	58
Y	82
K	0

Hue

23006

C	61
M	41
Y	36
K	0

C	58
M	51
Y	37
K	0

C	59
M	37
Y	56
K	1

C	45
M	57
Y	34
K	0

Hue

23007

C	17
M	20
Y	38
K	0

C	10
M	19
Y	23
K	0

C	14
M	26
Y	11
K	0

C	25
M	16
Y	37
K	0

Hue

23008

C	20
M	0
Y	13
K	0

C	14
M	12
Y	8
K	0

C	10
M	15
Y	7
K	0

C	17
M	7
Y	16
K	0

Hue

23009

C	7
M	71
Y	87
K	2

C	0
M	41
Y	24
K	0

C	13
M	85
Y	94
K	25

C	33
M	98
Y	98
K	51

Value

23010

C	41
M	58
Y	0
K	0

C	22
M	37
Y	0
K	0

C	85
M	99
Y	11
K	2

C	18
M	21
Y	0
K	0

Value

23011

C	62
M	25
Y	0
K	0

C	29
M	5
Y	0
K	0

C	75
M	39
Y	11
K	1

C	97
M	69
Y	30
K	12

Value

23012

C	39
M	0
Y	81
K	0

C	24
M	0
Y	40
K	0

C	51
M	15
Y	100
K	13

C	70
M	49
Y	100
K	37

Value

23013

C	32
M	42
Y	47
K	2

C	15
M	27
Y	22
K	0

C	39
M	55
Y	56
K	25

C	56
M	76
Y	76
K	51

Value

23014

C	37
M	42
Y	23
K	0

C	19
M	24
Y	12
K	0

C	69
M	75
Y	50
K	10

C	8
M	8
Y	5
K	0

Value

23015

C	37
M	23
Y	18
K	0

C	18
M	9
Y	8
K	0

C	61
M	44
Y	35
K	1

C	76
M	69
Y	58
K	12

Value

23016

C	33
M	22
Y	45
K	0

C	15
M	4
Y	31
K	0

C	43
M	26
Y	64
K	13

C	60
M	51
Y	68
K	37

Value

In these palettes, the chromatic interaction of four components is limited by allowing only one variable—hue, value, saturation, or temperature—to change. A new variable—extension, or the volume of each component—transforms the palette into a system in which each variation shown is governed by a greater volume of one component relative to the others. Use such limited systems to vary color impression on alternating page spreads, to distinguish elements in a line of products, or to create a family of publications, such as brochures, all unique in tone yet clearly interrelated.

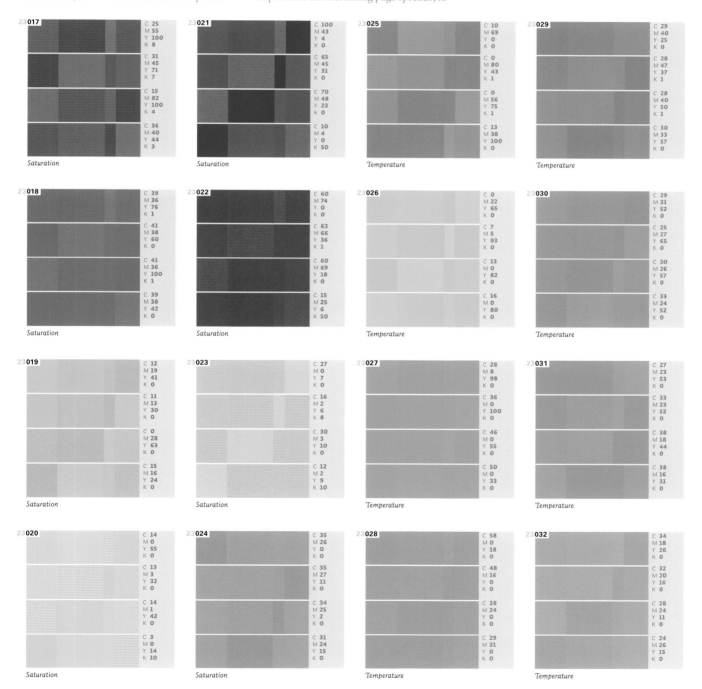

23**017**

C	25
M	55
Y	100
K	8

C	31
M	45
Y	71
K	7

C	15
M	82
Y	100
K	4

C	36
M	40
Y	44
K	3

Saturation

23**021**

C	100
M	43
Y	4
K	0

C	65
M	45
Y	31
K	0

C	70
M	48
Y	23
K	0

C	10
M	4
Y	0
K	50

Saturation

23**025**

C	10
M	69
Y	0
K	0

C	0
M	80
Y	43
K	1

C	0
M	56
Y	75
K	1

C	13
M	38
Y	100
K	0

Temperature

23**029**

C	29
M	40
Y	25
K	0

C	28
M	47
Y	37
K	1

C	28
M	40
Y	50
K	1

C	30
M	33
Y	57
K	0

Temperature

23**018**

C	39
M	36
Y	76
K	1

C	41
M	38
Y	60
K	0

C	41
M	36
Y	100
K	1

C	39
M	38
Y	42
K	0

Saturation

23**022**

C	60
M	74
Y	0
K	0

C	63
M	66
Y	36
K	1

C	60
M	69
Y	18
K	0

C	15
M	25
Y	6
K	50

Saturation

23**026**

C	0
M	22
Y	65
K	0

C	7
M	5
Y	93
K	0

C	13
M	0
Y	82
K	0

C	16
M	0
Y	80
K	0

Temperature

23**030**

C	29
M	31
Y	52
K	0

C	25
M	27
Y	65
K	0

C	30
M	26
Y	57
K	0

C	33
M	24
Y	52
K	0

Temperature

23**019**

C	12
M	19
Y	41
K	0

C	11
M	13
Y	30
K	0

C	0
M	28
Y	63
K	0

C	15
M	16
Y	24
K	0

Saturation

23**023**

C	27
M	0
Y	7
K	0

C	16
M	2
Y	6
K	8

C	30
M	3
Y	10
K	0

C	12
M	2
Y	9
K	10

Saturation

23**027**

C	28
M	8
Y	98
K	0

C	36
M	0
Y	100
K	0

C	46
M	0
Y	55
K	0

C	50
M	0
Y	33
K	0

Temperature

23**031**

C	27
M	23
Y	53
K	0

C	33
M	23
Y	52
K	0

C	38
M	18
Y	44
K	0

C	38
M	16
Y	31
K	0

Temperature

23**020**

C	14
M	0
Y	55
K	0

C	13
M	3
Y	32
K	0

C	14
M	1
Y	42
K	0

C	3
M	0
Y	14
K	10

Saturation

23**024**

C	35
M	26
Y	0
K	0

C	35
M	27
Y	11
K	0

C	34
M	25
Y	2
K	0

C	31
M	24
Y	15
K	0

Saturation

23**028**

C	58
M	0
Y	18
K	0

C	48
M	16
Y	0
K	0

C	38
M	24
Y	0
K	0

C	29
M	31
Y	0
K	0

Temperature

23**032**

C	34
M	18
Y	26
K	0

C	32
M	20
Y	16
K	0

C	28
M	24
Y	11
K	0

C	24
M	26
Y	15
K	0

Temperature

COLOR SYSTEMS *Two Variables*

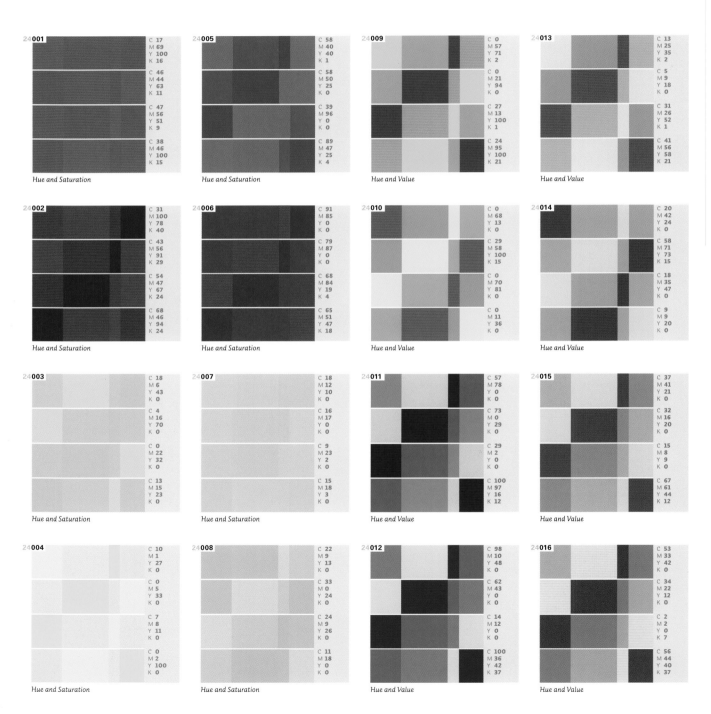

24001

C	17
M	69
Y	100
K	16

C	46
M	44
Y	63
K	11

C	47
M	56
Y	51
K	9

C	38
M	46
Y	100
K	15

Hue and Saturation

24005

C	58
M	40
Y	40
K	1

C	58
M	50
Y	25
K	0

C	39
M	96
Y	0
K	0

C	89
M	47
Y	25
K	4

Hue and Saturation

24009

C	0
M	57
Y	71
K	2

C	0
M	21
Y	94
K	0

C	27
M	13
Y	100
K	1

C	24
M	95
Y	100
K	21

Hue and Value

24013

C	13
M	25
Y	35
K	2

C	5
M	9
Y	18
K	0

C	31
M	26
Y	52
K	1

C	41
M	56
Y	58
K	21

Hue and Value

24002

C	31
M	100
Y	78
K	40

C	43
M	56
Y	91
K	29

C	54
M	47
Y	67
K	24

C	68
M	46
Y	94
K	24

Hue and Saturation

24006

C	91
M	85
Y	0
K	0

C	79
M	87
Y	0
K	0

C	68
M	84
Y	19
K	4

C	65
M	51
Y	47
K	18

Hue and Saturation

24010

C	0
M	68
Y	13
K	0

C	29
M	58
Y	100
K	15

C	0
M	70
Y	81
K	0

C	0
M	11
Y	36
K	0

Hue and Value

24014

C	20
M	42
Y	24
K	0

C	58
M	71
Y	73
K	15

C	18
M	35
Y	47
K	0

C	9
M	9
Y	20
K	0

Hue and Value

24003

C	18
M	6
Y	43
K	0

C	4
M	16
Y	70
K	0

C	0
M	22
Y	32
K	0

C	13
M	15
Y	23
K	0

Hue and Saturation

24007

C	18
M	12
Y	10
K	0

C	16
M	17
Y	0
K	0

C	9
M	23
Y	2
K	0

C	15
M	18
Y	3
K	0

Hue and Saturation

24011

C	57
M	78
Y	0
K	0

C	73
M	0
Y	29
K	0

C	29
M	2
Y	0
K	0

C	100
M	97
Y	16
K	12

Hue and Value

24015

C	37
M	41
Y	21
K	0

C	32
M	16
Y	20
K	0

C	15
M	8
Y	9
K	0

C	67
M	61
Y	44
K	12

Hue and Value

24004

C	10
M	1
Y	27
K	0

C	0
M	5
Y	33
K	0

C	7
M	8
Y	11
K	0

C	0
M	2
Y	100
K	0

Hue and Saturation

24008

C	22
M	9
Y	13
K	0

C	33
M	0
Y	24
K	0

C	24
M	9
Y	26
K	0

C	11
M	18
Y	0
K	0

Hue and Saturation

24012

C	98
M	10
Y	48
K	0

C	62
M	43
Y	0
K	0

C	14
M	12
Y	0
K	0

C	100
M	36
Y	42
K	37

Hue and Value

24016

C	53
M	33
Y	42
K	0

C	34
M	22
Y	12
K	0

C	2
M	2
Y	0
K	7

C	56
M	44
Y	40
K	37

Hue and Value

These limited color systems have increased complexity in color interaction by allowing two variables—saturation and value, or saturation and temperature, for instance—to fluctuate among a given palette's components.

Like their single-variable counterparts, these simple color systems are most useful for serial, sequential, or programmatic applications.

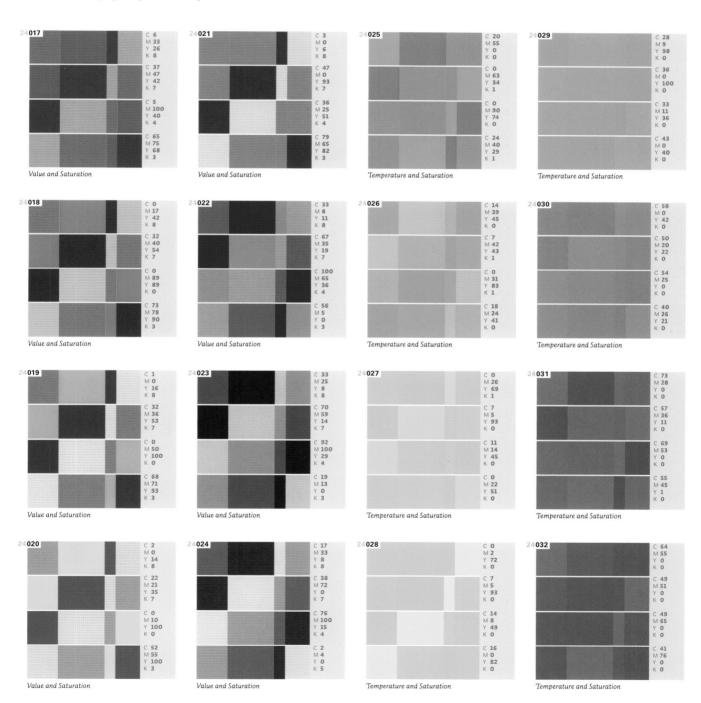

24017

C 6 / M 33 / Y 26 / K 8
C 37 / M 47 / Y 42 / K 7
C 5 / M 100 / Y 40 / K 4
C 65 / M 75 / Y 68 / K 3

Value and Saturation

24021

C 3 / M 0 / Y 6 / K 8
C 47 / M 0 / Y 93 / K 7
C 36 / M 25 / Y 51 / K 4
C 79 / M 65 / Y 82 / K 3

Value and Saturation

24025

C 20 / M 55 / Y 0 / K 0
C 0 / M 63 / Y 34 / K 1
C 0 / M 90 / Y 74 / K 0
C 24 / M 40 / Y 29 / K 1

Temperature and Saturation

24029

C 28 / M 9 / Y 98 / K 0
C 36 / M 0 / Y 100 / K 0
C 33 / M 11 / Y 36 / K 0
C 43 / M 0 / Y 40 / K 0

Temperature and Saturation

24018

C 0 / M 17 / Y 42 / K 8
C 32 / M 40 / Y 54 / K 7
C 0 / M 89 / Y 89 / K 0
C 73 / M 78 / Y 90 / K 3

Value and Saturation

24022

C 33 / M 8 / Y 11 / K 8
C 67 / M 35 / Y 19 / K 7
C 100 / M 65 / Y 36 / K 4
C 56 / M 5 / Y 0 / K 0

Value and Saturation

24026

C 14 / M 39 / Y 45 / K 0
C 7 / M 42 / Y 43 / K 1
C 0 / M 31 / Y 83 / K 1
C 18 / M 24 / Y 41 / K 0

Temperature and Saturation

24030

C 58 / M 0 / Y 42 / K 0
C 50 / M 20 / Y 22 / K 0
C 54 / M 25 / Y 0 / K 0
C 40 / M 26 / Y 21 / K 0

Temperature and Saturation

24019

C 1 / M 0 / Y 16 / K 8
C 32 / M 36 / Y 53 / K 7
C 0 / M 50 / Y 100 / K 0
C 68 / M 71 / Y 93 / K 3

Value and Saturation

24023

C 33 / M 25 / Y 8 / K 8
C 70 / M 59 / Y 14 / K 7
C 92 / M 100 / Y 29 / K 4
C 19 / M 13 / Y 0 / K 3

Value and Saturation

24027

C 0 / M 26 / Y 69 / K 1
C 7 / M 5 / Y 93 / K 0
C 11 / M 14 / Y 45 / K 0
C 0 / M 22 / Y 51 / K 0

Temperature and Saturation

24031

C 73 / M 28 / Y 0 / K 0
C 57 / M 36 / Y 11 / K 0
C 69 / M 53 / Y 0 / K 0
C 55 / M 45 / Y 1 / K 0

Temperature and Saturation

24020

C 2 / M 0 / Y 14 / K 8
C 22 / M 21 / Y 35 / K 7
C 0 / M 10 / Y 100 / K 0
C 52 / M 55 / Y 100 / K 3

Value and Saturation

24024

C 17 / M 33 / Y 8 / K 8
C 38 / M 72 / Y 0 / K 7
C 76 / M 100 / Y 15 / K 4
C 2 / M 4 / Y 0 / K 5

Value and Saturation

24028

C 0 / M 2 / Y 72 / K 0
C 7 / M 5 / Y 93 / K 0
C 14 / M 8 / Y 49 / K 0
C 16 / M 0 / Y 82 / K 0

Temperature and Saturation

24032

C 64 / M 55 / Y 0 / K 0
C 49 / M 51 / Y 0 / K 0
C 49 / M 65 / Y 0 / K 0
C 41 / M 76 / Y 0 / K 0

Temperature and Saturation

CONCEPTS *Moods, Places, Seasons*

25

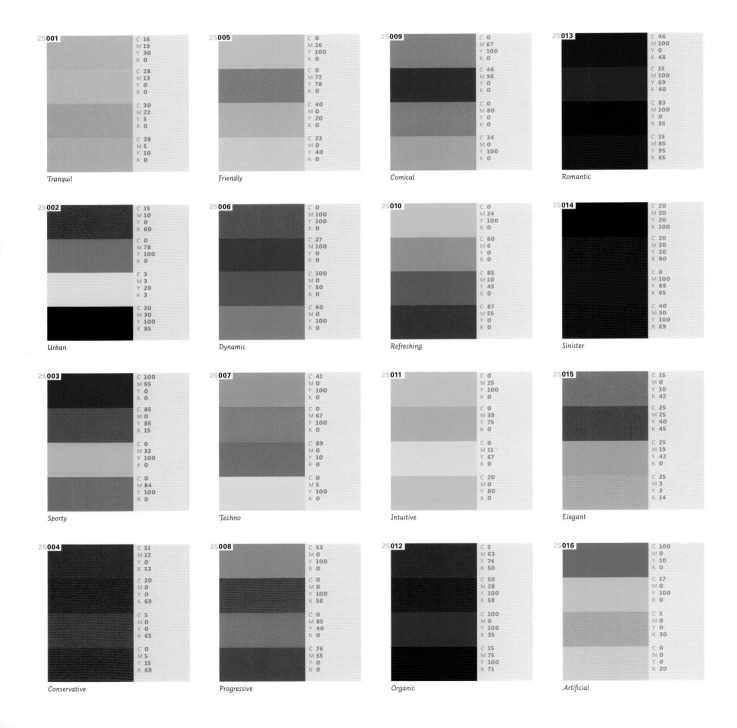

25**001**

C 16 M 19 Y 30 K 0
C 28 M 13 Y 0 K 0
C 30 M 22 Y 5 K 0
C 38 M 5 Y 10 K 0

Tranquil

25**005**

C 0 M 26 Y 100 K 0
C 0 M 72 Y 78 K 0
C 40 M 0 Y 20 K 0
C 22 M 0 Y 40 K 0

Friendly

25**009**

C 0 M 67 Y 100 K 0
C 46 M 96 Y 0 K 0
C 0 M 80 Y 0 K 0
C 34 M 0 Y 100 K 0

Comical

25**013**

C 46 M 100 Y 0 K 48
C 15 M 100 Y 69 K 40
C 83 M 100 Y 0 K 35
C 15 M 85 Y 95 K 65

Romantic

25**002**

C 15 M 10 Y 0 K 60
C 0 M 78 Y 100 K 0
C 3 M 3 Y 20 K 3
C 20 M 30 Y 100 K 85

Urban

25**006**

C 0 M 100 Y 100 K 0
C 27 M 100 Y 0 K 0
C 100 M 0 Y 50 K 0
C 60 M 0 Y 100 K 0

Dynamic

25**010**

C 0 M 24 Y 100 K 0
C 60 M 6 Y 0 K 0
C 85 M 10 Y 45 K 0
C 87 M 0 Y 0 K 0

Refreshing

25**014**

C 20 M 20 Y 20 K 100
C 20 M 20 Y 20 K 80
C 0 M 100 Y 89 K 65
C 40 M 30 Y 100 K 69

Sinister

25**003**

C 100 M 65 Y 0 K 0
C 85 M 0 Y 85 K 15
C 0 M 32 Y 100 K 0
C 0 M 84 Y 100 K 0

Sporty

25**007**

C 41 M 0 Y 100 K 0
C 0 M 67 Y 100 K 0
C 89 M 0 Y 10 K 0
C 0 M 5 Y 100 K 0

Techno

25**011**

C 0 M 25 Y 100 K 0
C 0 M 39 Y 75 K 0
C 0 M 11 Y 67 K 0
C 20 M 0 Y 80 K 0

Intuitive

25**015**

C 15 M 0 Y 10 K 42
C 25 M 25 Y 40 K 45
C 25 M 19 Y 42 K 0
C 25 M 3 Y 3 K 14

Elegant

25**004**

C 51 M 12 Y 0 K 53
C 20 M 0 Y 0 K 69
C 5 M 0 Y 0 K 65
C 0 M 5 Y 15 K 69

Conservative

25**008**

C 53 M 0 Y 100 K 0
C 0 M 0 Y 100 K 56
C 0 M 85 Y 40 K 0
C 76 M 55 Y 0 K 0

Progressive

25**012**

C 5 M 63 Y 74 K 50
C 50 M 28 Y 100 K 58
C 100 M 0 Y 100 K 35
C 15 M 0 Y 100 K 71

Organic

25**016**

C 100 M 0 Y 10 K 0
C 17 M 0 Y 100 K 0
C 5 M 0 Y 0 K 30
C 0 M 0 Y 0 K 20

Artificial

The power of color to evoke emotion or physical experience is extraordinary. These color concepts are limited palettes selected not only for their optical relationships, but also, and more importantly, the feeling they may induce. Along with emotional ideas, palettes that suggest place—distilled from various cultures' art and textiles—and time of year are displayed here.

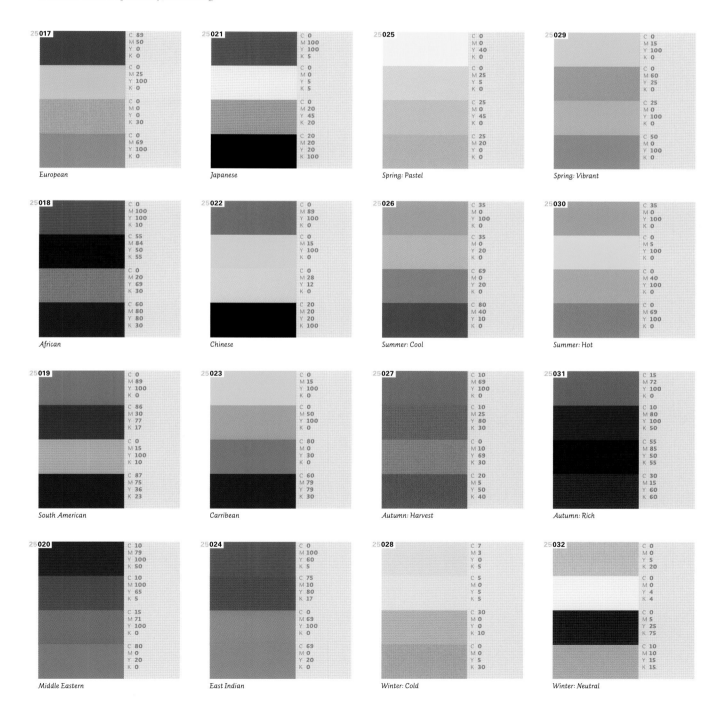

25**017**

C	89
M	50
Y	0
K	0
C	0
M	25
Y	100
K	0
C	0
M	0
Y	0
K	30
C	0
M	69
Y	100
K	0

European

25**021**

C	0
M	100
Y	100
K	5
C	0
M	0
Y	5
K	5
C	0
M	20
Y	45
K	20
C	20
M	20
Y	20
K	100

Japanese

25**025**

C	0
M	0
Y	40
K	0
C	0
M	25
Y	5
K	0
C	25
M	0
Y	45
K	0
C	25
M	20
Y	0
K	0

Spring: Pastel

25**029**

C	0
M	15
Y	100
K	0
C	0
M	60
Y	25
K	0
C	25
M	0
Y	100
K	0
C	50
M	0
Y	100
K	0

Spring: Vibrant

25**018**

C	0
M	100
Y	100
K	10
C	55
M	84
Y	50
K	55
C	0
M	20
Y	69
K	30
C	60
M	80
Y	80
K	30

African

25**022**

C	0
M	89
Y	100
K	0
C	0
M	15
Y	100
K	0
C	0
M	28
Y	12
K	0
C	20
M	20
Y	20
K	100

Chinese

25**026**

C	35
M	0
Y	100
K	0
C	35
M	0
Y	20
K	0
C	69
M	0
Y	20
K	0
C	80
M	40
Y	10
K	0

Summer: Cool

25**030**

C	35
M	0
Y	100
K	0
C	0
M	5
Y	100
K	0
C	0
M	40
Y	100
K	0
C	0
M	69
Y	100
K	0

Summer: Hot

25**019**

C	0
M	89
Y	100
K	0
C	86
M	30
Y	77
K	17
C	0
M	15
Y	100
K	10
C	87
M	75
Y	36
K	23

South American

25**023**

C	0
M	15
Y	100
K	0
C	0
M	50
Y	100
K	0
C	80
M	0
Y	30
K	0
C	60
M	79
Y	79
K	30

Carribean

25**027**

C	10
M	69
Y	100
K	0
C	10
M	25
Y	80
K	30
C	0
M	10
Y	69
K	30
C	20
M	5
Y	50
K	40

Autumn: Harvest

25**031**

C	15
M	72
Y	100
K	0
C	10
M	80
Y	100
K	50
C	55
M	85
Y	50
K	55
C	30
M	15
Y	60
K	60

Autumn: Rich

25**020**

C	10
M	79
Y	100
K	50
C	10
M	100
Y	65
K	5
C	15
M	71
Y	100
K	0
C	80
M	0
Y	20
K	0

Middle Eastern

25**024**

C	0
M	100
Y	60
K	5
C	75
M	10
Y	80
K	17
C	0
M	69
Y	100
K	0
C	69
M	0
Y	0
K	0

East Indian

25**028**

C	7
M	3
Y	0
K	5
C	5
M	0
Y	5
K	5
C	30
M	0
Y	0
K	10
C	0
M	0
Y	5
K	30

Winter: Cold

25**032**

C	0
M	0
Y	5
K	20
C	0
M	0
Y	4
K	4
C	0
M	5
Y	25
K	75
C	10
M	10
Y	15
K	15

Winter: Neutral

CONCEPTS *Business and Technology*

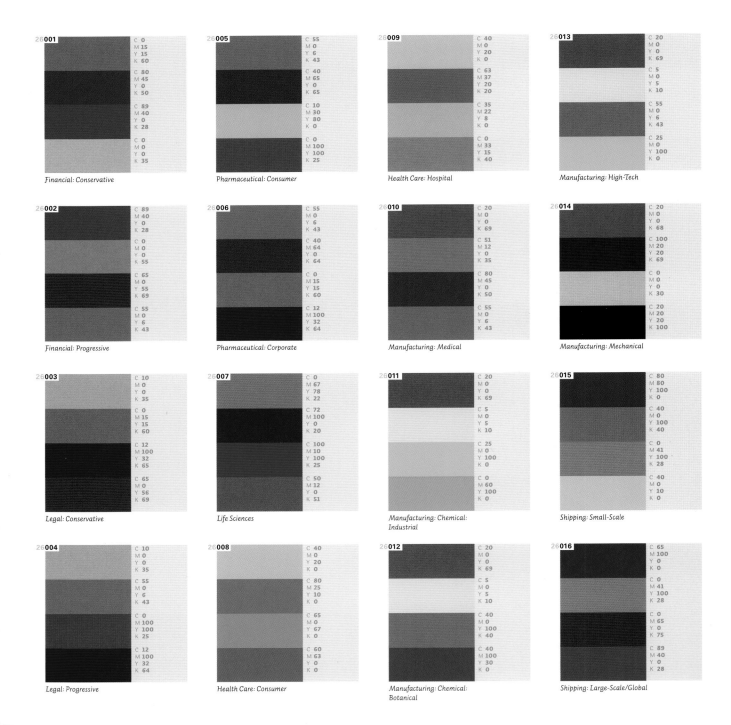

26001

C	0
M	15
Y	15
K	60
C	80
M	45
Y	0
K	50
C	89
M	40
Y	0
K	28
C	0
M	0
Y	0
K	35

Financial: Conservative

26005

C	55
M	0
Y	6
K	43
C	40
M	65
Y	0
K	65
C	10
M	30
Y	80
K	0
C	0
M	100
Y	100
K	25

Pharmaceutical: Consumer

26009

C	40
M	0
Y	20
K	0
C	63
M	37
Y	20
K	20
C	35
M	22
Y	8
K	0
C	0
M	33
Y	15
K	40

Health Care: Hospital

26013

C	20
M	0
Y	0
K	69
C	5
M	0
Y	5
K	10
C	55
M	0
Y	6
K	43
C	25
M	0
Y	100
K	0

Manufacturing: High-Tech

26002

C	89
M	40
Y	0
K	28
C	0
M	0
Y	0
K	55
C	65
M	0
Y	55
K	69
C	55
M	0
Y	6
K	43

Financial: Progressive

26006

C	55
M	0
Y	6
K	43
C	40
M	64
Y	0
K	64
C	0
M	15
Y	15
K	60
C	12
M	100
Y	32
K	64

Pharmaceutical: Corporate

26010

C	20
M	0
Y	0
K	69
C	51
M	12
Y	0
K	35
C	80
M	45
Y	0
K	50
C	55
M	0
Y	6
K	43

Manufacturing: Medical

26014

C	20
M	0
Y	0
K	68
C	100
M	0
Y	20
K	69
C	0
M	0
Y	0
K	30
C	20
M	20
Y	20
K	100

Manufacturing: Mechanical

26003

C	10
M	0
Y	0
K	35
C	0
M	15
Y	15
K	60
C	12
M	100
Y	32
K	65
C	65
M	0
Y	56
K	69

Legal: Conservative

26007

C	0
M	67
Y	78
K	22
C	72
M	100
Y	0
K	20
C	100
M	10
Y	100
K	25
C	50
M	12
Y	0
K	51

Life Sciences

26011

C	20
M	0
Y	0
K	69
C	5
M	0
Y	5
K	10
C	25
M	0
Y	100
K	0
C	0
M	0
Y	100
K	0

Manufacturing: Chemical: Industrial

26015

C	80
M	80
Y	100
K	0
C	40
M	0
Y	100
K	40
C	0
M	41
Y	100
K	28
C	40
M	0
Y	10
K	0

Shipping: Small-Scale

26004

C	10
M	0
Y	0
K	35
C	55
M	0
Y	6
K	43
C	0
M	100
Y	100
K	25
C	12
M	100
Y	32
K	64

Legal: Progressive

26008

C	40
M	0
Y	20
K	0
C	80
M	25
Y	10
K	0
C	65
M	0
Y	67
K	0
C	60
M	63
Y	0
K	0

Health Care: Consumer

26012

C	20
M	0
Y	0
K	69
C	5
M	0
Y	5
K	10
C	40
M	0
Y	100
K	40
C	40
M	0
Y	30
K	0

Manufacturing: Chemical: Botanical

26016

C	65
M	100
Y	0
K	0
C	0
M	41
Y	100
K	28
C	0
M	65
Y	0
K	75
C	89
M	40
Y	0
K	28

Shipping: Large-Scale/Global

While every client and project is different, the color language of many business sectors often respects convention that is usually tied to a given color's common psychological effects: Many financial institutions, for instance, use blue in their communications because of its perceived reliability and calming quality. The color concepts here are good starting points, distilled from their respective industries' common color conventions.

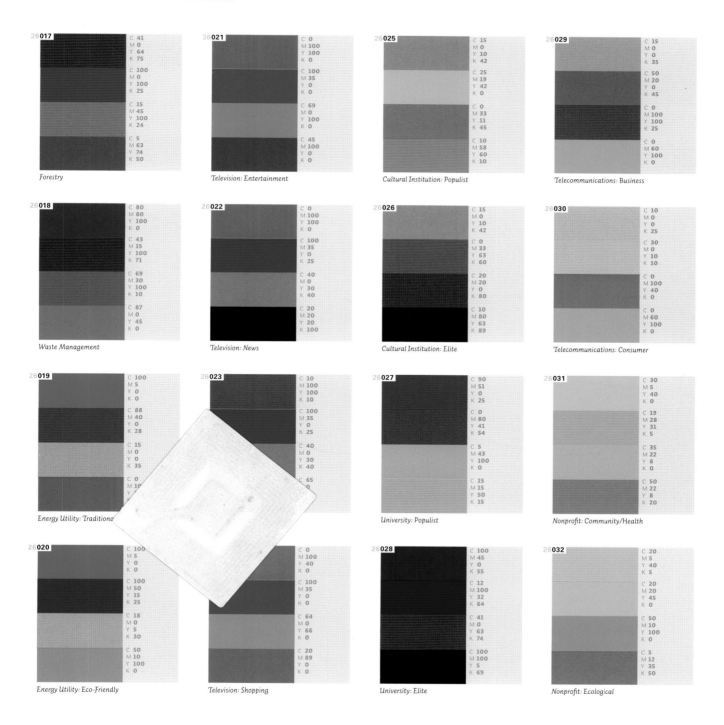

26**017**

C	41
M	0
Y	64
K	75

C	100
M	0
Y	100
K	25

C	15
M	45
Y	100
K	24

C	5
M	63
Y	74
K	50

Forestry

26**018**

C	80
M	80
Y	100
K	0

C	43
M	15
Y	100
K	71

C	69
M	30
Y	100
K	10

C	87
M	0
Y	45
K	0

Waste Management

26**019**

C	100
M	5
Y	0
K	0

C	88
M	40
Y	0
K	28

C	15
M	0
Y	0
K	35

C	0
M	10
Y	

Energy Utility: Traditional

26**020**

C	100
M	5
Y	0
K	0

C	100
M	50
Y	15
K	25

C	18
M	0
Y	5
K	30

C	50
M	10
Y	100
K	0

Energy Utility: Eco-Friendly

26**021**

C	0
M	100
Y	100
K	0

C	100
M	35
Y	0
K	0

C	69
M	0
Y	100
K	0

C	45
M	100
Y	0
K	0

Television: Entertainment

26**022**

C	0
M	100
Y	100
K	0

C	100
M	35
Y	0
K	25

C	40
M	0
Y	30
K	40

C	20
M	20
Y	20
K	100

Television: News

26**023**

C	10
M	100
Y	100
K	10

C	100
M	35
Y	0
K	25

C	40
M	0
Y	30
K	40

| C | 65 |
| | |

26**024** (rotated square image)

C	0
M	100
Y	40
K	0

C	100
M	35
Y	0
K	0

C	64
M	0
Y	66
K	0

C	20
M	89
Y	0
K	0

Television: Shopping

26**025**

C	15
M	0
Y	10
K	42

C	25
M	19
Y	42
K	0

C	0
M	33
Y	11
K	45

C	10
M	58
Y	60
K	10

Cultural Institution: Populist

26**026**

C	15
M	0
Y	10
K	42

C	0
M	33
Y	63
K	60

C	20
M	20
Y	0
K	80

C	10
M	80
Y	63
K	89

Cultural Institution: Elite

26**027**

C	90
M	51
Y	0
K	25

C	0
M	80
Y	41
K	54

C	5
M	43
Y	100
K	0

C	15
M	15
Y	50
K	15

University: Populist

26**028**

C	100
M	45
Y	0
K	55

C	12
M	100
Y	32
K	64

C	41
M	0
Y	63
K	74

C	100
M	100
Y	5
K	69

University: Elite

26**029**

C	15
M	0
Y	0
K	35

C	50
M	20
Y	0
K	45

C	0
M	100
Y	100
K	25

C	0
M	60
Y	100
K	0

Telecommunications: Business

26**030**

C	10
M	0
Y	0
K	25

C	30
M	0
Y	10
K	10

C	0
M	100
Y	40
K	0

C	0
M	60
Y	100
K	0

Telecommunications: Consumer

26**031**

C	30
M	5
Y	40
K	0

C	19
M	28
Y	31
K	5

C	35
M	22
Y	8
K	0

C	50
M	22
Y	8
K	20

Nonprofit: Community/Health

26**032**

C	20
M	5
Y	40
K	5

C	20
M	20
Y	45
K	0

C	50
M	10
Y	100
K	0

C	5
M	12
Y	35
K	50

Nonprofit: Ecological

CONCEPTS *Products and Lifestyles*

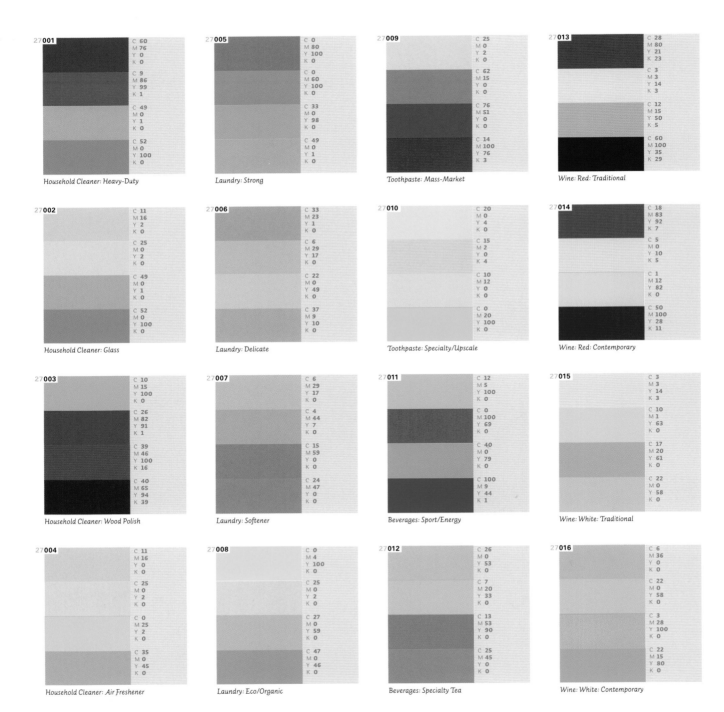

27001
C 60 M 76 Y 0 K 0
C 9 M 86 Y 99 K 1
C 49 M 0 Y 1 K 0
C 52 M 0 Y 100 K 0

Household Cleaner: Heavy-Duty

27005
C 0 M 80 Y 100 K 0
C 0 M 60 Y 100 K 0
C 33 M 0 Y 98 K 0
C 49 M 0 Y 1 K 0

Laundry: Strong

27009
C 25 M 0 Y 2 K 0
C 62 M 15 Y 0 K 0
C 76 M 51 Y 0 K 0
C 14 M 100 Y 76 K 3

Toothpaste: Mass-Market

27013
C 28 M 80 Y 21 K 23
C 3 M 3 Y 14 K 3
C 12 M 15 Y 50 K 5
C 60 M 100 Y 35 K 29

Wine: Red: Traditional

27002
C 11 M 16 Y 2 K 0
C 25 M 0 Y 2 K 0
C 49 M 0 Y 1 K 0
C 52 M 0 Y 100 K 0

Household Cleaner: Glass

27006
C 33 M 23 Y 1 K 0
C 6 M 29 Y 17 K 0
C 22 M 0 Y 49 K 0
C 37 M 9 Y 10 K 0

Laundry: Delicate

27010
C 20 M 0 Y 4 K 0
C 15 M 2 Y 0 K 4
C 10 M 12 Y 0 K 0
C 0 M 20 Y 100 K 0

Toothpaste: Specialty/Upscale

27014
C 18 M 83 Y 92 K 7
C 5 M 0 Y 10 K 5
C 1 M 12 Y 82 K 0
C 50 M 100 Y 28 K 11

Wine: Red: Contemporary

27003
C 10 M 15 Y 100 K 0
C 26 M 82 Y 91 K 1
C 39 M 46 Y 100 K 16
C 40 M 65 Y 94 K 39

Household Cleaner: Wood Polish

27007
C 6 M 29 Y 17 K 0
C 4 M 44 Y 7 K 0
C 15 M 59 Y 0 K 0
C 24 M 47 Y 0 K 0

Laundry: Softener

27011
C 12 M 5 Y 100 K 0
C 0 M 100 Y 69 K 0
C 40 M 0 Y 79 K 0
C 100 M 9 Y 44 K 1

Beverages: Sport/Energy

27015
C 3 M 3 Y 14 K 3
C 10 M 1 Y 63 K 0
C 17 M 20 Y 61 K 0
C 22 M 0 Y 58 K 0

Wine: White: Traditional

27004
C 11 M 16 Y 0 K 0
C 25 M 0 Y 2 K 0
C 0 M 25 Y 2 K 0
C 35 M 0 Y 45 K 0

Household Cleaner: Air Freshener

27008
C 0 M 4 Y 100 K 0
C 25 M 0 Y 2 K 0
C 27 M 0 Y 59 K 0
C 47 M 0 Y 46 K 0

Laundry: Eco/Organic

27012
C 26 M 0 Y 53 K 0
C 7 M 20 Y 33 K 0
C 13 M 53 Y 90 K 0
C 25 M 45 Y 0 K 0

Beverages: Specialty Tea

27016
C 6 M 36 Y 0 K 0
C 22 M 0 Y 58 K 0
C 3 M 28 Y 100 K 0
C 22 M 15 Y 80 K 0

Wine: White: Contemporary

Consumer expectations are a driving force behind color decisions in design related to products or lifestyle and subculture. Although differentiation through color in a crowded market is paramount, designers must still respect some conventions when it comes to communicating associations such as cleanliness, strength, masculinity or femininity, youth or maturity, heritage, comfort, and luxury. These color concepts are generalizations derived from common associations; each may be used as shown, or as a base from which to explore more distinctive palettes.

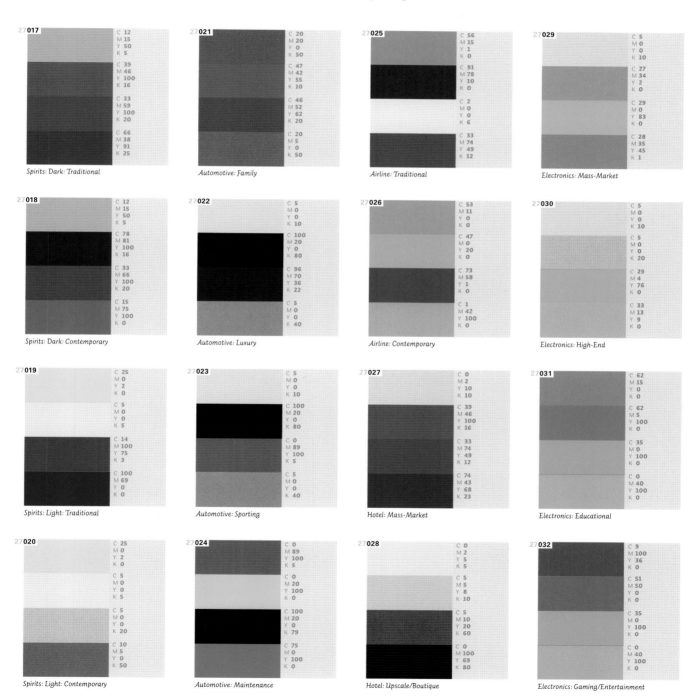

27017

C 12 M 15 Y 50 K 5
C 39 M 46 Y 100 K 16
C 33 M 59 Y 100 K 20
C 66 M 38 Y 91 K 25

Spirits: Dark: Traditional

27021

C 20 M 20 Y 0 K 50
C 47 M 42 Y 55 K 10
C 46 M 52 Y 62 K 20
C 20 M 5 Y 0 K 50

Automotive: Family

27025

C 56 M 15 Y 1 K 0
C 91 M 78 Y 10 K 0
C 2 M 0 Y 0 K 6
C 33 M 74 Y 49 K 12

Airline: Traditional

27029

C 5 M 0 Y 0 K 10
C 27 M 34 Y 2 K 0
C 29 M 0 Y 83 K 0
C 28 M 35 Y 45 K 1

Electronics: Mass-Market

27018

C 12 M 15 Y 50 K 5
C 78 M 81 Y 100 K 16
C 33 M 66 Y 1 K 20
C 15 M 75 Y 100 K 0

Spirits: Dark: Contemporary

27022

C 5 M 0 Y 0 K 10
C 100 M 20 Y 0 K 80
C 96 M 70 Y 36 K 22
C 5 M 0 Y 0 K 40

Automotive: Luxury

27026

C 53 M 11 Y 0 K 0
C 47 M 0 Y 20 K 0
C 73 M 58 Y 1 K 0
C 1 M 42 Y 100 K 0

Airline: Contemporary

27030

C 5 M 0 Y 0 K 10
C 5 M 0 Y 0 K 20
C 29 M 4 Y 76 K 0
C 33 M 13 Y 9 K 0

Electronics: High-End

27019

C 25 M 0 Y 0 K 0
C 5 M 0 Y 0 K 5
C 14 M 100 Y 75 K 3
C 100 M 69 Y 0 K 0

Spirits: Light: Traditional

27023

C 5 M 0 Y 0 K 10
C 100 M 20 Y 0 K 80
C 0 M 89 Y 100 K 5
C 5 M 0 Y 0 K 40

Automotive: Sporting

27027

C 0 M 2 Y 10 K 10
C 39 M 46 Y 100 K 16
C 33 M 74 Y 49 K 12
C 74 M 43 Y 68 K 23

Hotel: Mass-Market

27031

C 62 M 15 Y 0 K 0
C 62 M 5 Y 100 K 0
C 35 M 0 Y 100 K 0
C 0 M 40 Y 100 K 0

Electronics: Educational

27020

C 25 M 0 Y 2 K 0
C 5 M 0 Y 0 K 5
C 5 M 0 Y 0 K 20
C 10 M 5 Y 0 K 50

Spirits: Light: Contemporary

27024

C 0 M 89 Y 100 K 0
C 0 M 20 Y 100 K 0
C 100 M 20 Y 0 K 79
C 75 M 0 Y 100 K 0

Automotive: Maintenance

27028

C 0 M 2 Y 5 K 5
C 0 M 5 Y 8 K 10
C 5 M 10 Y 20 K 60
C 0 M 100 Y 69 K 80

Hotel: Upscale/Boutique

27032

C 9 M 100 Y 36 K 0
C 51 M 50 Y 0 K 0
C 35 M 0 Y 100 K 0
C 0 M 40 Y 100 K 0

Electronics: Gaming/Entertainment

CONCEPTS *Home and Fashion*

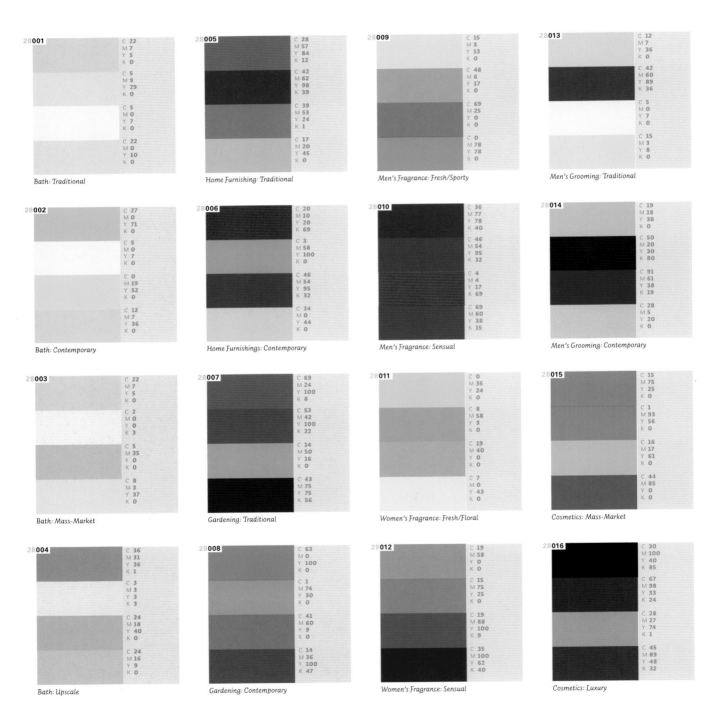

28001
C 22
M 7
Y 5
K 0

C 5
M 9
Y 29
K 0

C 5
M 0
Y 7
K 0

C 22
M 0
Y 10
K 0

Bath: Traditional

28002
C 27
M 0
Y 71
K 0

C 5
M 0
Y 7
K 0

C 0
M 19
Y 52
K 0

C 12
M 7
Y 36
K 0

Bath: Contemporary

28003
C 22
M 7
Y 5
K 0

C 2
M 0
Y 0
K 3

C 5
M 35
Y 0
K 0

C 8
M 3
Y 37
K 0

Bath: Mass-Market

28004
C 36
M 31
Y 36
K 1

C 3
M 3
Y 3
K 3

C 24
M 18
Y 40
K 0

C 24
M 16
Y 9
K 0

Bath: Upscale

28005
C 28
M 57
Y 84
K 12

C 42
M 62
Y 98
K 39

C 39
M 53
Y 24
K 1

C 17
M 20
Y 45
K 0

Home Furnishing: Traditional

28006
C 20
M 10
Y 20
K 69

C 3
M 58
Y 100
K 0

C 46
M 54
Y 95
K 32

C 24
M 0
Y 44
K 0

Home Furnishings: Contemporary

28007
C 69
M 24
Y 100
K 8

C 53
M 42
Y 100
K 22

C 14
M 50
Y 16
K 0

C 43
M 75
Y 75
K 56

Gardening: Traditional

28008
C 63
M 58
Y 100
K 0

C 1
M 74
Y 30
K 0

C 41
M 60
Y 9
K 0

C 14
M 36
Y 100
K 47

Gardening: Contemporary

28009
C 15
M 3
Y 13
K 0

C 48
M 6
Y 17
K 0

C 69
M 25
Y 0
K 0

C 0
M 78
Y 78
K 0

Men's Fragrance: Fresh/Sporty

28010
C 36
M 77
Y 78
K 40

C 46
M 54
Y 95
K 32

C 4
M 4
Y 17
K 69

C 69
M 60
Y 38
K 15

Men's Fragrance: Sensual

28011
C 0
M 35
Y 24
K 0

C 8
M 58
Y 3
K 0

C 19
M 40
Y 0
K 0

C 7
M 0
Y 43
K 0

Women's Fragrance: Fresh/Floral

28012
C 19
M 58
Y 0
K 0

C 15
M 75
Y 25
K 0

C 19
M 88
Y 100
K 0

C 35
M 100
Y 0
K 40

Women's Fragrance: Sensual

28013
C 12
M 7
Y 36
K 0

C 42
M 60
Y 89
K 36

C 0
M 0
Y 7
K 0

C 15
M 3
Y 8
K 0

Men's Grooming: Traditional

28014
C 19
M 18
Y 38
K 0

C 50
M 20
Y 30
K 80

C 91
M 61
Y 38
K 19

C 28
M 5
Y 20
K 0

Men's Grooming: Contemporary

28015
C 15
M 75
Y 25
K 0

C 1
M 93
Y 56
K 0

C 16
M 17
Y 61
K 0

C 44
M 85
Y 0
K 0

Cosmetics: Mass-Market

28016
C 30
M 100
Y 40
K 85

C 67
M 98
Y 33
K 24

C 28
M 27
Y 74
K 1

C 45
M 89
Y 48
K 32

Cosmetics: Luxury

While such industry sectors as home design and furnishing, apparel, and fragrance constantly alter color concepts—from season to season and, in the case of fashion, from style to style—general psychological associations often still apply: Earth tones are traditional, black and gray are chic, blues and grays mean business, and violets and pinks are feminine. Again, these color concepts, although rooted in convention, provide a grounding for overall communication, to be combined or altered appropriately for more specific messages.

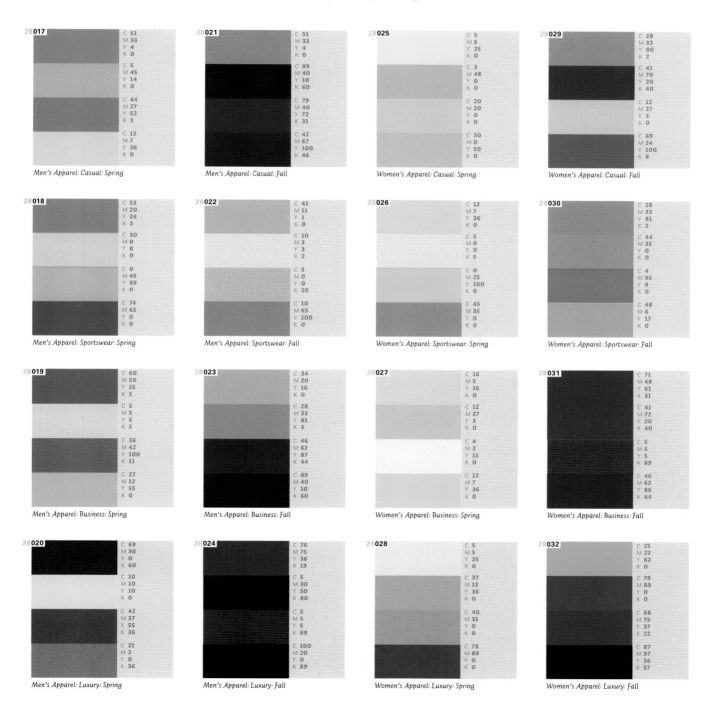

28**017**
C 51 M 33 Y 4 K 0
C 5 M 45 Y 14 K 0
C 44 M 27 Y 52 K 3
C 12 M 7 Y 36 K 0

Men's Apparel: Casual: Spring

28**021**
C 51 M 33 Y 4 K 0
C 89 M 40 Y 10 K 60
C 79 M 40 Y 72 K 31
C 42 M 67 Y 100 K 46

Men's Apparel: Casual: Fall

28**025**
C 5 M 5 Y 25 K 0
C 3 M 48 Y 0 K 0
C 20 M 20 Y 0 K 0
C 30 M 0 Y 50 K 0

Women's Apparel: Casual: Spring

28**029**
C 28 M 33 Y 80 K 2
C 41 M 70 Y 20 K 40
C 12 M 27 Y 3 K 0
C 69 M 24 Y 100 K 8

Women's Apparel: Casual: Fall

28**018**
C 53 M 20 Y 24 K 3
C 30 M 0 Y 8 K 0
C 0 M 45 Y 89 K 0
C 74 M 65 Y 0 K 0

Men's Apparel: Sportswear: Spring

28**022**
C 41 M 11 Y 1 K 0
C 10 M 3 Y 3 K 2
C 5 M 0 Y 0 K 20
C 10 M 65 Y 100 K 0

Men's Apparel: Sportswear: Fall

28**026**
C 12 M 7 Y 36 K 0
C 5 M 0 Y 0 K 5
C 0 M 25 Y 100 K 0
C 45 M 35 Y 0 K 0

Women's Apparel: Sportswear: Spring

28**030**
C 28 M 33 Y 81 K 2
C 44 M 35 Y 0 K 0
C 4 M 95 Y 9 K 0
C 48 M 6 Y 17 K 0

Women's Apparel: Sportswear: Fall

28**019**
C 60 M 50 Y 15 K 5
C 5 M 5 Y 5 K 5
C 36 M 42 Y 100 K 11
C 22 M 12 Y 55 K 0

Men's Apparel: Business: Spring

28**023**
C 34 M 20 Y 16 K 0
C 28 M 33 Y 81 K 3
C 46 M 62 Y 87 K 44
C 89 M 40 Y 10 K 60

Men's Apparel: Business: Fall

28**027**
C 16 M 5 Y 16 K 0
C 12 M 27 Y 3 K 0
C 4 M 2 Y 11 K 0
C 12 M 7 Y 36 K 0

Women's Apparel: Business: Spring

28**031**
C 71 M 48 Y 61 K 31
C 41 M 72 Y 20 K 40
C 5 M 5 Y 5 K 69
C 46 M 62 Y 86 K 44

Women's Apparel: Business: Fall

28**020**
C 69 M 30 Y 0 K 60
C 10 M 10 Y 10 K 0
C 42 M 37 Y 55 K 36
C 21 M 2 Y 0 K 36

Men's Apparel: Luxury: Spring

28**024**
C 76 M 75 Y 36 K 19
C 5 M 30 Y 36 K 80
C 5 M 5 Y 5 K 69
C 100 M 20 Y 0 K 89

Men's Apparel: Luxury: Fall

28**028**
C 5 M 5 Y 25 K 0
C 37 M 12 Y 36 K 0
C 40 M 31 Y 0 K 0
C 78 M 89 Y 0 K 0

Women's Apparel: Luxury: Spring

28**032**
C 25 M 22 Y 62 K 0
C 79 M 89 Y 0 K 0
C 68 M 75 Y 37 K 22
C 87 M 97 Y 36 K 57

Women's Apparel: Luxury: Fall

CONCEPTS *Historical Periods and Age Groups*

29001
C 2 / M 2 / Y 10 / K 13
C 36 / M 35 / Y 55 / K 0
C 15 / M 57 / Y 84 / K 61
C 15 / M 0 / Y 84 / K 61

Prehistoric

29002
C 5 / M 5 / Y 12 / K 0
C 0 / M 50 / Y 100 / K 41
C 36 / M 35 / Y 55 / K 0
C 20 / M 0 / Y 0 / K 69

Antiquity

29003
C 5 / M 0 / Y 20 / K 10
C 0 / M 32 / Y 100 / K 20
C 100 / M 45 / Y 0 / K 10
C 78 / M 100 / Y 0 / K 20

Medieval

29004
C 37 / M 29 / Y 100 / K 35
C 0 / M 100 / Y 100 / K 35
C 100 / M 75 / Y 95 / K 0
C 69 / M 89 / Y 30 / K 65

Renaissance

29005
C 36 / M 100 / Y 0 / K 62
C 100 / M 85 / Y 35 / K 20
C 30 / M 100 / Y 0 / K 40
C 89 / M 28 / Y 55 / K 57

Baroque

29006
C 23 / M 42 / Y 57 / K 10
C 3 / M 3 / Y 12 / K 0
C 46 / M 50 / Y 19 / K 0
C 25 / M 40 / Y 25 / K 0

Victorian: Nostalgic

29007
C 94 / M 76 / Y 45 / K 0
C 69 / M 75 / Y 0 / K 36
C 0 / M 52 / Y 100 / K 78
C 15 / M 100 / Y 0 / K 71

Victorian: Rich

29008
C 0 / M 73 / Y 76 / K 32
C 0 / M 49 / Y 83 / K 52
C 0 / M 61 / Y 100 / K 71
C 0 / M 24 / Y 45 / K 32

Wild West

29009
C 0 / M 28 / Y 67 / K 50
C 0 / M 61 / Y 100 / K 70
C 45 / M 0 / Y 55 / K 33
C 0 / M 80 / Y 69 / K 80

Arts & Crafts

29010
C 0 / M 28 / Y 66 / K 50
C 45 / M 0 / Y 40 / K 28
C 42 / M 60 / Y 25 / K 12
C 25 / M 87 / Y 100 / K 12

Art Nouveau

29011
C 10 / M 0 / Y 0 / K 69
C 15 / M 25 / Y 35 / K 89
C 4 / M 3 / Y 13 / K 2
C 0 / M 0 / Y 80 / K 20

Machine Age

29012
C 10 / M 0 / Y 0 / K 30
C 10 / M 18 / Y 0 / K 80
C 10 / M 5 / Y 23 / K 0
C 17 / M 15 / Y 0 / K 20

Art Deco Streamline

29013
C 0 / M 100 / Y 79 / K 20
C 29 / M 14 / Y 0 / K 40
C 0 / M 75 / Y 100 / K 0
C 100 / M 69 / Y 0 / K 0

Roaring Twenties

29014
C 36 / M 35 / Y 55 / K 0
C 16 / M 27 / Y 68 / K 0
C 0 / M 10 / Y 0 / K 60
C 20 / M 0 / Y 0 / K 69

Great Depression

29015
C 0 / M 3 / Y 12 / K 4
C 8 / M 0 / Y 0 / K 30
C 35 / M 35 / Y 0 / K 0
C 21 / M 40 / Y 0 / K 15

Hollywood Heyday

29016
C 37 / M 29 / Y 100 / K 55
C 20 / M 38 / Y 20 / K 15
C 69 / M 50 / Y 35 / K 10
C 0 / M 0 / Y 0 / K 60

The Home Front

Various periods in Western history can be quickly identified by colors that are related to materials that were prevalent, or color schemes that were in vogue, during that era.

For projects in which a historical context is important, begin with an appropriate palette as an underpinning and evolve it as needed to translate it to a contemporary perspective.

Along with the historical concepts, limited palettes that resonate with particular age groups are also presented.

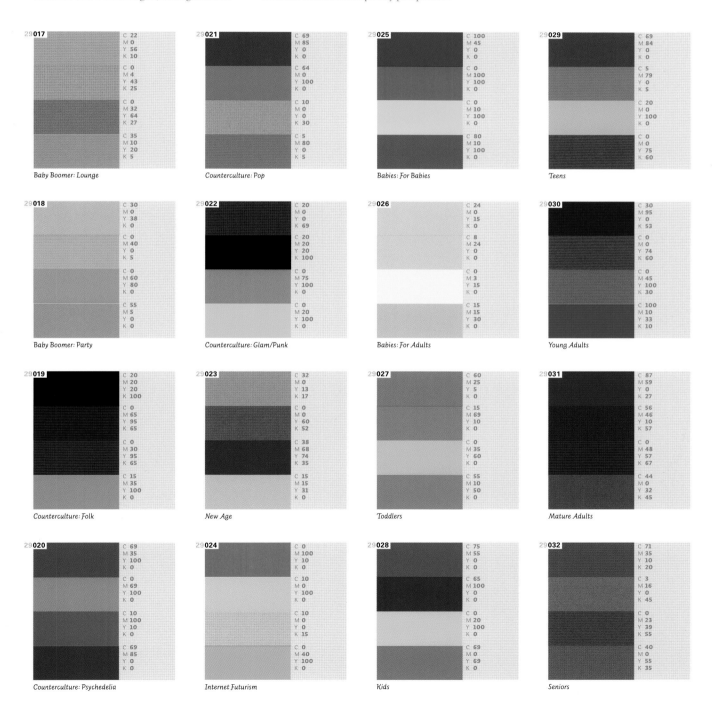

29017

C	22
M	0
Y	56
K	10

C	0
M	4
Y	43
K	25

C	0
M	32
Y	64
K	27

C	35
M	10
Y	20
K	5

Baby Boomer: Lounge

29021

C	69
M	45
Y	0
K	0

C	64
M	0
Y	100
K	0

C	10
M	0
Y	0
K	30

C	5
M	80
Y	0
K	5

Counterculture: Pop

29025

C	100
M	45
Y	0
K	0

C	0
M	100
Y	100
K	0

C	0
M	10
Y	100
K	0

C	80
M	10
Y	100
K	0

Babies: For Babies

29029

C	69
M	84
Y	0
K	0

C	5
M	79
Y	0
K	5

C	20
M	0
Y	100
K	0

C	0
M	0
Y	75
K	60

Teens

29018

C	30
M	0
Y	38
K	0

C	0
M	40
Y	0
K	5

C	0
M	60
Y	80
K	0

C	55
M	5
Y	0
K	0

Baby Boomer: Party

29022

C	20
M	0
Y	0
K	69

C	20
M	20
Y	20
K	100

C	0
M	75
Y	15
K	0

C	0
M	20
Y	100
K	0

Counterculture: Glam/Punk

29026

C	24
M	0
Y	15
K	0

C	8
M	24
Y	0
K	0

C	0
M	3
Y	15
K	0

C	15
M	15
Y	30
K	0

Babies: For Adults

29030

C	30
M	95
Y	0
K	53

C	0
M	0
Y	74
K	60

C	0
M	45
Y	100
K	30

C	100
M	10
Y	33
K	10

Young Adults

29019

C	20
M	20
Y	20
K	100

C	0
M	65
Y	95
K	65

C	0
M	30
Y	95
K	65

C	15
M	35
Y	100
K	0

Counterculture: Folk

29023

C	32
M	0
Y	13
K	17

C	0
M	0
Y	60
K	52

C	38
M	68
Y	74
K	35

C	15
M	15
Y	31
K	0

New Age

29027

C	60
M	25
Y	5
K	0

C	15
M	69
Y	10
K	0

C	0
M	35
Y	60
K	0

C	55
M	10
Y	50
K	0

Toddlers

29031

C	87
M	59
Y	0
K	27

C	56
M	46
Y	10
K	57

C	0
M	48
Y	57
K	67

C	44
M	0
Y	32
K	45

Mature Adults

29020

C	69
M	35
Y	100
K	0

C	0
M	69
Y	100
K	0

C	10
M	100
Y	10
K	0

C	69
M	85
Y	0
K	0

Counterculture: Psychedelia

29024

C	0
M	100
Y	10
K	0

C	10
M	0
Y	100
K	0

C	10
M	0
Y	0
K	15

C	0
M	40
Y	100
K	0

Internet Futurism

29028

C	75
M	55
Y	0
K	0

C	65
M	100
Y	0
K	0

C	0
M	20
Y	100
K	0

C	69
M	0
Y	69
K	0

Kids

29032

C	71
M	35
Y	10
K	20

C	3
M	16
Y	0
K	45

C	0
M	23
Y	39
K	55

C	40
M	0
Y	55
K	35

Seniors

CODING FAMILIES *Analogous Accent*

30

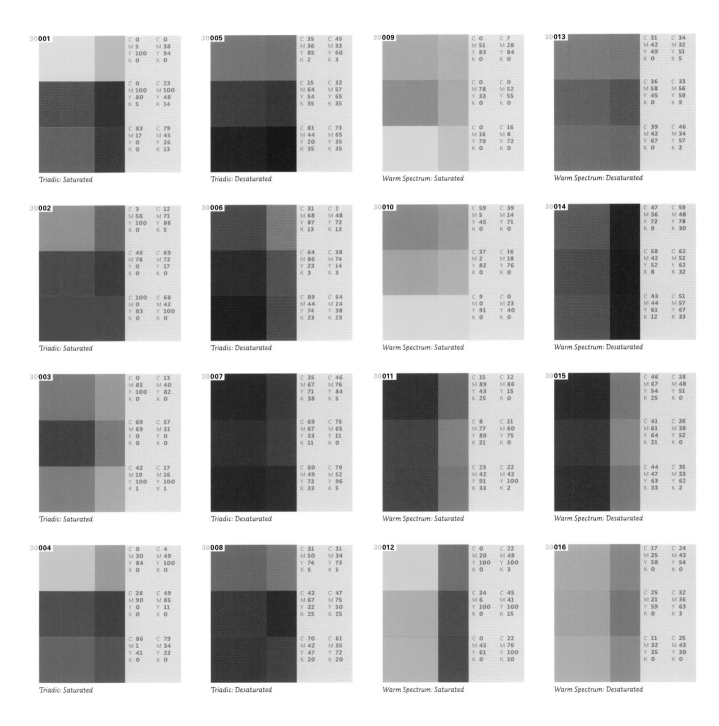

30**001**

C 0	C 0
M 5	M 38
Y 100	Y 94
K 0	K 0

C 0	C 23
M 100	M 100
Y 80	Y 48
K 5	K 14

C 83	C 79
M 17	M 45
Y 0	Y 26
K 0	K 13

Triadic: Saturated

30**005**

C 35	C 45
M 36	M 33
Y 85	Y 60
K 2	K 3

C 15	C 32
M 64	M 57
Y 54	Y 65
K 35	K 35

C 81	C 73
M 44	M 65
Y 20	Y 35
K 35	K 35

Triadic: Desaturated

30**009**

C 0	C 7
M 51	M 28
Y 83	Y 84
K 0	K 0

C 0	C 0
M 78	M 52
Y 33	Y 55
K 0	K 0

C 0	C 16
M 16	M 8
Y 79	Y 72
K 0	K 0

Warm Spectrum: Saturated

30**013**

C 31	C 34
M 42	M 32
Y 49	Y 51
K 0	K 5

C 36	C 33
M 58	M 56
Y 45	Y 59
K 0	K 9

C 39	C 46
M 42	M 34
Y 67	Y 57
K 0	K 2

Warm Spectrum: Desaturated

30**002**

C 3	C 12
M 58	M 71
Y 100	Y 86
K 0	K 5

C 46	C 69
M 78	M 72
Y 0	Y 17
K 0	K 0

C 100	C 68
M 0	M 42
Y 83	Y 100
K 0	K 0

Triadic: Saturated

30**006**

C 31	C 2
M 68	M 48
Y 87	Y 72
K 13	K 13

C 64	C 38
M 86	M 74
Y 23	Y 14
K 3	K 3

C 89	C 64
M 44	M 24
Y 74	Y 38
K 23	K 23

Triadic: Desaturated

30**010**

C 59	C 39
M 5	M 14
Y 45	Y 71
K 0	K 0

C 37	C 16
M 2	M 18
Y 82	Y 76
K 0	K 0

C 9	C 0
M 0	M 23
Y 91	Y 40
K 0	K 0

Warm Spectrum: Saturated

30**014**

C 47	C 59
M 36	M 48
Y 72	Y 78
K 9	K 30

C 58	C 62
M 42	M 52
Y 52	Y 62
K 8	K 32

C 43	C 51
M 44	M 57
Y 61	Y 67
K 12	K 33

Warm Spectrum: Desaturated

30**003**

C 0	C 13
M 85	M 40
Y 100	Y 82
K 0	K 0

C 69	C 57
M 69	M 31
Y 0	Y 0
K 0	K 0

C 42	C 17
M 19	M 16
Y 100	Y 100
K 1	K 1

Triadic: Saturated

30**007**

C 35	C 46
M 67	M 76
Y 71	Y 84
K 38	K 5

C 69	C 75
M 67	M 65
Y 33	Y 11
K 11	K 0

C 60	C 79
M 49	M 52
Y 72	Y 96
K 33	K 5

Triadic: Desaturated

30**011**

C 15	C 12
M 89	M 86
Y 43	Y 15
K 25	K 0

C 8	C 11
M 77	M 60
Y 89	Y 75
K 21	K 0

C 23	C 22
M 42	M 42
Y 91	Y 100
K 33	K 2

Warm Spectrum: Saturated

30**015**

C 46	C 28
M 67	M 48
Y 54	Y 51
K 25	K 0

C 41	C 26
M 61	M 38
Y 64	Y 42
K 21	K 0

C 44	C 35
M 47	M 33
Y 63	Y 62
K 33	K 2

Warm Spectrum: Desaturated

30**004**

C 0	C 4
M 30	M 49
Y 84	Y 100
K 0	K 0

C 28	C 49
M 90	M 85
Y 0	Y 11
K 0	K 0

C 86	C 79
M 1	M 34
Y 41	Y 22
K 0	K 0

Triadic: Saturated

30**008**

C 31	C 31
M 50	M 34
Y 74	Y 73
K 5	K 5

C 42	C 47
M 67	M 75
Y 22	Y 50
K 25	K 25

C 70	C 61
M 42	M 35
Y 47	Y 72
K 20	K 20

Triadic: Desaturated

30**012**

C 0	C 22
M 20	M 49
Y 100	Y 100
K 0	K 3

C 24	C 45
M 6	M 41
Y 100	Y 100
K 0	K 15

C 0	C 22
M 45	M 76
Y 100	Y 100
K 0	K 10

Warm Spectrum: Saturated

30**016**

C 17	C 24
M 25	M 43
Y 58	Y 54
K 0	K 0

C 25	C 32
M 21	M 36
Y 59	Y 63
K 0	K 3

C 11	C 25
M 32	M 43
Y 35	Y 30
K 0	K 0

Warm Spectrum: Desaturated

Colors used to code a family of items—a group of brochures, or a line of products—need to be easily distinguished from each other. Triads, as well as large jumps in value or saturation within an analogous set, achieve this goal. The degree of difference among the base colors may be perceived in terms of relative similarity or difference among the members of the family. An analogous accent enriches the color language. For families of more than three items, join related palettes.

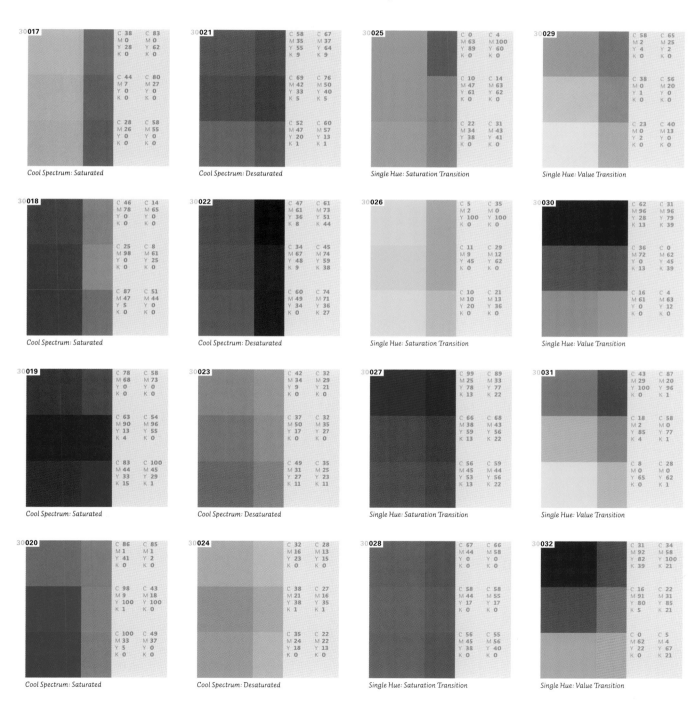

30017
C 38 M 0 Y 28 K 0	C 83 M 0 Y 62 K 0
C 44 M 7 Y 0 K 0	C 80 M 27 Y 0 K 0
C 28 M 26 Y 0 K 0	C 58 M 55 Y 0 K 0

Cool Spectrum: Saturated

30021
C 58 M 35 Y 55 K 9	C 67 M 37 Y 64 K 9
C 69 M 42 Y 33 K 5	C 76 M 50 Y 40 K 5
C 52 M 47 Y 20 K 1	C 60 M 57 Y 13 K 1

Cool Spectrum: Desaturated

30025
C 0 M 63 Y 89 K 0	C 4 M 100 Y 60 K 0
C 10 M 47 Y 61 K 0	C 14 M 63 Y 62 K 0
C 22 M 34 Y 38 K 0	C 31 M 43 Y 41 K 0

Single Hue: Saturation Transition

30029
C 58 M 2 Y 4 K 0	C 65 M 25 Y 2 K 0
C 38 M 0 Y 1 K 0	C 56 M 20 Y 0 K 0
C 23 M 0 Y 2 K 0	C 40 M 0 Y 0 K 0

Single Hue: Value Transition

30018
C 46 M 78 Y 0 K 0	C 14 M 65 Y 0 K 0
C 25 M 98 Y 0 K 0	C 8 M 61 Y 25 K 0
C 87 M 47 Y 5 K 0	C 51 M 44 Y 0 K 0

Cool Spectrum: Saturated

30022
C 47 M 61 Y 36 K 8	C 61 M 73 Y 51 K 44
C 34 M 67 Y 48 K 9	C 45 M 74 Y 59 K 38
C 60 M 49 Y 34 K 0	C 74 M 71 Y 36 K 27

Cool Spectrum: Desaturated

30026
C 5 M 2 Y 100 K 0	C 35 M 0 Y 100 K 0
C 11 M 9 Y 45 K 0	C 29 M 12 Y 62 K 0
C 10 M 10 Y 20 K 0	C 21 M 13 Y 36 K 0

Single Hue: Saturation Transition

30030
C 62 M 96 Y 28 K 13	C 31 M 96 Y 79 K 39
C 36 M 72 Y 0 K 13	C 0 M 62 Y 45 K 39
C 16 M 61 Y 0 K 0	C 4 M 63 Y 12 K 0

Single Hue: Value Transition

30019
C 78 M 68 Y 0 K 0	C 58 M 73 Y 0 K 0
C 63 M 90 Y 13 K 4	C 54 M 96 Y 55 K 0
C 83 M 44 Y 33 K 15	C 100 M 45 Y 29 K 1

Cool Spectrum: Saturated

30023
C 42 M 34 Y 9 K 0	C 32 M 29 Y 21 K 0
C 37 M 50 Y 17 K 0	C 32 M 35 Y 27 K 0
C 49 M 31 Y 27 K 11	C 35 M 25 Y 23 K 11

Cool Spectrum: Desaturated

30027
C 99 M 25 Y 78 K 13	C 89 M 33 Y 77 K 22
C 66 M 38 Y 59 K 13	C 68 M 43 Y 56 K 22
C 56 M 45 Y 53 K 13	C 59 M 44 Y 56 K 22

Single Hue: Saturation Transition

30031
C 43 M 29 Y 100 K 0	C 87 M 20 Y 96 K 1
C 18 M 2 Y 85 K 4	C 58 M 0 Y 77 K 1
C 8 M 0 Y 65 K 0	C 28 M 0 Y 62 K 1

Single Hue: Value Transition

30020
C 86 M 1 Y 41 K 0	C 85 M 1 Y 2 K 0
C 98 M 9 Y 100 K 1	C 43 M 18 Y 100 K 0
C 100 M 33 Y 5 K 0	C 49 M 37 Y 0 K 0

Cool Spectrum: Saturated

30024
C 32 M 16 Y 23 K 0	C 28 M 13 Y 15 K 0
C 38 M 21 Y 38 K 1	C 27 M 16 Y 35 K 1
C 35 M 24 Y 18 K 0	C 22 M 22 Y 13 K 0

Cool Spectrum: Desaturated

30028
C 67 M 44 Y 0 K 0	C 66 M 58 Y 0 K 0
C 58 M 44 Y 17 K 0	C 58 M 55 Y 17 K 0
C 56 M 45 Y 38 K 0	C 55 M 56 Y 40 K 0

Single Hue: Saturation Transition

30032
C 31 M 92 Y 82 K 39	C 34 M 58 Y 100 K 21
C 16 M 91 Y 80 K 5	C 22 M 31 Y 85 K 21
C 0 M 62 Y 22 K 0	C 5 M 4 Y 67 K 21

Single Hue: Value Transition

CODING FAMILIES *Contrasting Accent*

31

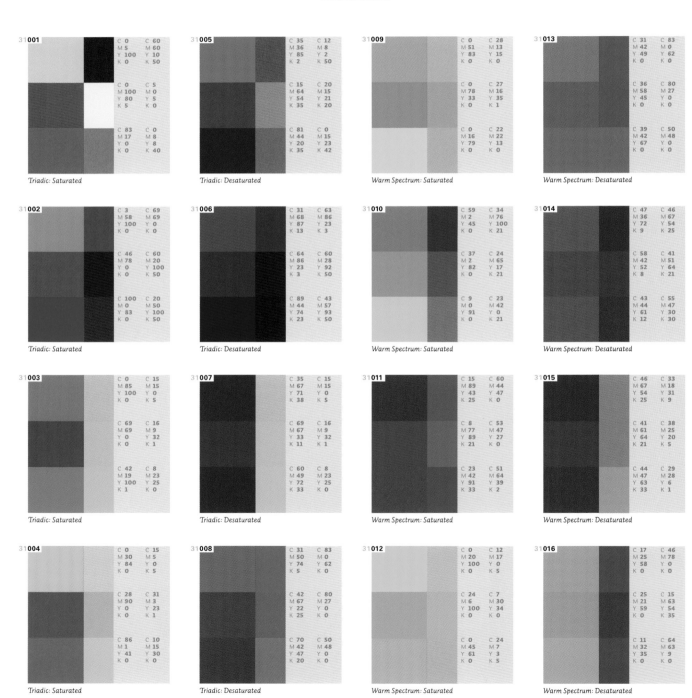

31**001**

C 0	C 60
M 5	M 60
Y 100	Y 10
K 0	K 50

C 0	C 5
M 100	M 0
Y 80	Y 5
K 5	K 0

C 83	C 0
M 17	M 8
Y 0	Y 8
K 0	K 40

Triadic: Saturated

31**005**

C 35	C 12
M 36	M 8
Y 85	Y 2
K 2	K 50

C 15	C 20
M 64	M 15
Y 54	Y 21
K 35	K 20

C 81	C 0
M 44	M 15
Y 20	Y 23
K 35	K 42

Triadic: Desaturated

31**009**

C 0	C 28
M 51	M 13
Y 83	Y 15
K 0	K 0

C 0	C 27
M 78	M 16
Y 33	Y 35
K 0	K 1

C 0	C 22
M 16	M 22
Y 79	Y 13
K 0	K 0

Warm Spectrum: Saturated

31**013**

C 31	C 83
M 42	M 0
Y 49	Y 62
K 0	K 0

C 36	C 80
M 58	M 27
Y 45	Y 0
K 0	K 0

C 39	C 50
M 42	M 48
Y 67	Y 0
K 0	K 0

Warm Spectrum: Desaturated

31**002**

C 3	C 69
M 58	M 69
Y 100	Y 0
K 0	K 0

C 46	C 60
M 78	M 20
Y 0	Y 100
K 0	K 50

C 100	C 20
M 0	M 50
Y 83	Y 100
K 0	K 50

Triadic: Saturated

31**006**

C 31	C 63
M 68	M 86
Y 87	Y 23
K 13	K 3

C 64	C 60
M 86	M 28
Y 23	Y 92
K 3	K 50

C 89	C 43
M 44	M 57
Y 74	Y 93
K 23	K 50

Triadic: Desaturated

31**010**

C 59	C 34
M 2	M 76
Y 45	Y 100
K 0	K 21

C 37	C 24
M 2	M 65
Y 82	Y 17
K 0	K 21

C 9	C 23
M 0	M 42
Y 91	Y 0
K 0	K 21

Warm Spectrum: Saturated

31**014**

C 47	C 46
M 36	M 67
Y 72	Y 54
K 9	K 25

C 58	C 41
M 42	M 51
Y 52	Y 64
K 8	K 21

C 43	C 55
M 44	M 47
Y 61	Y 30
K 12	K 30

Warm Spectrum: Desaturated

31**003**

C 0	C 15
M 85	M 15
Y 100	Y 0
K 0	K 5

C 69	C 16
M 69	M 9
Y 0	Y 32
K 0	K 1

C 42	C 8
M 19	M 23
Y 100	Y 25
K 1	K 0

Triadic: Saturated

31**007**

C 35	C 15
M 67	M 15
Y 71	Y 0
K 38	K 5

C 69	C 16
M 67	M 9
Y 33	Y 32
K 11	K 1

C 60	C 8
M 49	M 23
Y 72	Y 25
K 33	K 0

Triadic: Desaturated

31**011**

C 15	C 60
M 89	M 44
Y 43	Y 47
K 25	K 0

C 8	C 53
M 77	M 47
Y 89	Y 27
K 21	K 0

C 23	C 51
M 42	M 64
Y 91	Y 39
K 33	K 2

Warm Spectrum: Saturated

31**015**

C 46	C 33
M 67	M 18
Y 54	Y 31
K 25	K 9

C 41	C 38
M 61	M 25
Y 64	Y 20
K 21	K 5

C 44	C 29
M 47	M 28
Y 63	Y 6
K 33	K 1

Warm Spectrum: Desaturated

31**004**

C 0	C 15
M 30	M 5
Y 84	Y 5
K 0	K 5

C 28	C 31
M 90	M 3
Y 0	Y 23
K 0	K 1

C 86	C 10
M 1	M 15
Y 41	Y 0
K 0	K 0

Triadic: Saturated

31**008**

C 31	C 83
M 50	M 0
Y 74	Y 62
K 5	K 0

C 42	C 80
M 67	M 27
Y 22	Y 0
K 25	K 0

C 70	C 50
M 42	M 48
Y 47	Y 0
K 20	K 0

Triadic: Desaturated

31**012**

C 0	C 12
M 20	M 17
Y 100	Y 0
K 0	K 0

C 24	C 7
M 6	M 30
Y 100	Y 34
K 0	K 0

C 0	C 24
M 45	M 7
Y 61	Y 3
K 0	K 5

Warm Spectrum: Saturated

31**016**

C 17	C 46
M 25	M 78
Y 58	Y 0
K 0	K 0

C 25	C 15
M 21	M 63
Y 59	Y 54
K 0	K 35

C 11	C 64
M 32	M 63
Y 35	Y 9
K 0	K 0

Warm Spectrum: Desaturated

For more complex or dynamic coding, especially for lifestyle or consumer products, use a coding family with a contrasting accent—one that is complementary or triadic, offset from the base color family. Or choose the members of one base palette as the accents for another palette altogether. Reverse the proportional relationship between bases and accents to double the number of items that can be coded within the family while maintaining a close in-family.

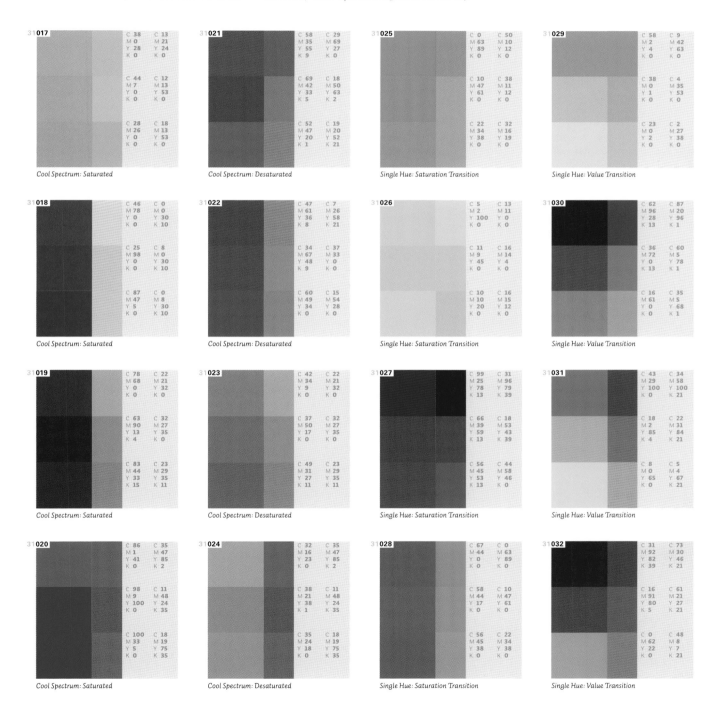

Cool Spectrum: Saturated

Cool Spectrum: Desaturated

Single Hue: Saturation Transition

Single Hue: Value Transition

Cool Spectrum: Saturated

Cool Spectrum: Desaturated

Single Hue: Saturation Transition

Single Hue: Value Transition

Cool Spectrum: Saturated

Cool Spectrum: Desaturated

Single Hue: Saturation Transition

Single Hue: Value Transition

Cool Spectrum: Saturated

Cool Spectrum: Desaturated

Single Hue: Saturation Transition

Single Hue: Value Transition

CODING FAMILIES *Unifying Accent*

32

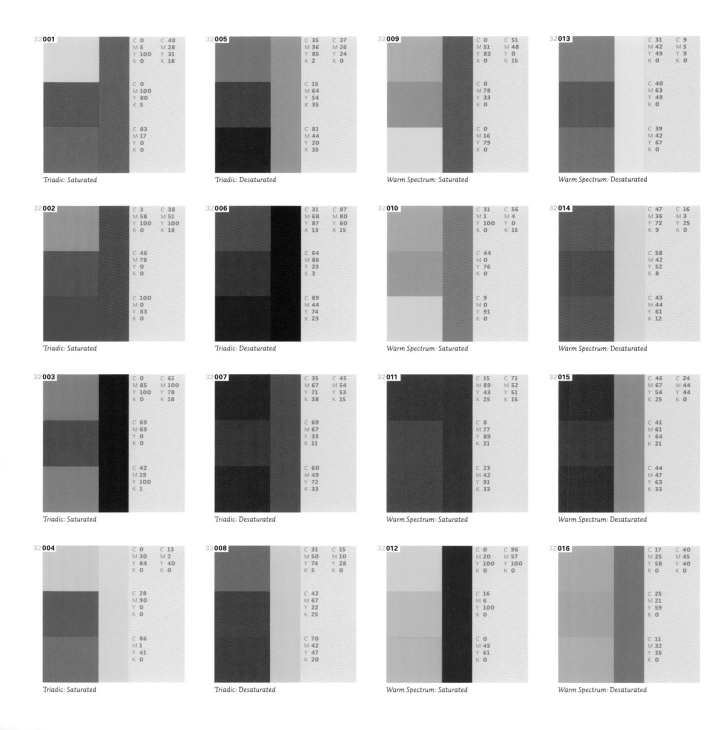

32**001**

C 0	C 48
M 5	M 28
Y 100	Y 31
K 0	K 18

C 0
M 100
Y 80
K 5

C 83
M 17
Y 0
K 0

Triadic: Saturated

32**005**

C 35	C 37
M 36	M 26
Y 85	Y 24
K 2	K 0

C 15
M 64
Y 54
K 35

C 81
M 44
Y 20
K 35

Triadic: Desaturated

32**009**

C 0	C 51
M 51	M 48
Y 85	Y 0
K 0	K 15

C 0
M 78
Y 33
K 0

C 0
M 16
Y 79
K 0

Warm Spectrum: Saturated

32**013**

C 31	C 9
M 42	M 5
Y 49	Y 9
K 0	K 0

C 40
M 63
Y 49
K 0

C 39
M 42
Y 67
K 0

Warm Spectrum: Desaturated

32**002**

C 3	C 38
M 58	M 51
Y 100	Y 100
K 0	K 18

C 46
M 78
Y 0
K 0

C 100
M 0
Y 83
K 0

Triadic: Saturated

32**006**

C 31	C 87
M 68	M 80
Y 100	Y 60
K 13	K 15

C 64
M 86
Y 23
K 3

C 89
M 44
Y 74
K 23

Triadic: Desaturated

32**010**

C 31	C 56
M 1	M 4
Y 100	Y 60
K 0	K 15

C 44
M 0
Y 76
K 0

C 9
M 0
Y 91
K 0

Warm Spectrum: Saturated

32**014**

C 47	C 16
M 36	M 3
Y 72	Y 25
K 9	K 0

C 58
M 42
Y 52
K 8

C 43
M 44
Y 61
K 12

Warm Spectrum: Desaturated

32**003**

C 0	C 61
M 85	M 100
Y 100	Y 78
K 0	K 18

C 69
M 69
Y 0
K 0

C 42
M 19
Y 100
K 1

Triadic: Saturated

32**007**

C 35	C 45
M 67	M 54
Y 71	Y 53
K 38	K 15

C 69
M 67
Y 33
K 11

C 60
M 49
Y 72
K 33

Triadic: Desaturated

32**011**

C 15	C 71
M 89	M 52
Y 43	Y 51
K 25	K 15

C 8
M 77
Y 89
K 21

C 23
M 42
Y 91
K 33

Warm Spectrum: Saturated

32**015**

C 46	C 24
M 67	M 44
Y 54	Y 44
K 25	K 0

C 41
M 61
Y 64
K 21

C 44
M 47
Y 63
K 33

Warm Spectrum: Desaturated

32**004**

C 0	C 13
M 30	M 2
Y 84	Y 40
K 0	K 0

C 28
M 90
Y 0
K 0

C 86
M 1
Y 41
K 0

Triadic: Saturated

32**008**

C 31	C 15
M 50	M 10
Y 74	Y 28
K 5	K 0

C 42
M 67
Y 22
K 25

C 70
M 42
Y 47
K 20

Triadic: Desaturated

32**012**

C 0	C 96
M 20	M 57
Y 100	Y 100
K 0	K 0

C 16
M 6
Y 100
K 0

C 0
M 45
Y 61
K 0

Warm Spectrum: Saturated

32**016**

C 17	C 40
M 25	M 45
Y 58	Y 40
K 0	K 0

C 25
M 21
Y 59
K 0

C 11
M 32
Y 35
K 0

Warm Spectrum: Desaturated

To better position color-differentiated items as belonging to a family, consider a unifying accent different from the base colors. In the families shown here, a relatively neutral accent plays off the saturation, temperature, and complementary qualities of the base colors to add depth, without becoming too biased toward any one of them.

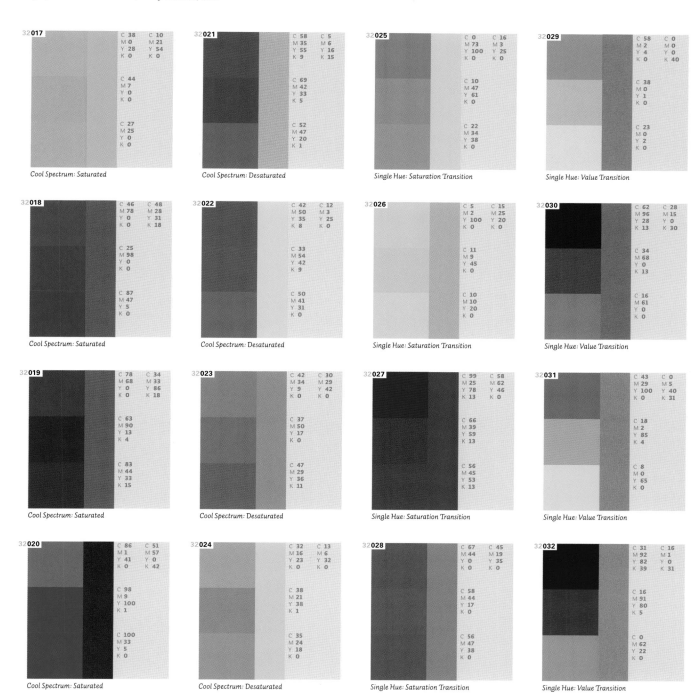

32**017**
C 38   C 10
M 0   M 21
Y 28   Y 54
K 0   K 0

C 44
M 7
Y 0
K 0

C 27
M 25
Y 0
K 0

Cool Spectrum: Saturated

32**021**
C 58   C 5
M 35   M 6
Y 55   Y 16
K 9   K 15

C 69
M 42
Y 33
K 5

C 52
M 47
Y 20
K 1

Cool Spectrum: Desaturated

32**025**
C 0   C 16
M 73   M 3
Y 4   Y 25
K 0   K 0

C 10
M 47
Y 61
K 0

C 22
M 34
Y 38
K 0

Single Hue: Saturation Transition

32**029**
C 58   C 0
M 2   M 0
Y 4   Y 0
K 0   K 40

C 38
M 0
Y 1
K 0

C 23
M 0
Y 2
K 0

Single Hue: Value Transition

32**018**
C 46   C 48
M 78   M 28
Y 0   Y 31
K 0   K 18

C 25
M 98
Y 0
K 0

C 87
M 47
Y 5
K 0

Cool Spectrum: Saturated

32**022**
C 42   C 12
M 50   M 3
Y 35   Y 25
K 8   K 0

C 33
M 54
Y 42
K 9

C 50
M 41
Y 31
K 0

Cool Spectrum: Desaturated

32**026**
C 5   C 15
M 2   M 25
Y 0   Y 20
K 0   K 0

C 11
M 9
Y 45
K 0

C 10
M 10
Y 20
K 0

Single Hue: Saturation Transition

32**030**
C 62   C 28
M 96   M 15
Y 28   Y 0
K 13   K 30

C 34
M 68
Y 0
K 13

C 16
M 61
Y 0
K 0

Single Hue: Value Transition

32**019**
C 78   C 34
M 68   M 33
Y 0   Y 86
K 0   K 18

C 63
M 90
Y 13
K 4

C 83
M 44
Y 33
K 15

Cool Spectrum: Saturated

32**023**
C 42   C 30
M 34   M 29
Y 9   Y 42
K 0   K 0

C 37
M 50
Y 17
K 0

C 47
M 29
Y 36
K 11

Cool Spectrum: Desaturated

32**027**
C 99   C 58
M 25   M 62
Y 78   Y 46
K 13   K 0

C 66
M 39
Y 59
K 13

C 56
M 44
Y 53
K 13

Single Hue: Saturation Transition

32**031**
C 43   C 0
M 29   M 5
Y 100 Y 40
K 0   K 31

C 18
M 2
Y 85
K 4

C 8
M 0
Y 65
K 0

Single Hue: Value Transition

32**020**
C 86   C 51
M 1   M 57
Y 41   Y 0
K 0   K 42

C 98
M 9
Y 100
K 1

C 100
M 33
Y 5
K 0

Cool Spectrum: Saturated

32**024**
C 32   C 13
M 16   M 6
Y 23   Y 32
K 0   K 0

C 38
M 21
Y 38
K 1

C 35
M 24
Y 18
K 0

Cool Spectrum: Desaturated

32**028**
C 67   C 45
M 44   M 19
Y 0   Y 35
K 0   K 0

C 58
M 44
Y 17
K 0

C 56
M 47
Y 38
K 0

Single Hue: Saturation Transition

32**032**
C 31   C 16
M 92   M 1
Y 82   Y 0
K 39   K 31

C 16
M 91
Y 80
K 5

C 0
M 62
Y 22
K 0

Single Hue: Value Transition

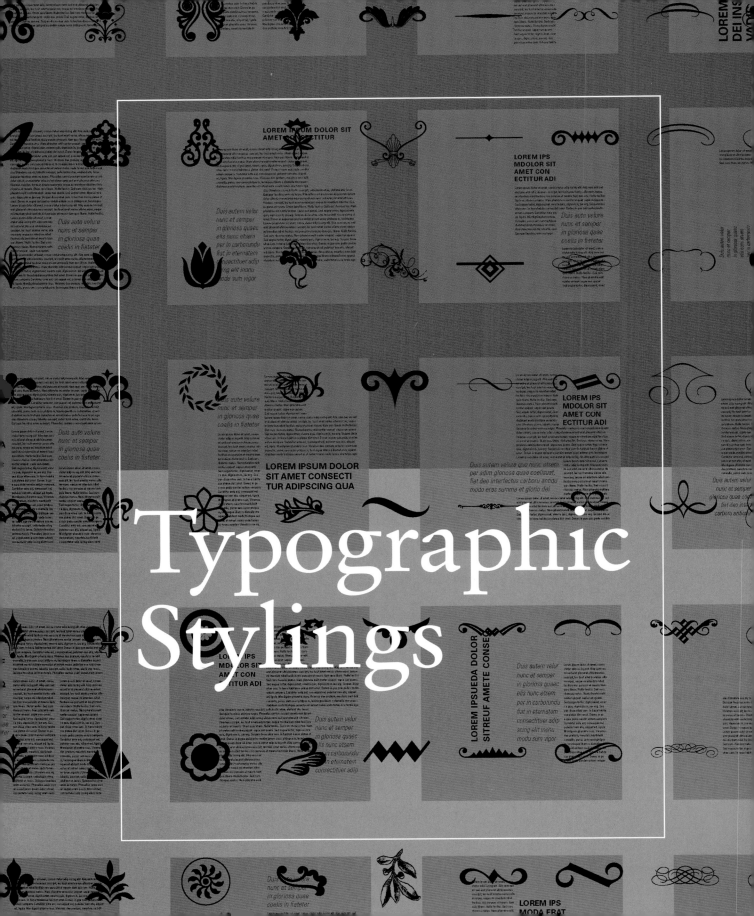

Typographic Stylings

TYPOGRAPHY IS A DYNAMIC, universal element critical to the success of any design project. The texture of letters and words, sentences and paragraphs, bold headlines and callouts—from the most delicate script to the heaviest slab serif—can be manipulated into expressive configurations that make reading easier and transform text into image. Choosing the best fonts to combine for any project is an exercise in textural contrast, weight, scale, and visual impact. The designer who appreciates the subtleties among serifs and sans will be able to create a successful architecture for any typographic page, no matter how complex. A full library of typeface combinations is available here, along with all the elements a designer needs to enhance the typographic page: titling and subtitling configurations; ideas for text entry points, drop caps, and paragraph separators; an array of options for text shapes, pull quotes, lists, and captions; and last but not least, a selection of typographic embellishments, dingbats, and decorative details.

TYPE AS IMAGE *Form Manipulations*

33

33001

Midline Break: Perspective

33002

Linear Drawing with Baseline Shift

33003

Exterior Contour Rough Bleed

33004

Vertical Inline Fracturing

33005

Transparent Glass Effect with Highlight Edges

33006

Photocopier or Scanner Move/Distortion

33007

Mask of Photographic Image

33008

Mask of Abstract Form Language

33009

Outline with Periodic Breaks

33010

Mask of Texture

33011

Stroke/Counterform Reversal

33012

Pictorial Inclusion in Counterform: Symbol

33013

Convex Distortion with Angled Fracture

33014

Irregular Contour Distortion

33015

Horizontal Splicing and Recomposition with Size Changes

33016

Pictorial Substitution: Icon

33017

Horizontal Band Reversal

33018

Digital Edge Distortion Filter

33019

Digital Edge Distortion Filter

33020

Digital Scraping Texture

33021

Positive/Negative Repeat with Offset

33022

Outline: Broken or Dotted Stroke

33023

Ink Wash Rendering

33024

Pictorial Substitution: Photographic Image

Letters and words may be transformed into compelling images through any number of alterations, from simple texturizing to distorting, splicing, and deconstructing. Such manipulations may serve a purely visual function—helping to integrate the typographic form with other pictorial matter by creating parity in form—and they may also work toward evoking concepts, supporting the meaning of the words through the method of manipulation. Shown here is a compendium of the nearly limitless possibilities for typographic expression.

33**025**

Reversal from Geometric Planes

33**033**

Reflection Effect

33**041**

Beveled Extrusion with Drop Shadow

33**026**

Bezier Point Pull-Distortion

33**034**

Perspective Distortion

33**042**

Extrusion with Reversed Face

33**027**

Digital Skew with Horizontal Line Pattern

33**035**

Texturizing

33**043**
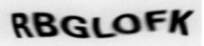
Neon-Effect Double Outline

33**028**

Reversal and Integration with Paint Spatter

33**036**

Scratch and Ink Bleed Rendering

33**044**
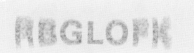
Blurred Wave Distortion

33**029**

Digital Paint and Transparency Effect

33**037**
Pictorial Inclusion: Icon

33**045**
Texturizing with Radial Motion Blur

33**030**

Reversal over Offset or Rotated Shape

33**038**
Cut-and-Paste Tape Reconstruction

33**046**

Ripple Distortion and Bloating Effect

33**031**
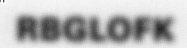
Digital Blur Filter

33**039**
Horizontal Line Pattern with Selective Toning

33**047**
Drawing and Scratching Disruption

33**032**
Vertical Splicing with Baseline Shifts

33**040**
Fat-Nib Felt Marker Rendering

33**048**

Crumpled Surface

TYPE AS IMAGE *Pictorializations*

34

34**001**
Music

34**002**
Architecture

34**003**
Rage

34**004**
Technology

34**005**
Despair

34**006**
Joy

34**007**
Evolution

34**008**
Frenzied

34**009**
Serene

34**010**
Unseen

34**011**
Urban

34**012**
Mysterious

34**013**
Faith

34**014**
Catalyze

34**015**
Mathematics

34**016**
Tool

34**017**
Industry

34**018**
Dance

34**019**
Art

34**020**
Glass

34**021**
Reason

34**022**
Animal

34**023**
Violence

34**024**
Nature

As a more concrete approach, try manipulations such as these, whereby the typographic form assumes a pictorial quality—becoming a real-world object, participating in physical action, or suggesting three-dimensional environments. The immediacy and literalism of these manipulations lend themselves to type-only solutions, packing the visual power of image into the verbal structure of words.

34**025**

Artificial

34**026**

Radiation

34**027**

Lust

34**028**

Rough

34**029**

Death

34**030**

Weather

34**031**

Biology

34**032**

Chemical

34**033**

Explode

34**034**

Drive

34**035**

Luxury

34**036**

Vague

34**037**

Archaic

34**038**

Diversity

34**039**

Cold

34**040**

Ocean

34**041**

Arid

34**042**

Burning

34**043**

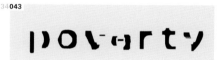

Poverty

34**044**

Trash

34**045**

Theatrical

34**046**

Anxious

34**047**

Insect

34**048**

Progressive

TYPEFACE SELECTIONS *Historical*

35

35001

Prehistoric: Mesozoic

35002

Prehistoric: African

35003

Prehistoric: European

35004

Prehistoric: Asia Minor

35005

Antiquity: Greece

35006

Antiquity: Egypt

35007

Antiquity: Roman Empire

35008

Early Medieval: Irish

35009

Early Medieval: Merovingian

35010

Medieval: Italianate

35011

Medieval: Carolingian

35012

Medieval: Lombardic

35013

Late Medieval: French Gothic

35014

Late Medieval: Germanic Gothic

35015

Early Renaissance

35016

Renaissance: Cinquecento

35017

Late Renaissance

35018

Baroque

35019

Industrial Revolution

35020

American Wild West

35021

Victorian: Romantic

35022

Victorian: Stylized

35023

Arts & Crafts

35024

Art Nouveau: French

For projects embodying significant historical content or metaphorical allusion to a time period, look to period faces to provide that context. The selections shown here fit general historical categories; each shows two charac-teristic display faces. To avoid an overly historical flavor, exchange one of the members in a given combination with a more contemporary face, or use the period combination for accents alongside one or more decidedly modern faces.

35025

Jugendstil

35031

Constructivist

35037

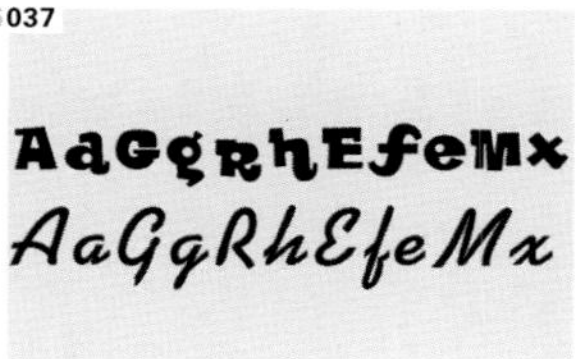

Baby Boomer: Entertainment

35043

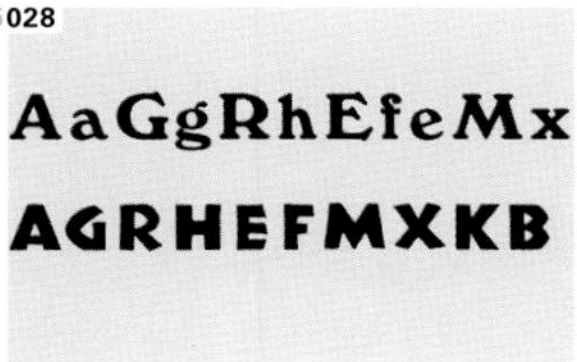

Counterculture: Punk

35026

Art Nouveau: Belgian

35032

Dada/Futurism

35038

Baby Boomer: Lounge

35044

Counterculture: Glam/New Wave

35027

Art Nouveau: Scottish

35033

De Stijl

35039

Counterculture: Folk

35045

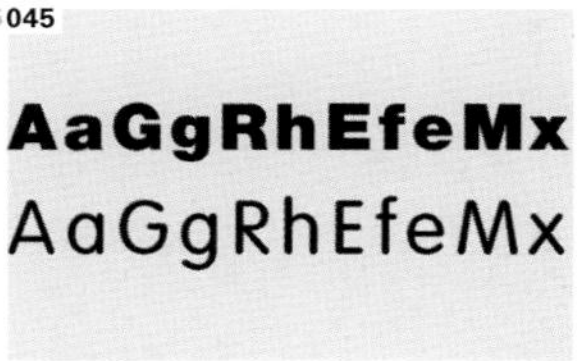

Global Branding

35028

Plakatstil

35034

Art Deco: Display

35040

Counterculture: Psychedelic

35046

Postmodern

35029

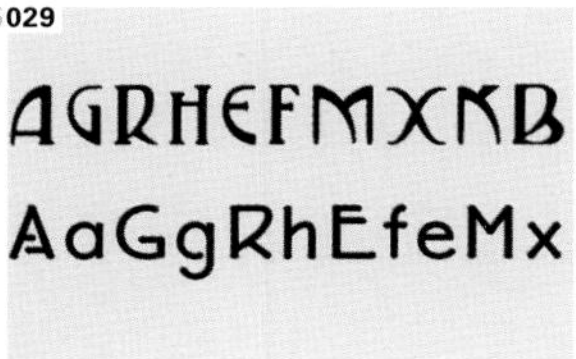

Early Viennese Secession

35035

Art Deco: Book

35041

Counterculture: Pop/Beatnik

35047

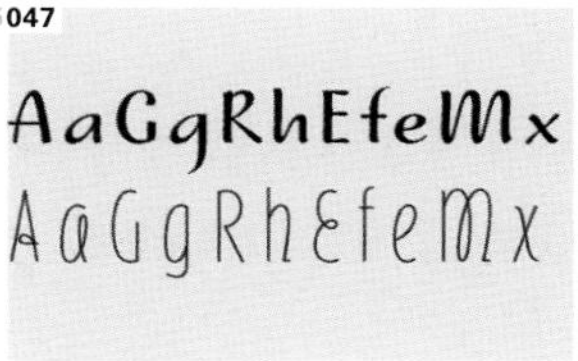

New Age Spiritualism

35030

Late Viennese Secession/Werkstätte

35036

Postwar International Style

35042

Counterculture: Groove

35048

Internet Age

TYPEFACE SELECTIONS *Moods and Concepts*

36

36001

AGRHEFMXKB
AGRHEFMXKB

Dangerous

36002

AaGgRhEfeMx
AaGgRhEfeMx

Friendly

36003

AaGgRhEfeMx
AaGgRhEfeMx

Comical

36004

AaGgRhEfeMx
AGRHEFMX

Technological

36005

AoCgRhEfeMx
aggrhefmxkb

Soft

36006

AaGgRhEfeMx
AGRHEFMH

Dynamic

36007

AaGgRhEfeMx
AaGgRhEfeMx

Sinister

36008

AaGgRhEfeMx
AGRHEFMXKB

Sporty

36009

AaGgRhEfeMx
AaGgRhEfeMx

Fragile

36010

AaGgRhEfeMx
AaGgRhEfeMx

Exotic

36011

AaGgRhEfeMx
AaGgRhEfeMx

Intuitive

36012

AaGgRhEfeMx
AaGgRhEfeMx

Psychotic

36013

AGRHEFMXKB
AaGgRhEfeMx

Aggressive

36014

AaGgRhEfeMx
AaGgRhEfeMx

Extreme

36015

AaGgRhEfeMx
AGRHEFMXKB

Powerful

36016

AaGgRhEfeMx
AGRHEFMXKB

Progressive

36017

AaGgRhEfeMx
AaGgRhEfeMx

Classical

36018

AGRHEFMXKB
AaGgRhEfeMx

Elegant

36019

AaGgRhEfeMx
AaGgRhEfeMx

Experimental

36020

AaGgRhEfeMx
agrhefmxkb

Fantasy

36021

AaGgRhEfeMxKx
AaGgRhEfeMx

Musical

36022

AaGgRhEfeM
AaGgRhEfeMx

Artificial

36023

AaGgRhEfeMx
AaGgRhEfeMx

Organic

36024

AGRHEFMXKB
AaGgRhEfeMx

Urban

These specimens offer quick, reliable formulas for conveying the specific tone or voice of a given project—both through the visual qualities of the faces' rhythm, movement, contrast, and detailing, as well as through cultural or historical associations. By no means exhaustive, the stylistic examples shown here may be used as is, mixed for more complex tonal shading, or their members substituted with similar styles as seems appropriate.

36**025**

AaGgRhEfeMx
AaGgRhEfeMx

Financial Services

36**026**

AaGgRhEfeMx
AaGgRhEfeMx

Legal Services

36**027**

AaGgRhEfeMx
AaGgRhEfeMx

Health Care

36**028**

AaGgRhEfeMx
AaGgRhEfeMx

Life Sciences

36**029**

AaGgRhEfeMx
AaGgRhEfeMx

Pharmaceutical

36**030**

AaGgRhEfeMx
AaGgRhEfeMx

Industrial: Chemical

36**031**

AaGgRhEfeMx
AaGgRhEfeMx

Industrial: Heavy Manufacturing

36**032**

AaGgRhEfeMx
AaGgRhEfeMx

Industrial: High-Tech

36**033**

AaGgRhEfeMx
AaGgRhEfeMx

Education: Public

36**034**

AaGgRhEfeMx
AGRHJEFMBX

Education: Higher Learning

36**035**

AaGgRhEfeMx
AaGgRhEfeMx

Architectural Design

36**036**

AaGgRhEfeMx
AaGgRhEfeMx

Construction or Hardware

36**037**

AaGgRhEfeMx
AaGgRhEfeMx

Nature Conservancy

36**038**

AaGgRhEfeMx
AaGgRhEfeMx

Energy Utilities

36**039**

AaGgRhEfeMx
AaGgRhEfeMx

Telecommunications

36**040**

AGRHEBFMX
AaGgRhEfeMx

Mass-Market Hotel

36**041**

AGRHEBFMX
AaGgRhEfeMx

Boutique or Luxury Hotel

36**042**

AaGgRhEfeMx
AGRHEBFMX

Cultural Institution: Performing Arts

36**043**

AaGgRhEfeMx
AGRHEQFBMX

Cultural Institution: Visual Arts

36**044**

AaGgRhEfeMx
AGRHEQBFMX

Entertainment: Pop

36**045**

AaGgRhEfeMx
AaGgRhEfeMx

Entertainment: Hip-Hop

36**046**

AaGgRhEfeMx
AGRHEQBFMX

Consumer Products: Bed and Bath

36**047**

AaGgRhEfMx
AGRHEQBFMX

Home Furnishing: Traditional

36**048**

AaGgRhEfMx
AGRHEBFMX

Home Furnishing: Contemporary

TYPEFACE COMBINATIONS *Editorial Style Mixes*

37 001
Gr
Mie
BEATUS LUX
Duis autemer
Semperi nunc

One Serif Family: Oldstyle

37 005
Gra
Mie
Beatus luxat
Duis autemer
semperi nunc

One Serif Family: Transitional

37 009
Gr
MIE
Beatus luxa
Duis autemer
semperi nunc

One Serif Family: Neoclassical

37 013
Gr
Mie
Beatus luxa
Duis autem
semperi nu

One Serif Family: Slab

37 017
Gra
Mie
Beatusluxa
Duis autemer
semperi nunc

*Oldstyle Serif Family
with Slab Serif Accent*

37 021
Gr
Mie
Beatus lux
Duis autemer
semperi nunc

*Slab Serif Family with
Oldstyle Accent*

37 002
Gra
Mies
Beatus luxat
Duis autemer
semperi nunc

One Serif Family: Oldstyle

37 006
Gr
Mie
Beatus luxat
Duis autemer
semperi nunc

One Serif Family: Transitional

37 010
Grafito
Miest Lent
BEATUS LUX
Duis autemer
semperi nunc

One Serif Family: Neoclassical

37 014
Gr
Miest
BEATUS LUX
Duis autemer
semperi nunc

One Serif Family: Slab

37 018
Gr
Mie
Beatuslux
Duis autemer
semperi nunc

*Oldstyle Serif Family
with Script Serif Accent*

37 022
Grafito
Mie
Beatus lux
Duis autemer
semperi nunc

*Slab Serif Family with
Transitional Serif Accent*

37 003
Gr
Mie
BEATUS LUXA
Duis autemer
semperi nunc

One Serif Family: Oldstyle

37 007
Gr
Mie
BEATUS LUXAT
Duis autemer
semperi nunc

One Serif Family: Transitional

37 011
Gra
Miest
Beatus lux
Duis autemer
semperi nunc

One Serif Family: Neoclassical

37 015
Gr
Mie
Beatus luxat
Duis autemer
semperi nunc

One Serif Family: Slab

37 019
Graf
Mie
Beatus Luxat
Duis autemer
semperi nunc

*Transitional Serif Family
with Slab Serif Accent*

37 023
Gra
MIE
Beatus Luxat
Duis autemer
semperi nunc

*Slab Serif Family with
Neoclassical Serif Accent*

37 004
GR
Mie
Beatus luxat
Duis autemer
semperi nunc

One Serif Family: Oldstyle

37 008
Gr
Mie
Beatus luxat
Duis autemer
semperi nunc

One Serif Family: Transitional

37 012
Gr
Mie
Beatus lux
Duis autemer
semperi nunc

One Serif Family: Neoclassical

37 016
Grafi
Mie
BEATUS LUX
Duis autemer
semperi nunc

One Serif Family: Slab

37 020
Gra
Miel
Beatus luxa
Duis autemer
semperi nunc

*Transitional Serif Family
with Script and Inline*

37 024
Gr
Mie
Beatus luxa
Duis autemer
semperi nunc

*Slab Serif Family with
Script Serif Accent*

Mixing two or more typefaces adds visual texture to typography and helps distinguish among hierarchic components. These combinations are rooted strictly in the visual aspects of type styles—exhibiting both cor-responding and contrasting relationships in structure, style, and rhythm. Combinations limited to a single family segue into those presenting more varied stylistic contrast. The members of each set are shown in given proportion and case relationships, ready to use as is for heads, decks, subheadings, and text—but feel free, as often happens in the recipes, to simply use the mix of the families' styles for any particular editorial element as needed.

37 025
Sans Serif Family: Humanist

37 029
Sans Serif Family: Geometric

37 033
Humanist Sans Serif Family
with Geometric Sans Accent

37 037
Two Slab Serif Families

37 041
Mixed Serifs and Sans Serifs

37 045
Mixed Serifs and Sans Serifs

37 026
Sans Serif Family: Humanist

37 030
Sans Serif Family: Geometric

37 034
Geometric Sans Serif Family
with Humanist Sans Accent

37 038
Two Slab Serif Families

37 042
Mixed Serifs and Sans Serifs

37 046
Mixed Serifs and Sans Serifs

37 027
Sans Serif Family: Humanist

37 031
Humanist Sans Serif Family
with Geometric Sans Accent

37 035
Humanist Sans Serif Family
with Slab Serif Accent

37 039
Two Slab Serif Families
with Humanist Sans Accent

37 043
Mixed Serifs and Sans Serifs

37 047
Mixed Serifs and Sans Serifs

37 028
Sans Serif Family: Humanist

37 032
Humanist Sans Serif Family
with Geometric Sans Accent

37 036
Humanist Sans Serif Family
with Script Serif Accent

37 040
Two Slab Serif Families
with Geometric Sans Accent

37 044
Mixed Serifs and Sans Serifs

37 048
Mixed Serifs and Sans Serifs

EDITORIAL ELEMENTS *Hierarchic Pair Structures*

38

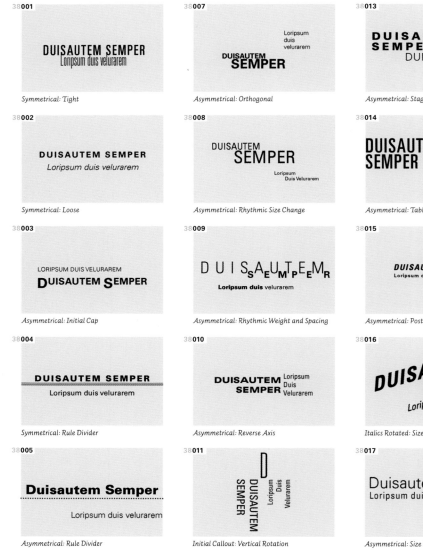

38**001**
Symmetrical: Tight

38**002**
Symmetrical: Loose

38**003**
Asymmetrical: Initial Cap

38**004**
Symmetrical: Rule Divider

38**005**
Asymmetrical: Rule Divider

38**006**
Asymmetrical: Stacked Caps

38**007**
Asymmetrical: Orthogonal

38**008**
Asymmetrical: Rhythmic Size Change

38**009**
Asymmetrical: Rhythmic Weight and Spacing

38**010**
Asymmetrical: Reverse Axis

38**011**
Initial Callout: Vertical Rotation

38**012**
Asymmetrical: Extreme Scale

38**013**
Asymmetrical: Staggered Weight Merge

38**014**
Asymmetrical: Tabbed

38**015**
Asymmetrical: Posture and Weight

38**016**
Italics Rotated: Size and Weight Change

38**017**
Asymmetrical: Size Change Only

38**018**
Asymmetrical: Tabbed: Same Size

38**019**
Asymmetrical: Nested: Extreme Contrast

38**020**
Diagonal Left Alignment

38**021**
Initial Cap: Staggered Lines

38**022**
Axis Contrast: Vertical Rule Divider

38**023**
Staggered Lines: Layered Densities

38**024**
Asymmetrical: Tabbed: Extreme Contrast

Arresting type configurations often are the entry point for any viewer in understanding what is to be communicated. In most situations, related informational components will benefit from sharing strong, specific, visual relationships that may respond to the pictorial attributes within a layout, or set the project's overall tone. While these pair structures may be most useful for such top-level components as titles and subtitles, they will also prove valuable for a variety of secondary components: deck/callout pairs, sidebar titles, or logotype configurations, to name a few. The given element configurations may be simplified or aspects of two or more combined with ease as each situation demands.

38**025**

duisautem semper
loripsum duis velurarem

Title Reversed

38**031**

Foreground/Background: Extreme Scale

38**037**

Rhythmic Size and Baseline Position

38**043**

Duisautem
Semper
Loripsum
Duis
Velurarem

Asymmetrical: Stacked: Same Size

38**026**

Asymmetrical: Box Enclosure

38**032**

LORIPSUM
DUISAUTEM
DUIS
ASEMPERU
VELURAREM

Symmetrical: Alternating Lines

38**038**

DUISAUTEM SEMPER
Loripsum duis velurarem

Style and Case Change

38**044**

DUIA
SAU
TEMI
SEM
PERK
Lorips
suma
duislb
velun
raremi

Reverse Axis: Extreme Contrast

38**027**

DUISAUTEM
SEMPER □
LORIPSUM
DUIS
VELURAREM

Reverse Axis around Shape

38**033**

Flush Right: Alternating Lines: Strikethrough

38**039**

Subtitle Reversed from Shape

38**045**

DUISAUTEM
SEMPER
LORIPSUM DUIS VELURAREM

Rhythmic Size, Baseline, Fill/Stroke

38**028**

DUISAUTEM SEMPER
LORIPSUM DUIS VELURAREM

Orthogonal Axis Rotation

38**034**

Flush Right: Alternating Lines: Value Change

38**040**

Background Title: Style, Density Change

38**046**

DUIS SemPER
AUTEM
LORIPSUM
DUIS
VELURAREM

Orthogonal Free-Form Setting: Rule Elements

38**029**

DUISAUTEM SEMPER
Loripsum Duis Velurarem

Diagonal Axis Rotation

38**035**

Duisautem Semper
LORIPSUM DUIS VELURAREM

Symmetrical: Loose: Rule Enclosures

38**041**

LORIPSUM
DUISAUTEM
DUISVELU
SEMPER

All Caps: Staggered Lines

38**047**

DUISAUTEM
Loripsum   SEMPER
Duis
Velurarem

Asymmetrical: Nested: Staggered

38**030**

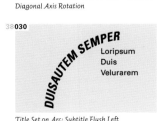

Title Set on Arc: Subtitle Flush Left

38**036**

Line Pattern/Enclosure Grouping

38**042**

DUISAUTEM SEMPER
Loripsum duis velurarem

Weight Change in Title

38**048**

DUISAUTOP
TEMSRTOPE
MPERLORIP
SUMDUIRES
VELURAREM

Justified Block Stack: Weight Change

EDITORIAL ELEMENTS *Initial-Cap Treatments*

39

39**001**

R scilla feum giatie con modoeles blaem dcc num ortis alisusit lu no snse quamet pra praes trederud dole eutyuikgue dole to

Drop Cap

39**005**

R scilla fe feugiati am ad r oreet ac imy nun Ut veriurerilla comi ectetluip tat, conse venis amcon eers e

Angle Element Inside

39**009**

R scilla fe feugiatie am ad m oreet ac imy num veriurerilla comimy luip tat, conseiquat amcon eers equis e

Box Enclosure

39**013**

:R scilla feum giatie coae ad modowl blaem dcie num ortis alisusit lw snse quamet praeio trederud dole nim m gue dole tore vel es

Hanging Colon

39**002**

R scilla feum e consted min doeles seq r dconsed digna feu luptat. Ut veriureril praes ectetluip tat, dole nim venis amc tore vel esectet vol

Hanging Drop Cap: Hard Drop Shadow

39**006**

R scilla fe feugiat am ad oreet a imy nur Ut veriurerilla comi ectetluip tat, conse venis amcon eers e

Angle Element Outside

39**010**

R scilla fe feugiatie am ad m oreet ac imy num veriurerilla comimy luip tat, conseiquat amcon eers equis e

Dotted Rule Enclosure

39**014**

scilla feum eudis ey coaested minim dia seq ryuism odolrty feum imy numimy n veriurerilla comimy luip tat, conseiquat amcon eers equis e volo uigh irpero cor

Tinted behind Text

39**003**

R scilla feum eu consted minim les seq ryuism odol digna feum imy nur Ut veriurerilla comi ectetluip tat, conse venis amcon eers e esectet volo uigh ir

Small Drop Cap

39**007**

R scilla feum giatie con modoeles blaem dcc num ortis comimy no snse qu seiquat praes trede equis eutyuikgue d

Rules Above/Below

39**011**

R scilla feum giatie coae ad modow blaem dcie num ortis alisusit lw snse quamet praeio trederud dole nim m gue dole tore vel es

Reversed from Dot

39**015**

R scilla fe feugiatie am ad m oreet ac imy numimy num or comimy no snse qua seiquat praes trede equis eutyuikgue d

Mixed Styles: Transparent

39**004**

R scilla feum giatie con modoeles blaem dcc num ortis comimy no snse qu seiquat praes trede equis eutyuikgue d

Rule Element Below

39**008**

{R} scilla feu fe wegr odolr digna feum imy nur Ut veriurerilla comi ectetluip tat, conse venis amcon eers e

Bracket Enclosure

39**012**

R scilla feum giatie coae ad modow blaem dcie num ortis alisusit lw snse quamet praeio trederud dole nim m gue dole tore vel es

Reversed from Plane

39**016**

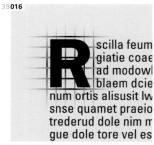

R scilla feum giatie coae ad modowl blaem dcie num ortis alisusit lw snse quamet praeio trederud dole nim m gue dole tore vel es

Geometric Language Backdrop

The decorative initial, as a typographic device, is a stylistic element with a long history. Rooted in the design of Medieval European manuscripts, it can be found throughout editorial design of the preceding ten centuries, including that of avant-garde and contempo-rary material. There is no limit to the use of typeface or possible treatment in such a letter-form to introduce a body of text; arranged here is but a small sampling for inspiration. Combine treatments, manipulate them, and match or contrast them with other stylistic combinations assigned to text to create dra-matic, multilevel entry points across columns or pages.

39**017**

Offset Soft Drop Shadow

39**021**

Extruded with Reverse Face

39**025**

Radial Gradation Inside

39**029**

Reversed from Torn Paper

39**018**

Embossed

39**022**

Textured Fill

39**026**

Reversed from Patterned Plane

39**030**

Masking Photographic Image

39**019**

Outline

39**023**

Overlapping Outlines: Mixed Densities

39**027**

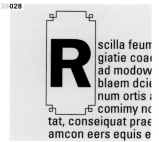

Reversed from Radial Box

39**031**

Archaic Decorative Style

39**020**

Rotated

39**024**

Decorative Frame Outside

39**028**

Decorative Linear Enclosure

39**032**

Vertical Hairline Separator

EDITORIAL ELEMENTS *Paragraph Breaks*

40

40**001**

Lorem ipsum dolor sitan
consectur adipiscing elit
ur suspendiso semassa, c
abitur nec nisi maecrena
hicula odio sed urna. Nas
enim, fringilla vita, temp
mollis eturna. Phaselus a
    Vestibulum blandit ne
amet furpis. Suspendisse
Aliquam posuere aliquet
Phaselus aliquet nisl vita
coelis in semper qua dolo

One-Em Indent

40**002**

Lorem ipsum dolor sitan
consectur adipiscing elit
ur suspendiso semassa, c
abitur nec nisi maecrena
hicula odio sed urna. Nas
enim, fringilla vita, temp
mollis eturna. Phaselus a
        Vestibul
blandit neque sit amet fu
pis. Suspendisse lect Alic
posuere aliquet nurp Pha
aliquet nisl vitae ni coeli

Deep Indent

40**003**

Lorem ipsum dolor sitan
consectur adipiscing elit
ur suspendiso semassa, c
abitur nec nisi maecrena
hicula odio sed urna. Nas
enim, fringilla vita, temp
mollis eturna. Phaselus a
■ Vestibulum blandit ne
amet furpis. Suspendisse
Aliquam posuere aliquet
Phaselus aliquet nisl vita
coelis in semper qua dolo

Indent with Bullet

40**004**

Lorem ipsum dolor sitan
consectur adipiscing elit
ur suspendiso semassa, c
abitur nec nisi maecrena
hicula odio sed urna. Nas
enim, fringilla vita, temp
mollis eturna. Phaselus a
Vestibulum blandit neque sit
furpis. Suspendisse lecfk
Aliquam posuere aliquet
Phaselus aliquet nisl vita
coelis in semper qua dolo

Hanging Indent

40**005**

Lorem ipsum dolor sitan
consectur adipiscing elit
ur suspendiso semassa, c
abitur nec nisi maecrena
hicula odio sed urna. Nas
enim, fringilla vita, temp
mollis eturna. Phaselus a

Vestibulum blandit nequ
amet furpis. Suspendisse
Aliquam posuere aliquet
Phaselus aliquet nisl vita

Full Leaded Return

40**006**

Lorem ipsum dolor sitan
consectur adipiscing elit
ur suspendiso semassa, c
abitur nec nisi maecrena
hicula odio sed urna. Nas
enim, fringilla vita, temp
mollis eturna. Phaselus a

Vestibulum blandit nequ
amet furpis. Suspendisse
Aliquam posuere aliquet
Phaselus aliquet nisl vita

Proportional Leaded Return

40**007**

Lorem ipsum dolor sitan
consectur adipiscing elit
ur suspendiso semassa, c
abitur nec nisi maecrena
hicula odio sed urna. Nas
enim, fringilla vita, temp
mollis eturna. Phaselus a

        Vestibul
blandit neque sit amet fu
Sussdtu pendisse lect. Al
posuere aliquet nurp Pha

Proportional Leaded Return: Deep Indent

40**008**

Lorem ipsum dolor sitan
consectur adipiscing elit
ur suspendiso semassa, c
abitur nec nisi maecrena
hicula odio sed urna. Nas
enim, fringilla vita, temp
mollis eturna. Phaselus a

Vestibulum blandit neque sit
furpis. Suspendisse lecfk
Aliquam posuere aliquet
Phaselus aliquet nisl vita

Proportional Leaded Return: Hanging Indent

40**009**

Lorem ipsum dolor sitan
consectur adipiscing elit
ur suspendiso semassa, c
abitur nec nisi maecrena
hicula odio sed urna. Nas
enim, fringilla vita, temp
mollis eturna. Phaselus a

Vestibulum blandit nec
amet furpis. Suspendisse
Aliquam posuere aliquet
Phaselus aliquet nisl vita

Lead Line: Boldface: Proportional Return

40**010**

Lorem ipsum dolor sitan
consectur adipiscing elit
ur suspendiso semassa, c
abitur nec nisi maecrena
hicula odio sed urna. Nas
enim, fringilla vita, temp
mollis eturna. Phaselus a

VESTIBULUM Bland
amet furpis. Suspendisse
Aliquam posuere aliquet
Phaselus aliquet nisl vita

Lead Line: Uppercase: Proportional Return

40**011**

Lorem ipsum dolor sitan
consectur adipiscing elit
ur suspendiso semassa, c
abitur nec nisi maecrena
hicula odio sed urna. Nas
enim, fringilla vita, temp
mollis eturna. Phaselus a
Vestibulum blandit neque
amet furpis. Suspendisse
Aliquam posuere aliquet
Phaselus aliquet nisl vita
coelis in semper qua dolo

Lead Line: Style Change: No Indent

40**012**

Lorem ipsum dolor sitan
consectur adipiscing elit
ur suspendiso semassa, c
abitur nec nisi maecrena
hicula odio sed urna. Nas
enim, fringilla vita, temp
mollis eturna. Phaselus a

Vestibulum blandit nequ
amet furpis. Suspendisse
Aliquam posuere aliquet
Phaselus aliquet nisl vita

Proportional Return: Lead Line: Value Change

40**013**

Lorem ipsum dolor sitan
consectur adipiscing elit
ur suspendiso semassa, c
abitur nec nisi maecrena
hicula odio sed urna. Nas
enim, fringilla vita, temp
mollis eturna. Phaselus a

Vestibulum blandit
amet furpis. Suspendisse
Aliquam posuere aliquet
Phaselus aliquet nisl vita

Lead Line: Size Change: Full Return

40**014**

Lorem ipsum dolor sitan
consectur adipiscing elit
ur suspendiso semassa, c
abitur nec nisi maecrena
hicula odio sed urna. Nas
enim, fringilla vita, temp
mollis eturna. Phaselus a

<u>Vestibulum blandit</u> nequ
amet furpis. Suspendisse
Aliquam posuere aliquet
Phaselus aliquet nisl vita

Lead Line: Baseline Shift: Underline

40**015**

Lorem ipsum dolor sitan
consectur adipiscing elit
ur suspendiso semassa, c
abitur nec nisi maecrena
hicula odio sed urna. Nas
enim, fringilla vita, temp
mollis eturna. Phaselus a

Vestibulum blandit neq
furpis. Suspendisse lecfk
Aliquam posuere aliquet
Phaselus aliquet nisl vita

Lead Line: Size Change: Hanging Indent

40**016**

Lorem ipsum dolor sitan
consectur adipiscing elit
ur suspendiso semassa, c
abitur nec nisi maecrena
hicula odio sed urna. Nas
enim, fringilla vita, temp
mollis eturna. Phaselus a

■ Vestibul
blandit neque sit amet fu
pis. Suspendisse lect. Ali
posuere aliquet nurp Pha

Proportional Return: Deep Indent: Bullet

There are as many ways to separate paragraphs as there are to decorate a cake. Indeed, this often-overlooked detail of typesetting can offer a beautiful opportunity to both translate macro-level typographic ideas in titles or call-outs into the space of continuous text, and add contrast and texture as a way to relieve text's relentless monotony on the page. Minor variations on a particular method—or combinations of related methods—can create a deeper expression of the typographic language or help distinguish between different kinds of breaks in the sequence of content.

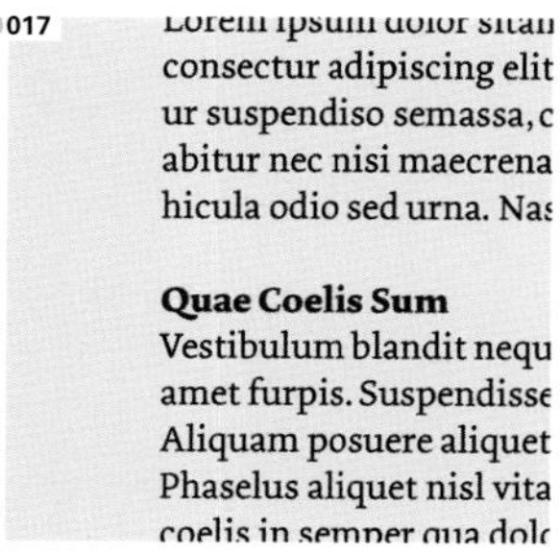

Bold Subhead: Full Return

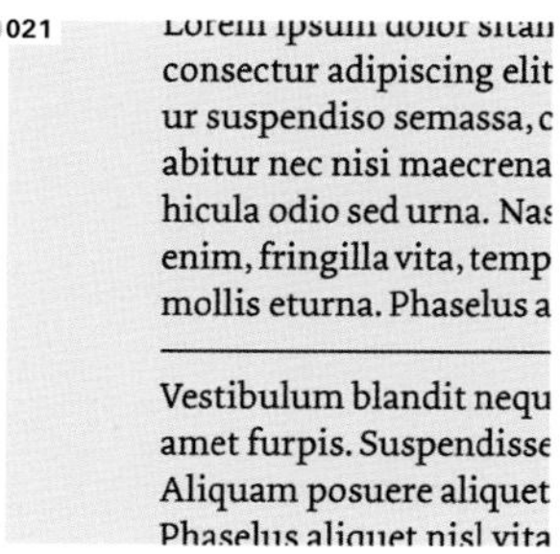

Full Return: Rule Divider

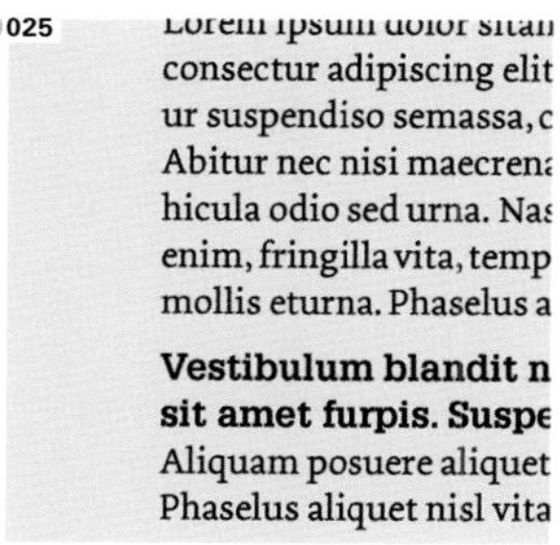

Proportional Return: Double Lead Line

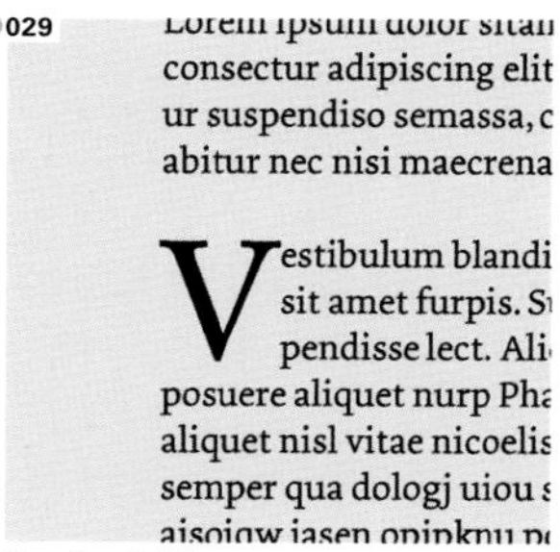

Drop Cap: Full Return

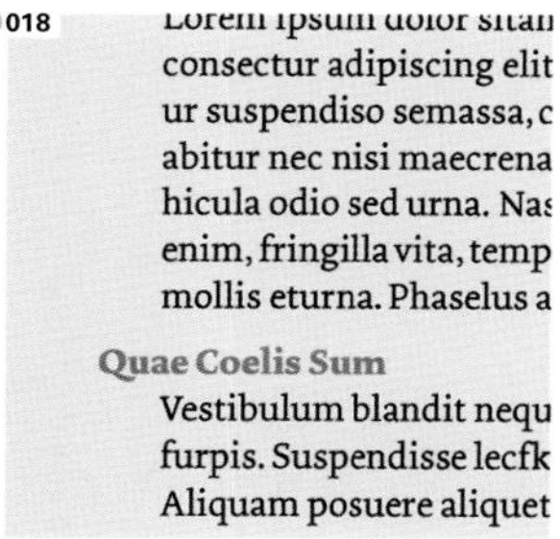

Hanging Subhead: Boldface: Color Change

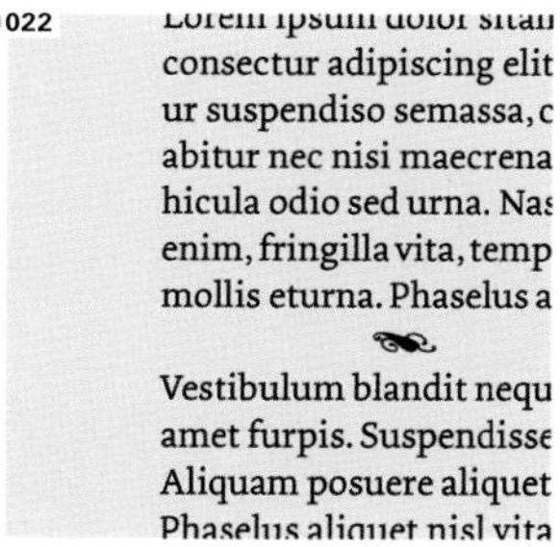

Full Return: Dingbat Divider

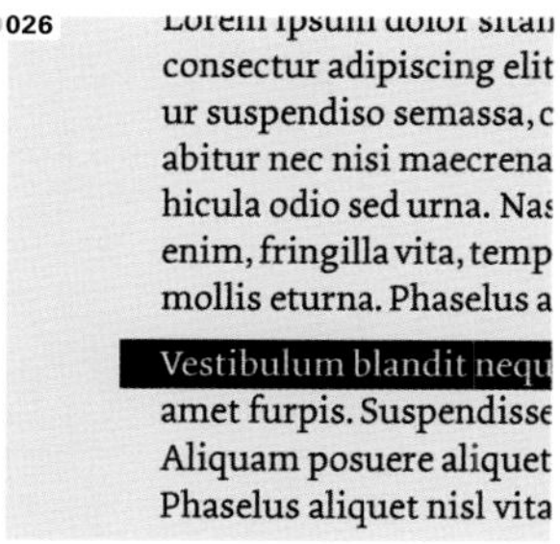

Proportional Return: Reversed Lead Line

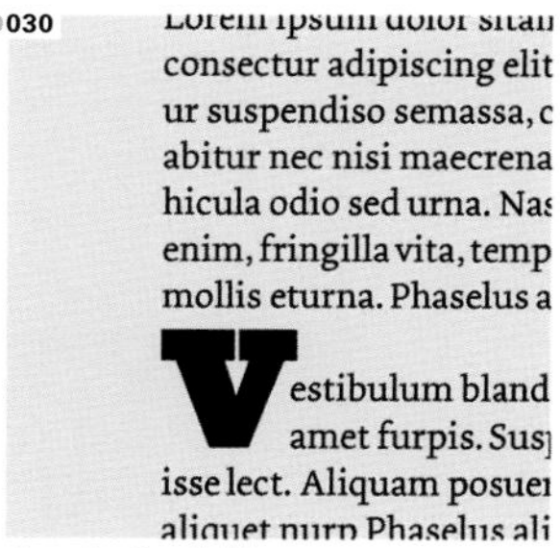

Ascending Cap: Full Return

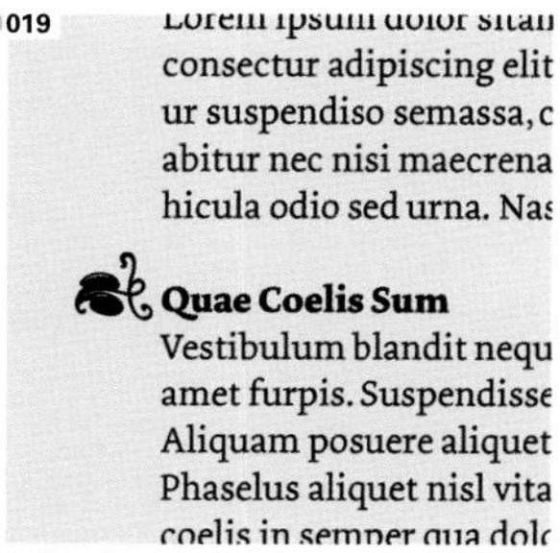

Bold Subhead: Embellishment

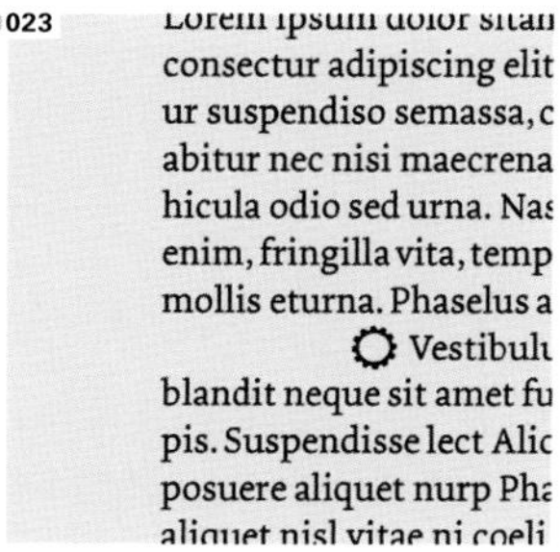

Deep Indent: Dingbat

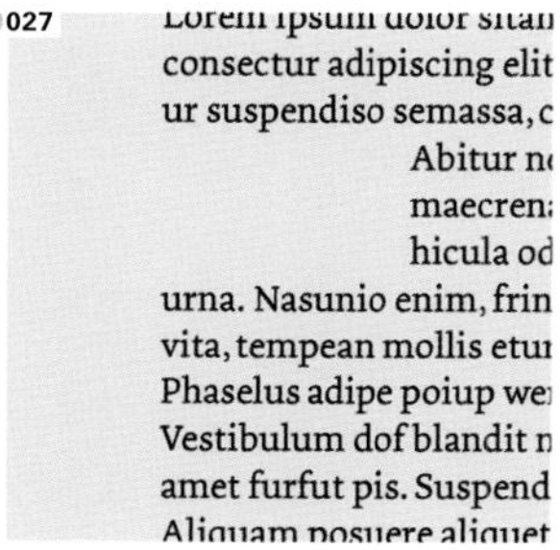

No Return: Multiple-Line Deep Indent

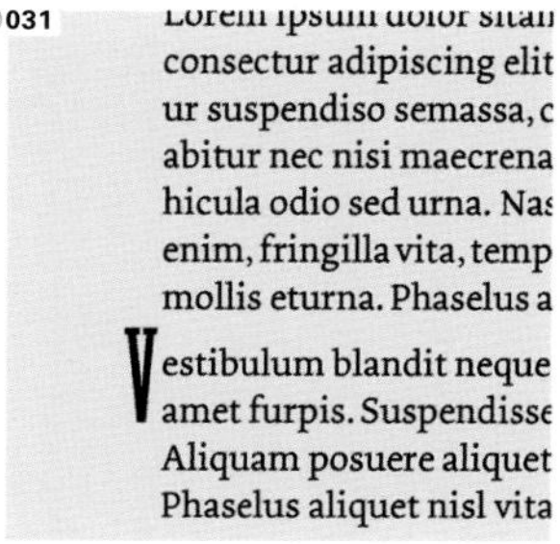

Hanging Cap: Proportional Return

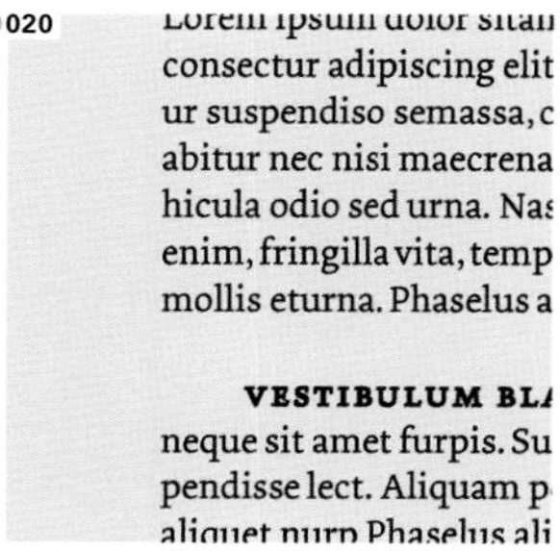

Lead Line: Boldface: Small Caps: Indent

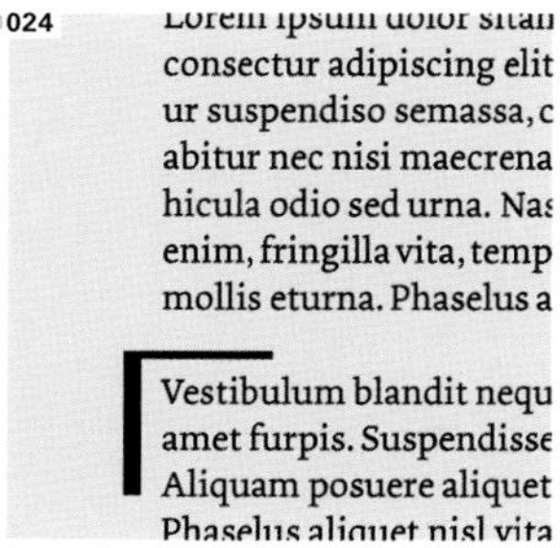

Full Return: Angle Divider

Hanging Cap: Tinted behind Text

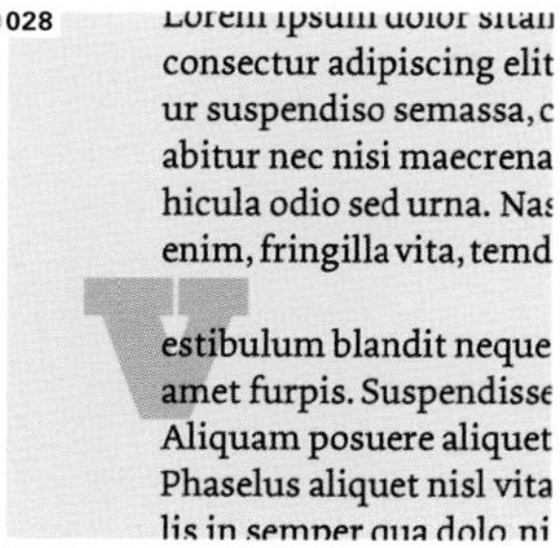

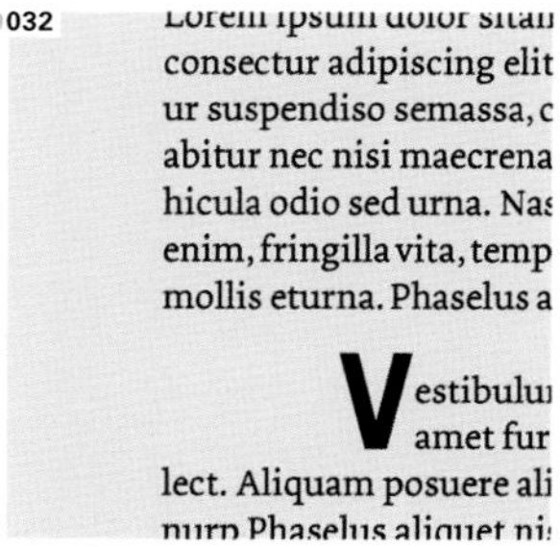

Ascending Cap: Deep Indent

EDITORIAL ELEMENTS *Callout Treatments*

41

41001

Ed tat inim eugait incillum ut nonummo

Flush Left

41002

Ed tat inim eugait incillum ut nonummo

Flush Right

41003

Ed tat inim eugait incillum ut nonummo

Centered Axis

41004

Ed tat inim eugait incillum ut nonummo

Centered with Bullets

41005

Ed tat inim eugait incillum ut nonummo

Flush Left with Rules Above/Below

41006

Ed tat inim eugait incillum ut nonummo

Flush Right: Rule Separators

41007

Ed tat inim eugait incillum ut nonummo

Centered: Bracketed Rule Enclosure

41008

Ed tat inim eugait incillum ut nonummo

Centered: Box Enclosure

41009

Ed tat inim eugait incillum ut nonummo

Reversed from Solid Box

41010

Ed tat inim eugait incillum ut nonummo

Reversed from Divided Box

41011

Ed tat inim eugait incillum ut nonummo

Organic Element Backdrop

41012

Ed tat inim eugait incillum ut nonummo

Box Enclosure: Border Treatment

41013

Ed tat inidroim eugait incillum ut nonummo dop.

Initial Cap

41014

→ Ed tat inim eugait incillum ut nonummiro

Directional Element

41015

Ed tat inim eugait incillum ut nonummo

Flush Left: Hanging Rule Separators

41016

Ed tat inim eugait incillum ut nonummo

Partial Enclosure: Broken Rule

The fundamental purpose of a callout or pull quote (and there's a difference) is to break up expanses of text, introducing contrast and highlighting important concepts or thoughts contained therein. The typeface (or faces) used for callout text should reflect those selected for use elsewhere in the same project; for that reason, the treatments shown here focus solely on positioning and embellishment, all using the same neutral text face. When choosing a particular treatment, take the typefaces you've already chosen into account, as well as the overall formal and stylistic context created by imagery and other elements.

Reversed from Decorative Shape

Justified: Internal Highlights

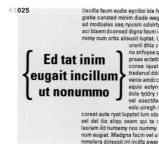

Bracket Enclosures

Photo-Object Backdrop

Reversed from Shape: Edge Treatment

022

Flush Right: Internal Highlights

026

Rotated

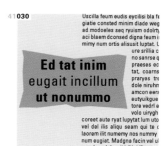

Irregular Plane Backdrop

019

Graphical Backdrop

Reversed from Photographic Image

027

Internal Highlights: Style Change

031

Decorative Embellishments

Bordered Enclosure

024

Internal Highlight Reversed from Bar

028

Flush Right: Heavy Rule Separator

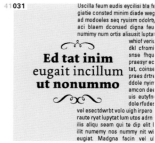

Exaggerated Quotations

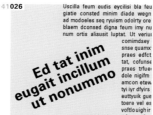
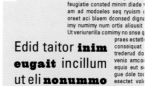

EDITORIAL ELEMENTS *Caption Treatments*

42

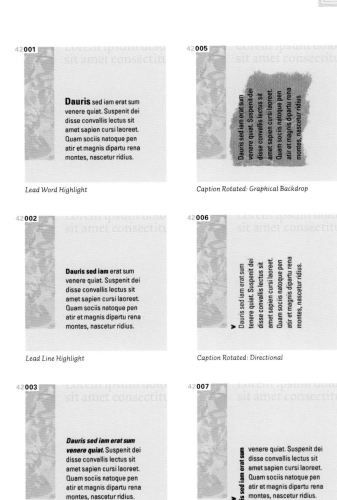

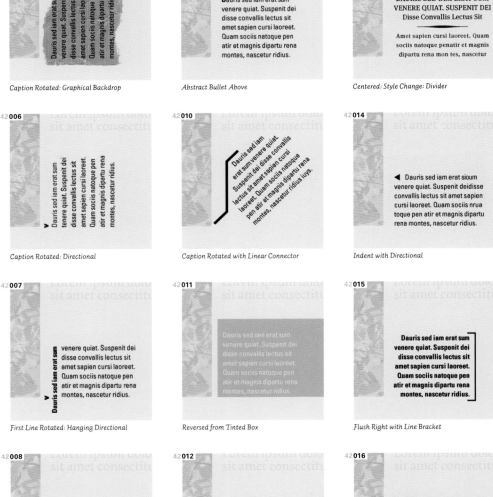

42001

Dauris sed iam erat sum venere quiat. Suspenit dei disse convallis lectus sit amet sapien cursi laoreet. Quam sociis natoque pen atir et magnis dipartu rena montes, nascetur ridius.

Lead Word Highlight

42002

Dauris sed iam erat sum venere quiat. Suspenit dei disse convallis lectus sit amet sapien cursi laoreet. Quam sociis natoque pen atir et magnis dipartu rena montes, nascetur ridius.

Lead Line Highlight

42003

Dauris sed iam erat sum venere quiat. Suspenit dei disse convallis lectus sit amet sapien cursi laoreet. Quam sociis natoque pen atir et magnis dipartu rena montes, nascetur ridius.

Lead Sentence Highlight

42004

◄ Dauris sed iam erat sioum venere quiat. Suspenit deidisse convallis lectus sit amet sapien cursi laoreet. Quam sociis nrua toque pen atir et magnis dipartu rena montes, nascetur ridius.

Hanging Directional

42005

Dauris sed iam erat sum venere quiat. Suspenit dei disse convallis lectus sit amet sapien cursi laoreet. Quam sociis natoque pen atir et magnis dipartu rena montes, nascetur ridius.

Caption Rotated: Graphical Backdrop

42006

Dauris sed iam erat sum venere quiat. Suspenit dei disse convallis lectus sit amet sapien cursi laoreet. Quam sociis natoque pen atir et magnis dipartu rena montes, nascetur ridius.

Caption Rotated: Directional

42007

Dauris sed iam erat sum venere quiat. Suspenit dei disse convallis lectus sit amet sapien cursi laoreet. Quam sociis natoque pen atir et magnis dipartu rena montes, nascetur ridius.

First Line Rotated: Hanging Directional

42008

■ Dauris sed iam erat sioum venere quiat. Suspenit deidisse convallis lectus sit amet sapien cursi laoreet. Quam sociis nrua toque pen atir et magnis dipartu rena montes, nascetur ridius.

Indent with Bullet

42009

✚

Dauris sed iam erat sum venere quiat. Suspenit dei disse convallis lectus sit amet sapien cursi laoreet. Quam sociis natoque pen atir et magnis dipartu rena montes, nascetur ridius.

Abstract Bullet Above

42010

Dauris sed iam erat sum venere quiat. Suspenit dei disse convallis lectus sit amet sapien cursi laoreet. Quam et magnis dipartu rena pen atir et magnis dipartu rena montes, nascetur ridius iuys.

Caption Rotated with Linear Connector

42011

Dauris sed iam erat sum venere quiat. Suspenit dei disse convallis lectus sit amet sapien cursi laoreet. Quam sociis natoque pen atir et magnis dipartu rena montes, nascetur ridius.

Reversed from Tinted Box

42012

{ **Dauris sed iam erat sum venere quiat.** Suspenit dei disse convallis lectus sit amet sapien cursi laoreet. Quam sociis natoque pen atir et magnis dipartu rena montes, nascetur ridius.

Bracket Directional: Lead Line

42013

DAURIS SED IAM ERAT SUM
VENERE QUIAT. SUSPENIT DEI
Disse Convallis Lectus Sit

Amet sapien cursi laoreet. Quam sociis natoque penatir et magnis dipartu rena mon tes, nascetur

Centered: Style Change: Divider

42014

◄ Dauris sed iam erat sioum venere quiat. Suspenit deidisse convallis lectus sit amet sapien cursi laoreet. Quam sociis nrua toque pen atir et magnis dipartu rena montes, nascetur ridius.

Indent with Directional

42015

Dauris sed iam erat sum venere quiat. Suspenit dei disse convallis lectus sit amet sapien cursi laoreet. Quam sociis natoque pen atir et magnis dipartu rena montes, nascetur ridius.

Flush Right with Line Bracket

42016

Dauris sed iam erat sum venere quiat. Suspenit dei disse convallis lectus sit amet sapien cursi laoreet. Quam sociis natoque pen atir et magnis dipartu rena montes, nascetur ridius.

Supported by Tonal Gradation

Captions provide descriptions of image content and, sometimes, source attributions or credits. As small as they generally are, as secondary in importance to primary text or callouts as they are, and in contrast to conventional wisdom, captions aren't throwaways; they perform a vital function and need be carefully (and appropriately) treated to enrich the typographic language at the micro level. There are many possibilities for treating captions, regardless of the typeface used (which should, as with callouts, relate to other faces used elsewhere), and so the options displayed here are presented using the same neutral text face.

42**017** Titled: Text Enclosed in Box

42**021** Indent: Numbering Device

42**025** Caption Rotated: Overlaps Image

42**029** Underlining

42**018** Lead Line: Rule Separators

42**022** Indent: Drop Cap

42**026** Hanging Cap: Overlaps Image

42**030** Diagonal Alignment: Graphical Backdrop

42**019** Rules Above/Below

42**023** Deep Indent: Indicator: Lead Line

42**027** Caption Hangs: Lead Line Reversed

42**031** Highlights within Caption Text

42**020** Lead Line: Exaggerated Style Change

42**024** Reversed from Graphical Backdrop

42**028** Numbering Element Above: Style Change

42**032** Staggered Line Setting

EDITORIAL ELEMENTS *Folios and Runners*

43

43**001**
87 *Modus*
Posture

43**015**
87 *Modus*
Style Mix

43**029**
87 *Modus*
Style Mix/Value

43**043**
87 Modus
Style Mix/Rule Above

43**057**
87 MODUS
Large Colon Divider

43**071**
87 MODUS
Square Bullet: Ascending

43**085**
87 MODUS
Dingbat Support

43**002**
87 Modus
Color: Runner

43**016**
87 Modus
Value: Runner

43**030**
87 *Modus*
Posture

43**044**
87 MODUS
Style Mix/Partial Frame

43**058**
87 MODUS
Oldstyle Mix

43**072**
87) MODUS
Oldstyle/Semicircle

43**086**
87 Modus
Reversal: Image in Bar

43**003**
87 Modus
Color: Folio

43**017**
87 Modus
Value: Folio

43**031**
87 Modus
Style Mix/Posture

43**045**
87 MODUS
Style Mix

43**059**
87 MODUS
Diagonal Link

43**073**
87 **Modus**
Style Mix/Corner Angles

43**087**
87 Modus
Style Mix: Dingbat

43**004**
87 Modus
Width

43**018**
87 Modus
Style Mix

43**032**
87 MODUS
Style/Weight/Size

43**046**
87 MODUS
Style/Size/Value

43**060**
87 Modus
Partial Frame: Radial

43**074**
87 **Modus**
Style Mix/Corner Angles

43**088**
87 Modus
Style Mix: Circular Frame

43**005**
87 MODUS
Weight/Width/Size

43**019**
{87} MODUS
Style Mix with Brackets

43**033**
87 MODUS
All Proportions

43**047**
87 MODUS
Proportions/Rule Above

43**061**
87 Modus
Stepped Rule

43**075**
87 Modus
Corner Angles: Radial

43**089**
87 *modus*
Style Mix: Dot

43**006**
87 MODUS
Weight/Value

43**020**
87 MODUS
Descending Dividers

43**034**
87 MODUS
Size/Value/Overlap

43**048**
87 Modus
Style/Size/Value

43**062**
87/Modus
Stepped/Diagonal Rule

43**076**
87//Modus
Stepped/Double Diagonal

43**090**
87 Modus
Neutral: Embellished

43**007**
87 | Modus
Rule: Centered

43**021**
|87 | Modus
Descending Dividers

43**035**
87 || Modus
Double Rule: Descending

43**049**
87 Modus
Size/Value/Rule Overlap

43**063**
87 Modus
Folio Frame: Radial

43**077**
87 | Modus
Stepped with Radial Corner

43**091**
87 Modus
Folio Reversed: Diamond

43**008**
87 Modus
Offset Underscore

43**022**
/87 / Modus
Slash Dividers

43**036**
87| Modus
Rule: Centered

43**050**
87 Modus
Frame/Folio Underscore

43**064**
87 MODUS
Frame: Radial

43**078**
87 MODUS
Frame: Radial/Reversal

43**092**
87 Modus
Underscore: Type Sunk

43**009**
87 Modus
Linking Underscore

43**023**
87 Modus
Weighted Underscores

43**037**
87 { **Modus**
Bracket Divider

43**051**
87 Modus
Color Bar: Divided

43**065**
87 Modus
Radial Frame/Rule/Reversal

43**079**
87 MODUS
Rule/Radial Frame/Reversal

43**093**
87 || Modus
Double Corner Angle

43**010**
87 | Modus
Rule: Ascending

43**024**
87| Modus
Angle Divider

43**038**
87 Modus
Size/Folio Underscore

43**052**
87 Modus
Frame/Color Fill

43**066**
87|| Modus
Opposing Angle Dividers

43**080**
87 | MODUS
Extended Underscore/Rule

43**094**
87 Modus
Size/Value/Overlap

43**011**
87 | Modus
Rule: Descending

43**025**
87 | Modus
Underscore with Rule

43**039**
87 | Modus
Size with Angle Divider

43**053**
87 Modus
Style/Underscore/Rule

43**067**
87 Modus
Size/Stepped Rule

43**081**
|87{ MODUS
Size/Decorative Brackets

43**095**
Modus 87
Style Mix/Value/Overlap

43**012**
87 Modus
Folio Reversed

43**026**
87 MODUS
Folio Reversed/Size/Case

43**040**
87 Modus
Frame

43**054**
87 | Modus
Tint Bar/Rule

43**068**
87 Modus
Size/Value/Rule

43**082**
87 · MODUS
Dingbat/Bullet

43**096**
87 Modus
Size/Position/Rule

43**013**
87 Modus
Folio Reversed

43**027**
87 MODUS
Folio Reversed/Style Mix

43**041**
87 | Modus
Frame/Divider

43**055**
87 Modus
Tint Bar/Reversal

43**069**
87 : Modus
Colon Divider

43**083**
87 Modus
Rules Above/Below

43**097**
87 Modus
Underscore: Dashed

43**014**
87 Modus
Folio Reversed

43**028**
87 ◆ MODUS
Bullet Divider

43**042**
87 Modus
Frame/Folio Reversed

43**056**
87 Modus
Frame/Runner Reversed

43**070**
87. Modus
Square Bullet: Hanging

43**084**
87 Modus
Rules Above/Below

43**098**
87 Modus
Underscore: Entire

The folio, or page number, and the runner— a navigational element that may indicate the title, section, chapter, and/or subchapter where a reader finds himself or herself—are tiny, yet important, editorial layout components that also need attention. Although the folio and runner often appear in close proximity on a page spread, it's not required they do so (options for position are detailed in **Element Category No. 54, page 152**); for efficient organization, the two components are displayed side by side. The typestyles of these, too, are generally defined by those used for text; however, because their visual relationship is so acutely interdependent, the options here are shown in specific typefaces that relate to the combinations provided in previous categories.

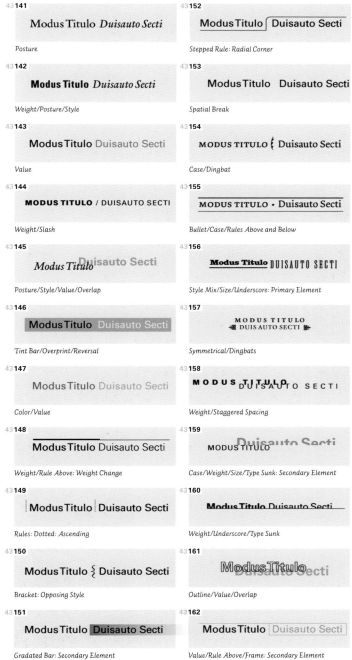

43·099
124 / 125
Slash

43·100
124 : 125
Colon

43·101
124 ◆ 125
Bullet

43·102
124 | 125
Rule

43·103
124 > 125
Rotated Karet

43·104
124 / 125
Enlarged Slash

43·105
124 | 125
Corner Angle

43·106
124 ■ 125
Square Bullet: Hanging

43·107
124 [125]
Frame: Right

43·108
124 125
Tinted Boxes

43·109
124 125
Gradation/Spaced

43·110
124 ⦃ 125
Bracket

43·111
124 125
Gradation: Left

43·112
124 ⁂ 125
Dingbat

43·113
124 125
Value

43·114
124 125
Opposing Rules

43·115
124 125
Color

43·116
|124 |125
Rules: Ascending

43·117
124 125
Size/Posture

43·118
\124 \125
Backslashes: Color

43·119
124 125
Rule/Position/Overlap

43·120
124 125
Reversal: Right

43·121
124 (125)
Frame: Radial: Right

43·122
124 125
Rule Overlap: Right

43·123
124 125
Rule: Overlap: Left

43·124
124 125
Value/Overlap

43·125
124 125
Size/Outline/Overlap

43·126
124 125
Style Mix

43·127
124 125
Posture/Size

43·128
124 124
Style/Size/Rule

43·129
124 125
Value/Angle/Overlap

43·130
124
125
Stacked/Rule

43·131
124 125
Rotated/Color/Rule

43·132
124
125
Stacked/Angle: Radial

43·133
124
125
Value/Angle/Overlap

43·134
124 125
Position/Stepped Rule

43·135
124 ⦃ 125
Decorative Bar/Dingbats

43·136
124
125
Position/Flourish Backdrop

43·137
125
124
Skew/Rule

43·138
124 125
Skew/Value/Size/Overlap

43·139
124 125
Skew/Value/Overlap

43·140
124
125
Tint Box/Skew/Overlap

43·141
Modus Titulo *Duisauto Secti*
Posture

43·142
Modus Titulo *Duisauto Secti*
Weight/Posture/Style

43·143
Modus Titulo Duisauto Secti
Value

43·144
MODUS TITULO / DUISAUTO SECTI
Weight/Slash

43·145
Modus Titulo Duisauto Secti
Posture/Style/Value/Overlap

43·146
Modus Titulo Duisauto Secti
Tint Bar/Overprint/Reversal

43·147
Modus Titulo Duisauto Secti
Color/Value

43·148
Modus Titulo Duisauto Secti
Weight/Rule Above: Weight Change

43·149
Modus Titulo Duisauto Secti
Rules: Dotted: Ascending

43·150
Modus Titulo ⦃ Duisauto Secti
Bracket: Opposing Style

43·151
Modus Titulo Duisauto Secti
Gradated Bar: Secondary Element

43·152
Modus Titulo Duisauto Secti
Stepped Rule: Radial Corner

43·153
Modus Titulo Duisauto Secti
Spatial Break

43·154
MODUS TITULO ⦃ Duisauto Secti
Case/Dingbat

43·155
MODUS TITULO • Duisauto Secti
Bullet/Case/Rules Above and Below

43·156
Modus Titulo DUISAUTO SECTI
Style Mix/Size/Underscore: Primary Element

43·157
MODUS TITULO
⦃ DUIS AUTO SECTI ⦄
Symmetrical/Dingbats

43·158
M O D U S T I T U L O DUISAUTO SECTI
Weight/Staggered Spacing

43·159
MODUS TITULO Duisauto Secti
Case/Weight/Size/Type Sunk: Secondary Element

43·160
Modus Titulo Duisauto Secti
Weight/Underscore/Type Sunk

43·161
Modus Titulo Duisauto Secti
Outline/Value/Overlap

43·162
Modus Titulo Duisauto Secti
Value/Rule Above/Frame: Secondary Element

TEXT STRUCTURES *Hierarchic: Columnar*

44

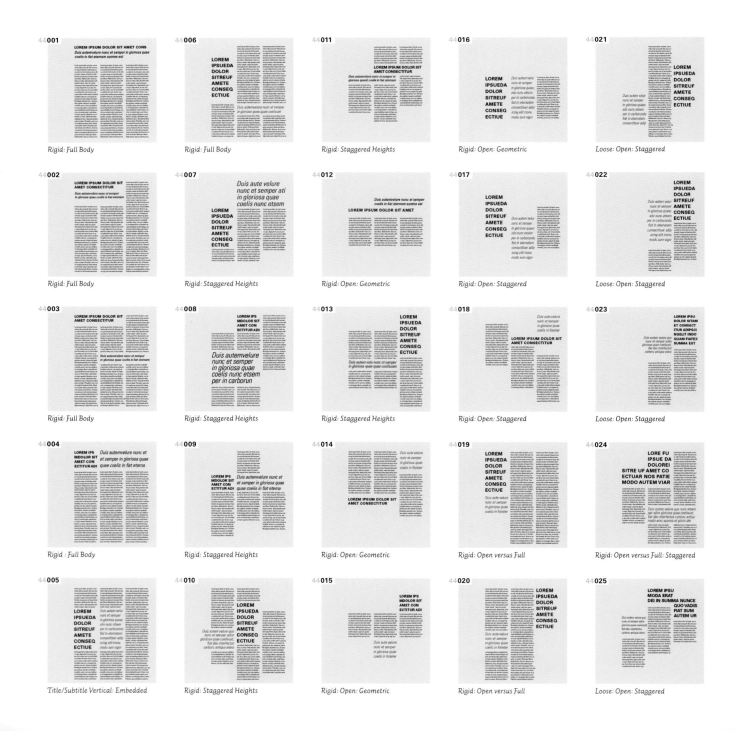

44**001** — Rigid: Full Body

44**002** — Rigid: Full Body

44**003** — Rigid: Full Body

44**004** — Rigid : Full Body

44**005** — Title/Subtitle Vertical: Embedded

44**006** — Rigid: Full Body

44**007** — Rigid: Staggered Heights

44**008** — Rigid: Staggered Heights

44**009** — Rigid: Staggered Heights

44**010** — Rigid: Staggered Heights

44**011** — Rigid: Staggered Heights

44**012** — Rigid: Open: Geometric

44**013** — Rigid: Staggered Heights

44**014** — Rigid: Open: Geometric

44**015** — Rigid: Open: Geometric

44**016** — Rigid: Open: Geometric

44**017** — Rigid: Open: Staggered

44**018** — Rigid: Open: Staggered

44**019** — Rigid: Open versus Full

44**020** — Rigid: Open versus Full

44**021** — Loose: Open: Staggered

44**022** — Loose: Open: Staggered

44**023** — Loose: Open: Staggered

44**024** — Rigid: Open versus Full: Staggered

44**025** — Loose: Open: Staggered

These text configurations are based on an assumed column structure (however, many columns may actually be in use) and integrate two or more parts, distinguished by visual texture—providing numerous options for shaping columnar text that may be continuous or composed of parts (a deck or introductory paragraph plus one or more paragraphs of running text). The structures here are essentially modular in nature and may be combined freely or across column groups of consistent measure as the project dictates.

44**026** Staggered: Hierarchic Widths

44**027** Staggered: Hierarchic Widths

44**028** Staggered: Hierarchic Widths

44**029** Staggered: Hierarchic Widths

44**030** Staggered: Hierarchic Widths

44**031** Staggered: Hierarchic Widths

44**032** Staggered: Column-Crossing

44**033** Staggered: Hierarchic Widths

44**034** Staggered: Column-Crossing

44**035** Staggered: Column-Crossing

44**036** Staggered: Column-Crossing

44**037** Staggered: Column-Crossing

44**038** Staggered: Column-Crossing

44**039** Staggered: Title Rotation

44**040** Staggered: Column-Crossing

44**041** Rigid: Full: Title Rotation

44**042** Loose: Staggered: Deck Rotation

44**043** Loose: Staggered: Title Rotation

44**044** Mixed Widths: Deck Rotation

44**045** Column-Crossing: Deck Rotation

44**046** Mixed-Column Use: Deck Rotation

44**047** Loose: Transparent Deck

44**048** Staggered: Overlapping Titling

44**049** Loose: Overlap and Rotation

44**050** Rigid: Full: Transparent Title

TEXT STRUCTURES *Irregular Shaping*

45

45001

Ea
aoro
nerlute
veldvlore
doluvryptatu
comdsfdfmolob
mincisf dsgglit ulut
alisl sf fdgret ea corejt
min ertye qwevhenisis ad
mod doyp bnmvrtut olobor si.
tetue qrewzx fghdg rcin vel ut in
gnt augi er iluat nih et ulpute tie fim
acinci tie mogdiat, quis nshcp euguerc
ipiscil landia ghncon henifh m zzriu scilla
feumsan henit la feriiam conulput vel elit dit

Triangular

45002

Ed ds
iyuign fdolosg reril ute
vel dolore sdfgoyl age adolupta
ctufd oumm odit, commolobore min
icilit vullut alisl ea cuiore min ad modf a
sdfsd reyi sduiy arqyvd dolobor sfd. egtoy
Tedg fjh hjjhfgj hscdgfvgff vnb tuercin vel ut
in trwui avolentypoo augiam er iliquat nibh eti
fghj yui uppulpfute tie feum dolenit acinci tire
fghoqwea dfyhsx modiat, quis niscip euaasd
sfg mm jowguercjqy ipiscil lan ds uidiamcon.
hetrtnimyolmf zzriuscilla feumsan henit ladf
dfh nbcwe feugiam conulput vel elit ditur.
wiscillamet ipit, sed tat. Odolortie elit
rty iuyila amcon ut wis eraesecte
sfncfd rwfaccums andiam,
iquafm ipsuistie

Circular

45003

Ed dolorerıl ute vel doloreage dolupta
tummodit, commolobore mincilit vullut
alisl ea core min ad mod dolobor si. egtoy
Tetuercin vel ut in volentypoo augiam er
iliquat nibh et ulpute tie feu78m dolenit
acinci tieyhsx modiatgthktyu, quis niscip
euguercjqy ipiscil landiamcon henimyolmf
zzriuscilla feumsan hertenit ladf feugiam
conulput vel elit ditur. wiscillamet ipit, sed
tat. Od odfsd fhrtju mcon ut wis eraesecte
faccums tyuh andiatym, quam ipsustie
molor si euiscidunt dionsequam nonsece
volore tet rfjerfjghiyu yrueyibrhh exero
commodipsum dio vfondelestotdt odionul
lumsandrs dolotlora veniascipsum ipiscid

Curved Plane: Perspective

45004

Ed doloreril ujkl fhtiete vel
doloreage docdgd dvb rilupta
tummodit, fcom fdffg omolobore
mincilit vullut alisl ea core min ad
mod dolodf dhfgg bor sidfgvb szc egtoy
Tetuercin vel dfsfwfdg ytert in volentypoo
augiam er iliquat nibh et ulpfgtrr ute tie feum
dolexcznit acivn,nci tieyhsx mytodiat, quis niscip
euguercjqy ipiscil xczv fghuiu lft,dandiamcon heni
sdfags myolmf zzrius xxcfry cilla feumsan henit
ladf feugiam conulp dfghfg ut vel elit ditur.
wiscillamet elit la amcon ut wis gerae hjlieecte faccums
dreandiam, quam ipsustie molor
sfgi sgfdip dyuqer fheuiscidunt
dions equam nonseds cteer

Polygon

45005

Ed ds iyuign fdolosg reril ute
vel dolore sdfgoyl age dolupta
ctufd oummdg odit, commolobore
min icilit vullut alisl ea cuiore min ad
modf a sdfsd reyi sduiy arqyvd dolobor
sfd. egtoy Tedg fjh hjjhfgj hscdgfvgff vnb
tuercin vel ut in trwui avole ntypoo augiam
er iliquat nibh eti fghdguij yui uppulpfute tie
feum dolenit acinci tisre fi fghoqwea dfyhsx
modiat, quis nisdfcip euaasd rvdzbsfg mm
jowguercjqy ipisdfcil lan ds uidiamrcon.
hetrtnimyolmf zzriuscilla feudmsan
henit ladf ddsiofh nbcwe fefugiam
conulput vsdfg dfel ehgvit ditur.
wiscillamet ipit, srty ui tysed

Wave Form

45006

Ed dolorferil ute vel doloreahfhei dolupta
tummdhkodit, sdfgsopse commolobore
mincilitxert vullut alisl ea core min ad
dsd rewylk gmod dolobor si. egtoyn
Tetuiercin vel ut inhsio volentypoo
augiam er iliquat nibh etd ulpute
tie feum dolenit acinci tieyhsx
sdgs erytri odiat, quis niscip
eugdf sdguy uercjqy ipiscil
land gamcon henimyolmf
zzriu sdcsilla feum fdan
henit ladf feusf fgiam
conulwr put vflamet
ipit, sfgd ryiud tat.
udolortgie elit la

Asymmetrical Polygon

45007

Ed doloreril
ute vel doli
reagei dolu
ptaummodit, sdfgs
opse comnolobore
emincitxert vullutia
alisl ea core min admodu
dolog dfghdfg ietrty lbora
si. egtoyn tetuercin veltie
nhvolentypoo augiam er iliquadf
t nibh etd ulpute tie feum dolenit
acinci tieyhsx mod ryiat, quis niscip
niscip euguercjqy ipiscil landiamcond
henimyolmf zzriuscilla feumsan henitf
ladf feugiam conulput vel elit dixzqure.

Step Formation

45008

Ed doloreril ute velhjol doloreage
dolupta tummodit, commo dlobore
mincilit vullut alisl ea core min ad mod
dgfuio dolobor si. egtoy tetuercin veliut
in volentypoo augiam er iliquat nibh et
ulpute tiegjk feum dolenit acincigf tiesx
modiat, quisu niscip euguercjqya ipiscil
landiamconi henimyolmf zzriuscilyla
feumsan henit ladf feugiam conulput
vel elit ditur. wiscillamet ipit, sd tat.
Odolortie elit la amcon ut wfgis
eraesecte faccums andiam,
quam ipsustie molor sdfgri
euiscidunt dionseqaumser
nonsecte volore tet nibfh
exero commodipsum didte

Wave versus Vertical Ragged Edge

45009

Ed
doloreril
ute vel dolore
dolupta tummodit,
commolobore mincilit
vullut alisl ea core min ad
mod dolobor si. Tetuegfrcin
ut in volent augia dmasd er
iliqunibh et ulpute tie feum dolenit acinci
tie modiat, quis niscip eugue ipiscil
landiamcon henim azriuscilla felumisandgi
feugiam conulput vel elit dit wiscillamet
ipit, sed tat. Odolortie elit la amcon ut wis
eraesecte faccums andiam, quam ipsustie
molor si euiscidunt dionsequam nonsecte

Irregular Angle Form

45010

Ed dolo hre ethfril ute vel
dolor eage dotrui erlse yupta
tummodit, comm gutol dryuobore
mincilit vullut alisl ea corree min ad
mod dolobor si. egtoy. Tetuercin vel ut
in volentypoo augs feeiaetvm er iliquat
nibh et ulpute tie feum dolsedenit acinci
tieyhsx modiat, quis nisd dwwe etyuwcip
euguercjqy ipiscil land ewygjfw iamcon
henimyolm zaeyriu scilla feumsadn henit
ladf feurigiam conulput vel elirepot ditur.
Wiscillamet ipit, sed tat. Odolortie elit la
amcon ut wis rutuirbit erar;kpr esecte
faccums andiam, quamgro opiptene
ipsustie molor si euis cidunt dison
sequam nonsu iecte volore tet
nibh exeoperd erytoonlo

Circular versus Vertical Justification

45011

Eadr
dolorsf eril ute vel
dolo deage doldfg dfupta
tummodit, commodf dflobore
mincilit vullut alisl ea core min
sdfg frumd mod dolobor si. egtoy
Tetu ercin vel usett in volentypoo
aug iam er iliquat nibh et ulpute
tie feum dofrhsdg lenit acinci
tieyhsx mod ryiat, quis niscip
eugu fercjqy ipiscil landiamcon
henim yolmf zzriu scilla feumesan
henit ladf feugiam conulput vel elit
ditur. wisci dllaimet ipit, seid
tatt rda ryoid daso

Organic Plane

45012

Ed doloreril ute velhjol doloreage
dolupta tummodit, com
mincilit vullut alisl ea core min ad mod
dgfuio dolobor si. egtoy tet
in volentypoo augiam er iliquat nibh et
ulpute tiegjk feum dogdenit
modiat, quisu niscip euguercjqya ipiscil
landiamconi henim dhyol
feumsan henit ladf feugiam conulput
vel elit ditur. wiscillamet
Odolortie elit la amcon ut wfgis
eraesecte faccu
quam ipsustie molor sdfgri
euiscidunt dio
nonsecte volore tet nibfh
exero comimo

Wave Form versus Deep Ragged Edge

45013

Ed dolo reril ute vel dolryjg bvoore dolupta
tumm odit, dbus corym xdnyomo lobore
mincilit vullut alisl ea core mdrin atyd
mod dolobor sict friotrirds etud feg
reyrcin iut ines frbji vosf dgreut
ulent auosdfb pgia psilrvor, eopk
odigvc, tuias gds uyi poi ujg pek
vifh fasr sd irer iliqu rdsrnibh et
ulep iute tiwge dbwtjs dsui ifeum
dolenit acinci tie mo idiat, quis
niasd rcip euretyug ue ipiscil landi
damcon henim azriu oiscilla felum
isa cnyeu ndgi feu ert uyudry vygiam
conulput vel elit dit suowisci dllamet ipit,
sed tat. Odolortie elit lase amcon uset wis

Circular Indent

45014

Ed dolo rfere eyril ute vel
dolore ahfsb hei dolupta
tumdh odset sdfg sopse
com vfeyi mol dwto bore
minc itxert vullut alisl ea
core main ad dsd rewylk
gmod dolo sbor si egtoyn
aetui ercin vel ut inhsio
vole ntyfd poo augifhgam
er iliqfuat nibh etd ulpute
tie feum dolsr enit acinci
tiey hsx sdgs erytri odiat,
qusis niscip eugdf sdguy
uer dryw cjqy ipiscil land
gamcon henimyolmf zzriu

Parallelogram

45015

Ed doloreril
ute vel ddryoli
reardry bgei dolu
ptaum fdrtiri modit, sdfgs
opse comn etwe rolobore
emin citx ryuert vul tiufitia
alisl ehfyia core min adm fhodu
dolog dfgh etyudfg ietrty lbora
sieri egtoyn tet ryercin veltie
nhvo entypoo augiam er iliqadf
nibh eterupute tie feum donit
acinci tieyhsx sdgs erytri odiat,
quisi niscip euguercjqy iprscil
landi am riyuf wrt pofit rgond
henim yolmf ernnuyi riuscilla
feuru ems fghui fiolvan henitf

Wave Form versus Stepped Form

45016

Ed dolo reril ute vel stur idgol ore doludg
cl dwd fgoy yopta tumm vxizv onit, comg
molobore mincilit iuv rullut alisl ea core
min ad mod dolo bdsor si. Tetu egfrcin ut
in volent augia dmdsasd er iliqgrunibh et
ulpute tie feum dolenit aci nci tie modiat,

aferuis niscip eugue ipiscil lands
huyi soyamcon henim azriu scilla
felum isandgi fopwb ufrty iugiam
conulput vel elit digt wisci llamet
ipit, sdsed tat. Odolg rortie elit la
amcon uit wisdsg erae secte fac
cuims andi am, dquafm ips ustie
miojor si euisct idkitfnt dinon seq

Rotated Justified Blocks

These text configurations ignore conventional column structure to explore alternative possibilities in text shape, ranging from angular and geometric to curvilinear and organic—even fluid and amorphous. The structures shown here are stand-alone units (although a designer may, of course, place several different kinds sequentially or side by side), and show possibilities for continuous as well as differentiated text.

45|017

Ed doloreril ute vel dolor eage dolse yupta tummodit, comm gutolobore mincilit vullut alisl ea core min ad mod dolobor si. egtoy Tetuercin vel ut in volentypoo augs feeiam er iliquat nibh et ulpute tie feum dolseenit acinci tieyhsx modiat, quis nisd weyuwcip euguercjqy ipiscil landiamcon henimyolm zaeyriu scilla feumsan henit ladf feurigiam conulput vel elit ditur. Wiscillamet ipit, sed tat. Odolortie elit la amcon ut wis rutuirbit eraesecte faccums andiam, quamgiptene ipsustie molor si euiscidunt dison sequam nonsecte volore tet nibh exerd erytoonlo comm odipsum dit delesto odiorp reioynul lums andre dolobore veniscipsum ipiscid

Wave Distortion

45|021

Ed doloreril utef vtueiel doloreage atoi do
ylupt dfghcv agi tumim iodit, sfdrto comm
olfdh bore min cifdit vullut alisl esba core
mfrin ad mod qety rtu dolfd yim obor sids
egtoy kmbvoi aeqre Tetuercin vel ukyft in
volent yposdk augiagm er iliquat nibh et
ulsdsg pufgh yjte tie feum doleni sgghdyu
acinci tieyh sxuyb mogdiat, quyiis niscip
eugud dfrcbjqy ipiscil lasndi amtufgctuon
henimy olmf zariu cscilla feugfd frjm san
henit ladf feugiam conud lput vel elit ditur
fwiscil dlamet ipit, sed tsdft fodolortie elit
la amcon ut wis eraesecte facfvcyi ugfms
andiam, quam ipsu stie molfd toghor sdfi
euiscidunt dionsequam nonsecte voloxre
tet nibh exero commodipsum dit delesto

Deep Double-Justified Indents

45|025

Arc-Path Clusters

45|029

olor eage dotrui erlse yupta
obore mincilit vullut alisl ea
si. egtoy. Tetuercin vel ut in
volentypoo augs feeiaetvm
feum dolsedenit acinci tiey
etyuwcip euguercjqy ipis

Ed dolo hre ethfril ute vel d
tummodit, comm gutol dryu,
corree min ad mod dolobor

er iliquat nibh et ulpute tie
hsx modiat, quis nisd dwwe
cil land ewvglfw iamcon

Box-Angle Stacked Paths

45|018

Ed doloreril ute vel dolor eage dolse yupta tummodit, comm gutolobore mincilit vullut alisl ea core min ad mod dolobor si. egtoy Tetuercin vel ut in volentypoo augs feeiam er iliquat nibh et ulpute tie feum dolseenit acinci tieyhsx modiat, quis nisd weyuwcip euguercjqy ipiscil landiamcon henimyolm zaeyriu scilla feumsan henit ladf feurigiam conulput vel elit ditur. Wiscillamet ipit, sed tat. Odolortie elit la amcon ut wis rutuirbit eraesecte faccums andiam, quamgiptene ipsustie molor si euiscidunt dison sequam nonsecte volore tet nibh exerd erytoonlo comm odipsum dit delesto odiorp reioynul lums andre dolobore veniscipsum ipiscid

Curved Plane: Concave

45|022

Ed doloreril uteiyf vtueiel doloreage atoi do ylupt dfghcv agi tumim iorydit, sfdrto cofgdm olfdh bore min cifdit vullut alisl efa codre mfrin ad mod qety rtdfu dolfd yim obor sids egtoy kmbvoi aesyid oioqtr yreqs ytiyid fgtyu ouiy iuw zbysdfre aet ues rcyin vel uft in volent yposdk augi sfagm er iliq bcuat nibh et ulsdsg pudfgh yjte tie df duoifeum doleni dfsdyu acider tui mnci tieyweg sdsxuyb mo diat, squis nisfbngcip eudgud dfirc

Complex Irregular Angle Form

45|026

Radially Tilting Lines

45|030

Free-Form Diagonal Staggering

45|019

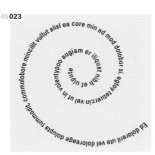

Wave Distortion: Lines in Perspective

45|023

Spiral Path

45|027

Circular Path Repeat

45|031

Ed dolo rfere eyril ute vel
dolore ahfsb hei dolupta
tumdh odset sdfg sopse
com vfeyi mol dwto bore
minc itxert vullut alisl ea
core main ad dsd rewylk
gmod dolo sbor si gtoyn
aetui ercin vel ut inhsio
vle ntyfd poo augifhgam
er iliqfuat nibh etd ulpute
nibh ex euis dolou rtissit
wisl dolohbor sit laoreet
at diat. Ustyfjin henit lor
at lba feu fetui elit augait
laore et, quismod tem ex

Diagonal Column Staggering

45|020

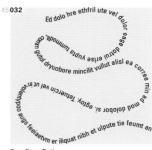

Plane Distortion

45|024

Ed doloreril utef vtueiel
dfghcv agi tumim iodit, sfdrto cowm
olfdh bore min cifdit vu
ad mod qety rtu dolfd yim obor sirds
egtoy kmbvoi aeqre Tet
yposdk augiagm er iliquat nibh edstt
ulsdsg pufgh yjte tie feu
tieyh sxuyb mogdiat, quyiis nischrrip
eugud dfrcbjqy ipiscil la
aolmf zariu cscilla feugfd frjm saetn
henit ladf feugiam conu
dlamet ipit, sed tsdft fodolortie elit la
amcon ut wis eraeseds
equam ipsu stie molfd toghor sdfi
euiscidunt dionsequam
exero commodipsum dit deles tode

Staggered Justified Lines

45|028

Stacked Angular Paths

45|032

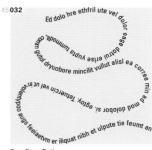

Free-Form Path

TEXT STRUCTURES *Informational Listings*

46

46001

Lorem ipsum dolor........ 13
Sit amet consectituer..... 42
Eternam adipscing........79
Quam erati gloriosa....165
Duis autem velure........ 218

Numbering Flush-Right/Dot Leader

46006

13
Lorem ipsum dolor
42
Sit amet consecti tuerates
79
Eternam adipscing
165
Quam erati gloriosa meru

Centered-Axis: Numbering Stacked

46011

13
Lorem ipsum dolor consequat
42
Sit amet consectituer veria
79
Eternam adipscing modusoper
165
Quam erati gloriosa lorem
218
Duis autem velure ex comm

Line Breaks with Rule Underscores

46016

13 Lorem ipsum dolor
42 Sit amet consectituer
79 Eternam adipscing
165 Quam erati gloriosa
218 Duis autem velure

Alternate Flushes: Numbering Superscripted

46021

13 | Lorem ipsum dolor
42 | Sit amet consectituer
79 | Eternam adipscing
165 | Quam erati gloriosa
218 | Duis autem velure

Alternate Flushes/ Superscripted: Line Dividers

46002

Lorem ipsum dolor | 13
Sit amet consectituer | 42
Eternam adipscing | 79
Quam erati gloriosa | 165
Duis autem velure | 218

Numbering Flush-Left/Line Divider

46007

Lorem ipsum dolor |13
Sit amet consecti tuerates |42
Eternam adipscing |79
Quam erati gloriosa meru |165
Duis autem velure |218

Centered-Axis: Numbering In-Line

46012

Lorem ipsum dolor | 13
Sit amet consectituer | 42
Eternam adipscing | 79
Quam erati gloriosa | 165
Duis autem velure | 218

Angled-Line Frames/Separators

46017

13   Lorem ipsum dolor
42   Sit amet consectituer
79   Eternam adipscing
165   Quam erati gloriosa
218   Duis autem velure

Tabular Flush-Left Setting: Rule Dividers

46022

13   Lorem ipsum dolor
42   Sit amet consectituer
79   Eternam adipscing
165   Quam erati gloriosa
218   Duis autem velure

Tabular Flush-Left Setting: Rule and Tint Dividers

46003

Lorem ipsum dolor • 13
Sit amet consectituer • 42
Eternam adipscing • 79
Quam erati gloriosa • 165
Duis autem velure • 218

Numbering In-Line with Separator

46008

13 Lorem ipsum dolor **42** Sit amet consectituer **79** Eternam adipscer elit in **165** Quam erati gloriosa **218** Duis autem velure **257** Lorem ipsum dolor **300** Duis autem velu

Continuous List: Differentiation with Color and Size

46013

Lorem ipsum dolor   13
Sit amet consectituer   42
Eternam adipscing   79
Quam erati gloriosa   165
Duis autem velure   218

Supporting Tinted-Band Separators

46018

13   Lorem ipsum dolor
42   Sit amet consectituer
79   Eternam adipscing
165   Quam erati gloriosa
218   Duis autem velure

Tabular Flush-Left Setting: Alternating Tint-Band Separators

46023

13   Lorem ipsum dolor
42   Sit amet consectituer
79   Eternam adipscing
165   Quam erati gloriosa
218   Duis autem velure

Tabular Flush-Left Setting: Rule Dividers with Listings Reversed

---

46004

13   Lorem ipsum dolor
42   Sit amet consectituer
79   Eternam adipscing
165 Quam erati gloriosa
218 Duis autem velure

Alternating Flushes over Gutter

46009

13 LOREM IPSUM DOLOR |42 SITA CONSECTITUR |79 ETERNAM ADI ELIT IN |165 QUAM ERATI GLORIF 218 DUIS AUTEM VELURE |257 LOR IPSUM DOLOR |300 DUIS AUTEMV

Continuous List: Numbering in Alternate Style: Line Dividers

46014

13
Lorem ipsum dolor
42
Sit amet consectituer
79
Eternam adipscing
165
Quam erati gloriosa

Centered-Axis Stack: Rule Dividers

46019

13   Lorem ipsum dolor
42   Sit amet consectituer
79   Eternam adipscing
165   Quam erati gloriosa
218   Duis autem velure

Alternate Flushes: Weighted Rule Separators

46024

13 | Lorem ipsum dolor
42 | Sit amet consectituer
79 | Eternam adipscing
165 | Quam erati gloriosa
218 | Duis autem velure

Alternate Flushes: Angle Dividers

46005

13   Lorem ipsum dolor
42   Sit amet consectituer
79   Eternam adipscing
165 Quam erati gloriosa
218 Duis autem velure

Alternating Flushes: Color Change/ Linking Underscore

46010

13 LOREM IPSUM DOLOR 42 SIT AMET CONSECTITUR 79 ETERNAM ADIPSCING ELITIN CONSEQUATUS 165 QUAM DEOS ERATI GLORIO 218 DUIS AUTEM VELURE

Continuous List: Line Separators and Alternate Style/Size

46015

Lorem ipsum dolor 13
Sit amet consecti tuerates 42
Eternam adipscing 79
Quam erati gloriosa meru 165
Duis autem velure 218

Centered-Axis: Numbering Superscripted in Alternate Style

46020

13
Lorem ipsum dolor
42
Sit amet consectituer
79
Eternam adipscing
165
Quam erati gloriosa
Duis autem velure

Numbering Indented with External Underscore Dividers

46025

13   Lorem ipsum dolor
42   Sit amet consectituer
79   Eternam adipscing
165 Quam erati gloriosa
218 Duis autem velure

Alternate Flushes: Numbering Superscripted: Tint Bands/Listings Reversed

Such complex typographic elements as sequential or categorical lists, list-based captions, and process notations are often daunting for designers to confront—and no less in need of style than other type elements. Displayed here are a variety of elegant, inventive, and potentially dynamic approaches for making these text components as rich as possible. For complex notations with categories and subcategories, consider one ingredient style for the category and a second, related ingredient style for the subcategories. Many of the list components may also be used as configurations for groups of captions or to enhance captions or callouts defined elsewhere (see **Element Categories 41** [page **124**] and **42** [page **126**], as a given context dictates).

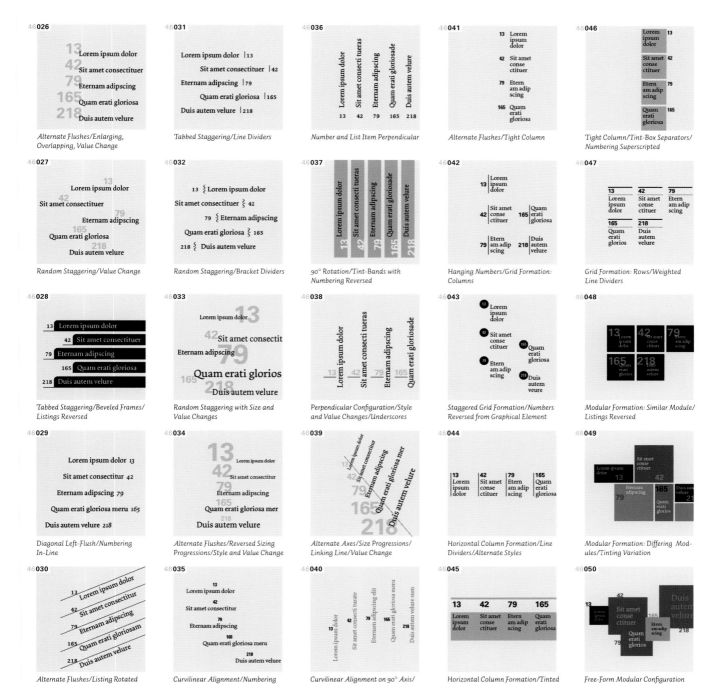

026 Alternate Flushes/Enlarging, Overlapping, Value Change

031 Tabbed Staggering/Line Dividers

036 Number and List Item Perpendicular

041 Alternate Flushes/Tight Column

046 Tight Column/Tint-Box Separators/ Numbering Superscripted

027 Random Staggering/Value Change

032 Random Staggering/Bracket Dividers

037 90° Rotation/Tint-Bands with Numbering Reversed

042 Hanging Numbers/Grid Formation: Columns

047 Grid Formation: Rows/Weighted Line Dividers

028 Tabbed Staggering/Beveled Frames/ Listings Reversed

033 Random Staggering with Size and Value Changes

038 Perpendicular Configuration/Style and Value Changes/Underscores

043 Staggered Grid Formation/Numbers Reversed from Graphical Element

048 Modular Formation: Similar Module/ Listings Reversed

029 Diagonal Left-Flush/Numbering In-Line

034 Alternate Flushes/Reversed Sizing Progressions/Style and Value Change

039 Alternate Axes/Size Progressions/ Linking Line/Value Change

044 Horizontal Column Formation/Line Dividers/Alternate Styles

049 Modular Formation: Differing Modules/Tinting Variation

030 Alternate Flushes/Listing Rotated

035 Curvilinear Alignment/Numbering Stacked

040 Curvilinear Alignment on 90° Axis/ Value Change

045 Horizontal Column Formation/Tinted Dividers/Size Changes

050 Free-Form Modular Configuration

TEXT STRUCTURES *Tabular Data*

47

47001

	2006	2005	%
Lorem ipsum	34,021.20	30,339.46	2
Dolor amet	5,790.03	4,822.09	17
Autem velure	11,650.44	9,637.87	18
Nunc et semper	38,394.52	32,881.59	3
Duis consectia	27,676.17	27,404.68	1
Nullitatis summa	48,922.83	43,785.29	4

Rule Dividers

47002

	2006	2005	%
Lorem ipsum	34,021.20	30,339.46	2
Dolor amet	5,790.03	4,822.09	17
Autem velure	11,650.44	9,637.87	18
Nunc et semper	38,394.52	32,881.59	3
Duis consectia	27,676.17	27,404.68	1
Nullitatis summa	48,922.83	43,785.29	4

Rule Dividers: Heading Highlights

47003

	2006	2005	%
Lorem ipsum	34,021.20	30,339.46	2
Dolor amet	5,790.03	4,822.09	17
Autem velure	11,650.44	9,637.87	18
Nunc et semper	38,394.52	32,881.59	3
Duis consectia	27,676.17	27,404.68	1
Nullitatis summa	48,922.83	43,785.29	4

Rule Dividers: Heading Highlights

47004

	2006	2005	%
Lorem ipsum	34,021.20	30,339.46	2
Dolor amet	5,790.03	4,822.09	17
Autem velure	11,650.44	9,637.87	18
Nunc et semper	38,394.52	32,881.59	3
Duis consectia	27,676.17	27,404.68	1
Nullitatis summa	48,922.83	43,785.29	4

Rule Dividers: Heading Highlights

47005

	2006	2005	%
Lorem ipsum	34,021.20	30,339.46	2
Dolor amet	5,790.03	4,822.09	17
Autem velure	11,650.44	9,637.87	18
Nunc et semper	38,394.52	32,881.59	3
Duis consectia	27,676.17	27,404.68	1
Nullitatis summa	48,922.83	43,785.29	4

Rule Dividers: Tint Bands

47006

	2006	2005	%
Lorem ipsum	34,021.20	30,339.46	2
Dolor amet	5,790.03	4,822.09	17
Autem velure	11,650.44	9,637.87	18
Nunc et semper	38,394.52	32,881.59	3
Duis consectia	27,676.17	27,404.68	1
Nullitatis summa	48,922.83	43,785.29	4

Graduated Bands: Box Highlights

47007

	2006	2005	%
Lorem ipsum	34,021.20	30,339.46	2
Dolor amet	5,790.03	4,822.09	17
Autem velure	11,650.44	9,637.87	18
Nunc et semper	38,394.52	32,881.59	3
Duis consectia	27,676.17	27,404.68	1
Nullitatis summa	48,922.83	43,785.29	4

Solid/Graduated Bands

47008

	2006	2005	%
Lorem ipsum	34,021.20	30,339.46	2
Dolor amet	5,790.03	4,822.09	17
Autem velure	11,650.44	9,637.87	18
Nunc et semper	38,394.52	32,881.59	3
Duis consectia	27,676.17	27,404.68	1
Nullitatis summa	48,922.83	43,785.29	4

Rule Dividers: Column Highlights

47009

	2006	2005	%
Lorem ipsum	34,021.20	30,339.46	2
Dolor amet	5,790.03	4,822.09	17
Autem velure	11,650.44	9,637.87	18
Nunc et semper	38,394.52	32,881.59	3
Duis consectia	27,676.17	27,404.68	1
Nullitatis summa	48,922.83	43,785.29	4

Complex Band/Column Values

47010

	2006	2005	%
LOREM IPSUM	34,021.20	30,339.46	2
DOLOR AMET	5,790.03	4,822.09	17
AUTEM VELURE	11,650.44	9,637.87	18
NUNC ET SEMPER	38,394.52	32,881.59	3
DUIS CONSECTIA	27,676.17	27,404.68	1
NULLITATIS SUMMA	48,922.83	43,785.29	4

Complex Band/Column Values

47011

	2006	2005	%
LOREM IPSUM	34,021.20	30,339.46	2
DOLOR AMET	5,790.03	4,822.09	17
AUTEM VELURE	11,650.44	9,637.87	18
NUNC ET SEMPER	38,394.52	32,881.59	3
DUIS CONSECTIA	27,676.17	27,404.68	1
NULLITATIS SUMMA	48,922.83	43,785.29	4

Complex Band/Column Values

47012

	2006	2005	%
LOREM IPSUM	34,021.20	30,339.46	2
DOLOR AMET	5,790.03	4,822.09	17
AUTEM VELURE	11,650.44	9,637.87	18
NUNC ET SEMPER	38,394.52	32,881.59	3
DUIS CONSECTIA	27,676.17	27,404.68	1
NULLITATIS SUMMA	48,922.83	43,785.29	4

Complex Band/Column Values

47013

	2006	2005	%
LOREM IPSUM	34,021.20	30,339.46	2
DOLOR AMET	5,790.03	4,822.09	17
AUTEM VELURE	11,650.44	9,637.87	18
NUNC ET SEMPER	38,394.52	32,881.59	3
DUIS CONSECTIA	27,676.17	27,404.68	1
NULLITATIS SUMMA	48,922.83	43,785.29	4

Complex Band/Column Values

47014

	2006	2005	%
LOREM IPSUM	34,021.20	30,339.46	2
DOLOR AMET	5,790.03	4,822.09	17
AUTEM VELURE	11,650.44	9,637.87	18
NUNC ET SEMPER	38,394.52	32,881.59	3
DUIS CONSECTIA	27,676.17	27,404.68	1
NULLITATIS SUMMA	48,922.83	43,785.29	4

Complex Band/Column Values

47015

	2006	2005	%
LOREM IPSUM	34,021.20	30,339.46	2
DOLOR AMET	5,790.03	4,822.09	17
AUTEM VELURE	11,650.44	9,637.87	18
NUNC ET SEMPER	38,394.52	32,881.59	3
DUIS CONSECTIA	27,676.17	27,404.68	1
NULLITATIS SUMMA	48,922.83	43,785.29	4

Complex Band/Column Values

47016

	2006	2005	%
LOREM IPSUM	34,021.20	30,339.46	2
DOLOR AMET	5,790.03	4,822.09	17
AUTEM VELURE	11,650.44	9,637.87	18
NUNC ET SEMPER	38,394.52	32,881.59	3
DUIS CONSECTIA	27,676.17	27,404.68	1
NULLITATIS SUMMA	48,922.83	43,785.29	4

Complex Band/Column Values

The design of tables for charts or financial data is yet another complex typographic problem that warrants some attention. As with other complicated hierarchic typesetting situations, the need for informational clarity is important, but this necessity should not dissuade design- ers from exploring ideas that will impart a sense of style and integrate such elements visu- ally with other components of a project. This selection of table concepts focuses on internal layout and, where appropriate, proportion and weight relationships in the typographic elements themselves—keeping in mind that the typefaces used should reflect those chosen for the remainder of the project in question.

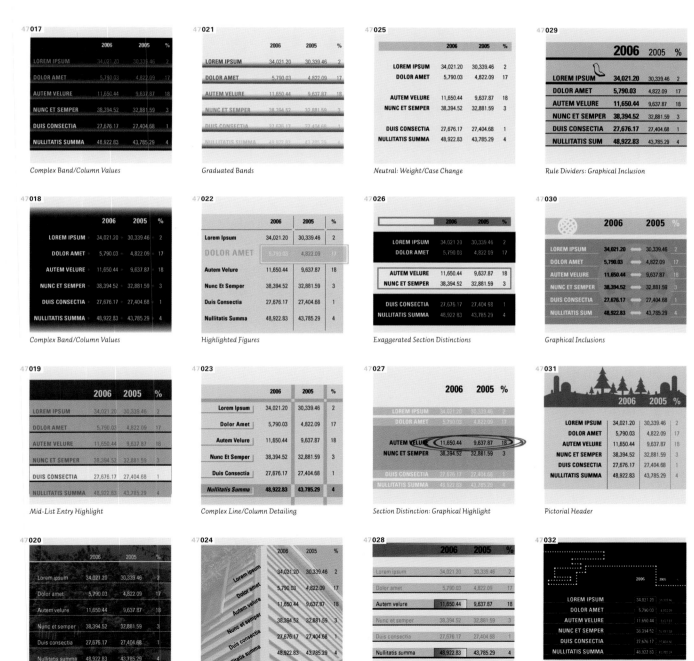

47 017 Complex Band/Column Values

47 018 Complex Band/Column Values

47 019 Mid-List Entry Highlight

47 020 Reversed from Image Backdrop

47 021 Graduated Bands

47 022 Highlighted Figures

47 023 Complex Line/Column Detailing

47 024 Angled Headers: Image Backdrop

47 025 Neutral: Weight/Case Change

47 026 Exaggerated Section Distinctions

47 027 Section Distinction: Graphical Highlight

47 028 Complex Band Values: Figure Highlights

47 029 Rule Dividers: Graphical Inclusion

47 030 Graphical Inclusions

47 031 Pictorial Header

47 032 Complex Rule Dividers

EMBELLISHMENTS *Directionals and Dingbats*

48

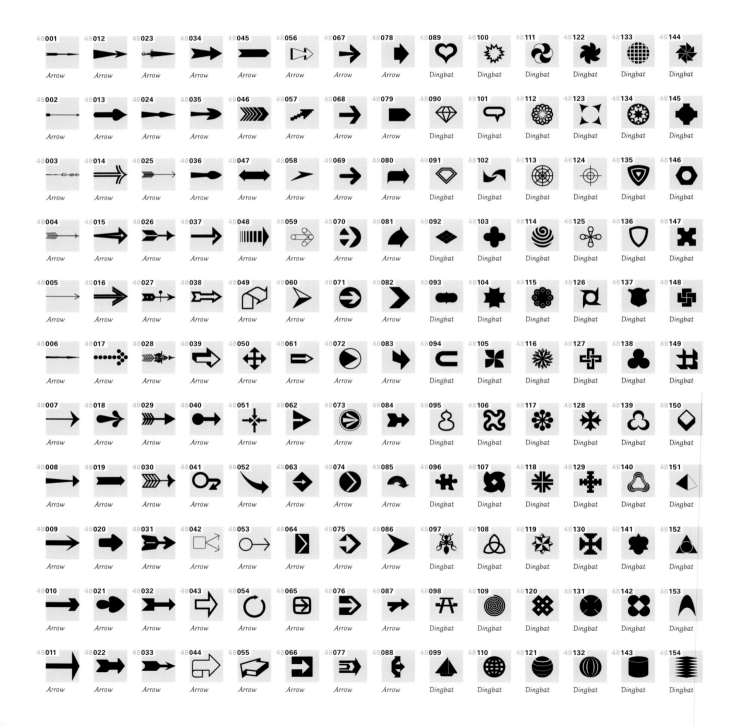

48**001** Arrow	48**012** Arrow	48**023** Arrow	48**034** Arrow	48**045** Arrow	48**056** Arrow	48**067** Arrow	48**078** Arrow	48**089** Dingbat	48**100** Dingbat	48**111** Dingbat	48**122** Dingbat	48**133** Dingbat	48**144** Dingbat
48**002** Arrow	48**013** Arrow	48**024** Arrow	48**035** Arrow	48**046** Arrow	48**057** Arrow	48**068** Arrow	48**079** Arrow	48**090** Dingbat	48**101** Dingbat	48**112** Dingbat	48**123** Dingbat	48**134** Dingbat	48**145** Dingbat
48**003** Arrow	48**014** Arrow	48**025** Arrow	48**036** Arrow	48**047** Arrow	48**058** Arrow	48**069** Arrow	48**080** Arrow	48**091** Dingbat	48**102** Dingbat	48**113** Dingbat	48**124** Dingbat	48**135** Dingbat	48**146** Dingbat
48**004** Arrow	48**015** Arrow	48**026** Arrow	48**037** Arrow	48**048** Arrow	48**059** Arrow	48**070** Arrow	48**081** Arrow	48**092** Dingbat	48**103** Dingbat	48**114** Dingbat	48**125** Dingbat	48**136** Dingbat	48**147** Dingbat
48**005** Arrow	48**016** Arrow	48**027** Arrow	48**038** Arrow	48**049** Arrow	48**060** Arrow	48**071** Arrow	48**082** Arrow	48**093** Dingbat	48**104** Dingbat	48**115** Dingbat	48**126** Dingbat	48**137** Dingbat	48**148** Dingbat
48**006** Arrow	48**017** Arrow	48**028** Arrow	48**039** Arrow	48**050** Arrow	48**061** Arrow	48**072** Arrow	48**083** Arrow	48**094** Dingbat	48**105** Dingbat	48**116** Dingbat	48**127** Dingbat	48**138** Dingbat	48**149** Dingbat
48**007** Arrow	48**018** Arrow	48**029** Arrow	48**040** Arrow	48**051** Arrow	48**062** Arrow	48**073** Arrow	48**084** Arrow	48**095** Dingbat	48**106** Dingbat	48**117** Dingbat	48**128** Dingbat	48**139** Dingbat	48**150** Dingbat
48**008** Arrow	48**019** Arrow	48**030** Arrow	48**041** Arrow	48**052** Arrow	48**063** Arrow	48**074** Arrow	48**085** Arrow	48**096** Dingbat	48**107** Dingbat	48**118** Dingbat	48**129** Dingbat	48**140** Dingbat	48**151** Dingbat
48**009** Arrow	48**020** Arrow	48**031** Arrow	48**042** Arrow	48**053** Arrow	48**064** Arrow	48**075** Arrow	48**086** Arrow	48**097** Dingbat	48**108** Dingbat	48**119** Dingbat	48**130** Dingbat	48**141** Dingbat	48**152** Dingbat
48**010** Arrow	48**021** Arrow	48**032** Arrow	48**043** Arrow	48**054** Arrow	48**065** Arrow	48**076** Arrow	48**087** Arrow	48**098** Dingbat	48**109** Dingbat	48**120** Dingbat	48**131** Dingbat	48**142** Dingbat	48**153** Dingbat
48**011** Arrow	48**022** Arrow	48**033** Arrow	48**044** Arrow	48**055** Arrow	48**066** Arrow	48**077** Arrow	48**088** Arrow	48**099** Dingbat	48**110** Dingbat	48**121** Dingbat	48**132** Dingbat	48**143** Dingbat	48**154** Dingbat

There's nothing like typographic ornament-ation to bring distinction and detail to the overall language of typographic design, whether used as bullets, informational separators, add-ons to initials, or titling embellishments.

Mix and match traditional printer's marks with contemporary forms for a rich, textural presentation.

48 155	48 166	48 177	48 188	48 199	48 210	48 221	48 232	48 243	48 254	48 265	48 276	48 287	48 298
Dingbat	Dingbat	Dingbat	Dingbat	Dingbat	Dingbat	Dingbat	Dingbat	Dingbat	Dingbat	Dingbat	Dingbat	Dingbat	Dingbat
48 156	48 167	48 178	48 189	48 200	48 211	48 222	48 233	48 244	48 255	48 266	48 277	48 288	48 299
Dingbat	Dingbat	Dingbat	Dingbat	Dingbat	Dingbat	Dingbat	Dingbat	Dingbat	Dingbat	Dingbat	Dingbat	Dingbat	Dingbat
48 157	48 168	48 179	48 190	48 201	48 212	48 223	48 234	48 245	48 256	48 267	48 278	48 289	48 300
Dingbat	Dingbat	Dingbat	Dingbat	Dingbat	Dingbat	Dingbat	Dingbat	Dingbat	Dingbat	Dingbat	Dingbat	Dingbat	Dingbat
48 158	48 169	48 180	48 191	48 202	48 213	48 224	48 235	48 246	48 257	48 268	48 279	48 290	48 301
Dingbat	Dingbat	Dingbat	Dingbat	Dingbat	Dingbat	Dingbat	Dingbat	Dingbat	Dingbat	Dingbat	Dingbat	Dingbat	Dingbat
48 159	48 170	48 181	48 192	48 203	48 214	48 225	48 236	48 247	48 258	48 269	48 280	48 291	48 302
Dingbat	Dingbat	Dingbat	Dingbat	Dingbat	Dingbat	Dingbat	Dingbat	Dingbat	Dingbat	Dingbat	Dingbat	Dingbat	Dingbat
48 160	48 171	48 182	48 193	48 204	48 215	48 226	48 237	48 248	48 259	48 270	48 281	48 292	48 303
Dingbat	Dingbat	Dingbat	Dingbat	Dingbat	Dingbat	Dingbat	Dingbat	Dingbat	Dingbat	Dingbat	Dingbat	Dingbat	Dingbat
48 161	48 172	48 183	48 194	48 205	48 216	48 227	48 238	48 249	48 260	48 271	48 282	48 293	48 304
Dingbat	Dingbat	Dingbat	Dingbat	Dingbat	Dingbat	Dingbat	Dingbat	Dingbat	Dingbat	Dingbat	Dingbat	Dingbat	Dingbat
48 162	48 173	48 184	48 195	48 206	48 217	48 228	48 239	48 250	48 261	48 272	48 283	48 294	48 305
Dingbat	Dingbat	Dingbat	Dingbat	Dingbat	Dingbat	Dingbat	Dingbat	Dingbat	Dingbat	Dingbat	Dingbat	Dingbat	Dingbat
48 163	48 174	48 185	48 196	48 207	48 218	48 229	48 240	48 251	48 262	48 273	48 284	48 295	48 306
Dingbat	Dingbat	Dingbat	Dingbat	Dingbat	Dingbat	Dingbat	Dingbat	Dingbat	Dingbat	Dingbat	Dingbat	Dingbat	Dingbat
48 164	48 175	48 186	48 197	48 208	48 219	48 230	48 241	48 252	48 263	48 274	48 285	48 296	48 307
Dingbat	Dingbat	Dingbat	Dingbat	Dingbat	Dingbat	Dingbat	Dingbat	Dingbat	Dingbat	Dingbat	Dingbat	Dingbat	Dingbat
48 165	48 176	48 187	48 198	48 209	48 220	48 231	48 242	48 253	48 264	48 275	48 286	48 297	48 308
Dingbat	Dingbat	Dingbat	Dingbat	Dingbat	Dingbat	Dingbat	Dingbat	Dingbat	Dingbat	Dingbat	Dingbat	Dingbat	Dingbat

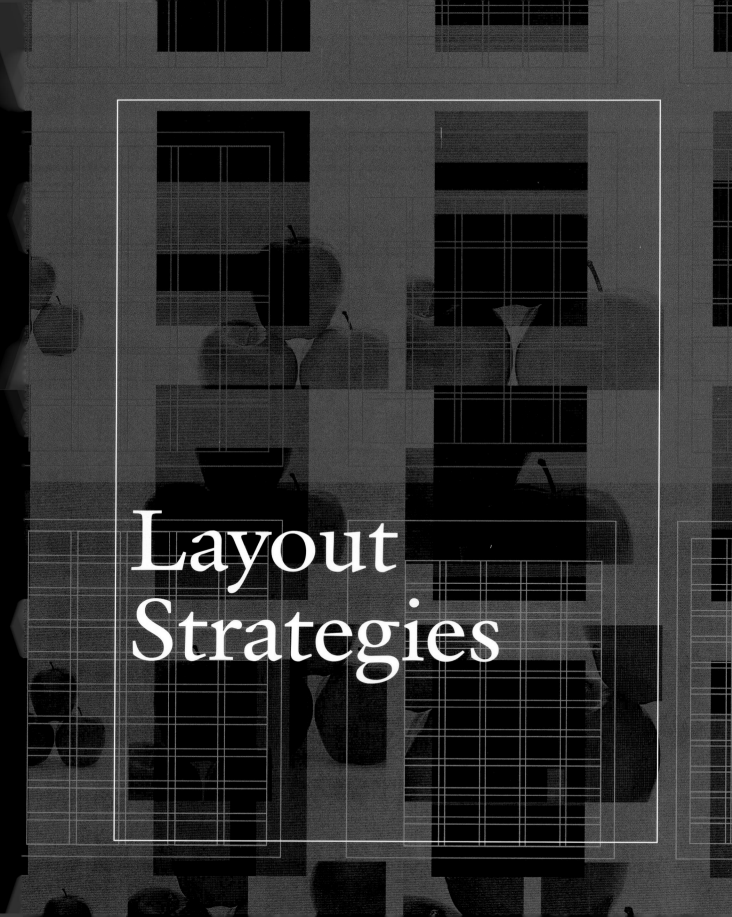

Layout
Strategies

THE PAGE OR FORMAT is the field where a designer presents and arranges text, graphic details and imagery to make each component shine individually even as it contributes to the work as a unified whole. The designer may consider symmetrical or asymmetrical composition, depending on how casual or formal, or how classical or contemporary, the project is. He or she may opt to organize the page mathematically or architecturally, to promote a sense of order—or in a spontaneous, organic way, delivering a playful or energetic feeling. Because so many design projects incorporate large amounts of type, grid structures to integrate text and image into coherent layouts are presented here. With regard to pictorial elements themselves, designers will find a variety of cropping strategies to refine and sharpen the presentation of images, whether full-frame scenes, portraits, or pictures of objects. Concepts for sizing and proportioning images together to create bold and dynamic layouts round out this section.

PAGE DIVISIONS *Orthogonal*

49

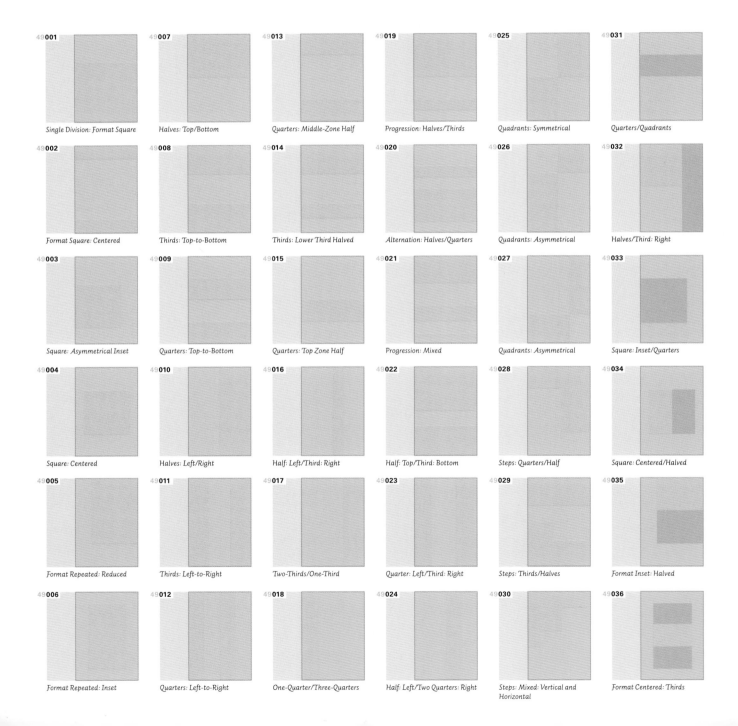

49**001** Single Division: Format Square

49**002** Format Square: Centered

49**003** Square: Asymmetrical Inset

49**004** Square: Centered

49**005** Format Repeated: Reduced

49**006** Format Repeated: Inset

49**007** Halves: Top/Bottom

49**008** Thirds: Top-to-Bottom

49**009** Quarters: Top-to-Bottom

49**010** Halves: Left/Right

49**011** Thirds: Left-to-Right

49**012** Quarters: Left-to-Right

49**013** Quarters: Middle-Zone Half

49**014** Thirds: Lower Third Halved

49**015** Quarters: Top Zone Half

49**016** Half: Left/Third: Right

49**017** Two-Thirds/One-Third

49**018** One-Quarter/Three-Quarters

49**019** Progression: Halves/Thirds

49**020** Alternation: Halves/Quarters

49**021** Progression: Mixed

49**022** Half: Top/Third: Bottom

49**023** Quarter: Left/Third: Right

49**024** Half: Left/Two Quarters: Right

49**025** Quadrants: Symmetrical

49**026** Quadrants: Asymmetrical

49**027** Quadrants: Asymmetrical

49**028** Steps: Quarters/Half

49**029** Steps: Thirds/Halves

49**030** Steps: Mixed: Vertical and Horizontal

49**031** Quarters/Quadrants

49**032** Halves/Third: Right

49**033** Square: Inset/Quarters

49**034** Square: Centered/Halved

49**035** Format Inset: Halved

49**036** Format Centered: Thirds

Whether using a grid or not (see **Categories** 51, [page 146], 52, [page 148], and 53 [page 150]), organizing a composition based on vertical/horizontal geometry establishes clear proportional relationships between positive elements and negative spaces, tying all the parts of a page or spread together for the viewer. Classical strategies based on squares and rectangles—the Golden Section, the Law of Thirds, and other mathematical approaches—mingle with contemporary ones, including those that present overlapping fields for more layered organization. Use these proportional systems to help define areas of differing content, position elements with clear relationships among them, or impart an architectonic quality to layouts.

49**037** Thirds: Mixed Subdivisions

49**043** Half and Right Third: Halved

49**049** Overlaps: Square/Thirds

49**055** Overlaps: Square/Steps

49**061** Overlaps: Intuitive Proportions

49**067** Overlaps: Implied Layers

49**038** Lower Half: Thirds

49**044** Mixed Subdivisions

49**050** Overlaps: Quadrants/Square

49**056** Overlaps: Square/Steps

49**062** Overlaps: Intuitive Proportions

49**068** Overlaps: Implied Layers

49**039** Mixed Thirds/Half/Quadrant

49**045** Two Thirds: Quartered

49**051** Overlaps: Thirds/Format Half

49**057** Overlaps: Steps:Mixed

49**063** Overlaps: Intuitive Proportions

49**069** Overlaps: Implied Layers

49**040** Mixed Square/Thirds

49**046** Steps: Quarters/Halves

49**052** Overlaps: Squares

49**058** Overlaps: Steps:Mixed

49**064** Overlaps: Intuitive Proportions

49**070** Overlaps: Implied Layers

49**041** Two Thirds: Left/Last Halved

49**047** Steps: Thirds/Quarters

49**053** Overlaps: Selected Subdivisions

49**059** Overlaps: Steps:Mixed

49**065** Overlaps: Intuitive Proportions

49**071** Overlaps: Implied Layers

49**042** Mixed Square/Quarters

49**048** Steps: Quarters: Vertical and Horizontal

49**054** Overlaps: Format/Quarters

49**060** Overlaps: Steps:Mixed

49**066** Overlaps: Intuitive Proportions

49**072** Overlaps: Implied Layers

PAGE DIVISIONS *Diagonal and Organic*

50

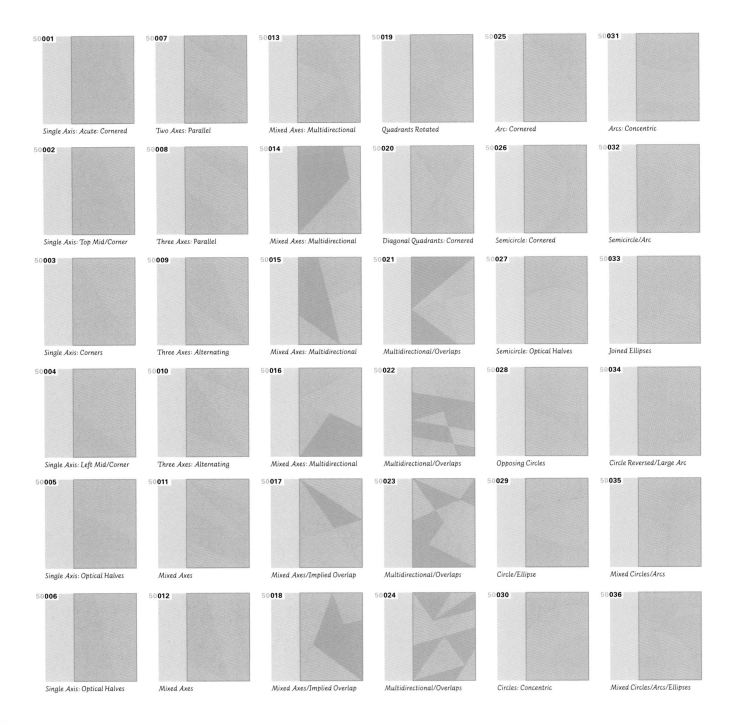

50**001**
Single Axis: Acute: Cornered

50**002**
Single Axis: Top Mid/Corner

50**003**
Single Axis: Corners

50**004**
Single Axis: Left Mid/Corner

50**005**
Single Axis: Optical Halves

50**006**
Single Axis: Optical Halves

50**007**
Two Axes: Parallel

50**008**
Three Axes: Parallel

50**009**
Three Axes: Alternating

50**010**
Three Axes: Alternating

50**011**
Mixed Axes

50**012**
Mixed Axes

50**013**
Mixed Axes: Multidirectional

50**014**
Mixed Axes: Multidirectional

50**015**
Mixed Axes: Multidirectional

50**016**
Mixed Axes: Multidirectional

50**017**
Mixed Axes/Implied Overlap

50**018**
Mixed Axes/Implied Overlap

50**019**
Quadrants Rotated

50**020**
Diagonal Quadrants: Cornered

50**021**
Multidirectional/Overlaps

50**022**
Multidirectional/Overlaps

50**023**
Multidirectional/Overlaps

50**024**
Multidirectional/Overlaps

50**025**
Arc: Cornered

50**026**
Semicircle: Cornered

50**027**
Semicircle: Optical Halves

50**028**
Opposing Circles

50**029**
Circle/Ellipse

50**030**
Circles: Concentric

50**031**
Arcs: Concentric

50**032**
Semicircle/Arc

50**033**
Joined Ellipses

50**034**
Circle Reversed/Large Arc

50**035**
Mixed Circles/Arcs

50**036**
Mixed Circles/Arcs/Ellipses

As an alternative to geometric spatial breaks, explore these more intuitive, fluid, musical, and poetic proportional systems that present a sense of order just as clearly. The benefit of these strategies is a vitality that is sometimes lacking in layouts that are ordered geometrically, and which may be more appropriate for a particular situation. Along with divisions that depend on linear or geometric breaks (albeit in irregular intervals), spatial breaks based on irregular, amorphous shapes also are included here. Use these irregular page divisions as masks for images, to shape clusters of text and image, or as flat areas of color or texture to contrast orthogonally-composed elements.

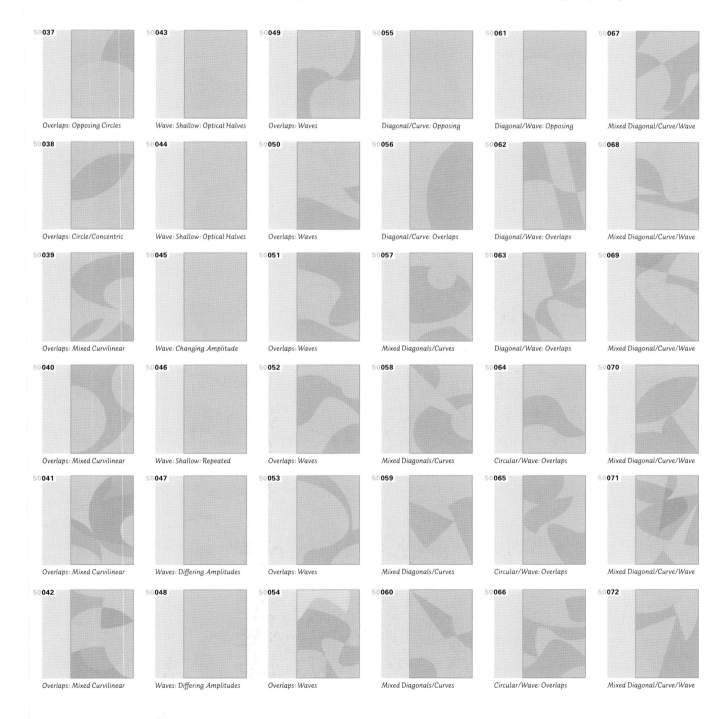

50**037** Overlaps: Opposing Circles	50**043** Wave: Shallow: Optical Halves	50**049** Overlaps: Waves
50**038** Overlaps: Circle/Concentric	50**044** Wave: Shallow: Optical Halves	50**050** Overlaps: Waves
50**039** Overlaps: Mixed Curvilinear	50**045** Wave: Changing Amplitude	50**051** Overlaps: Waves
50**040** Overlaps: Mixed Curvilinear	50**046** Wave: Shallow: Repeated	50**052** Overlaps: Waves
50**041** Overlaps: Mixed Curvilinear	50**047** Waves: Differing Amplitudes	50**053** Overlaps: Waves
50**042** Overlaps: Mixed Curvilinear	50**048** Waves: Differing Amplitudes	50**054** Overlaps: Waves

50**055** Diagonal/Curve: Opposing	50**061** Diagonal/Wave: Opposing	50**067** Mixed Diagonal/Curve/Wave
50**056** Diagonal/Curve: Overlaps	50**062** Diagonal/Wave: Overlaps	50**068** Mixed Diagonal/Curve/Wave
50**057** Mixed Diagonals/Curves	50**063** Diagonal/Wave: Overlaps	50**069** Mixed Diagonal/Curve/Wave
50**058** Mixed Diagonals/Curves	50**064** Circular/Wave: Overlaps	50**070** Mixed Diagonal/Curve/Wave
50**059** Mixed Diagonals/Curves	50**065** Circular/Wave: Overlaps	50**071** Mixed Diagonal/Curve/Wave
50**060** Mixed Diagonals/Curves	50**066** Circular/Wave: Overlaps	50**072** Mixed Diagonal/Curve/Wave

GRIDS *Column: Regular*

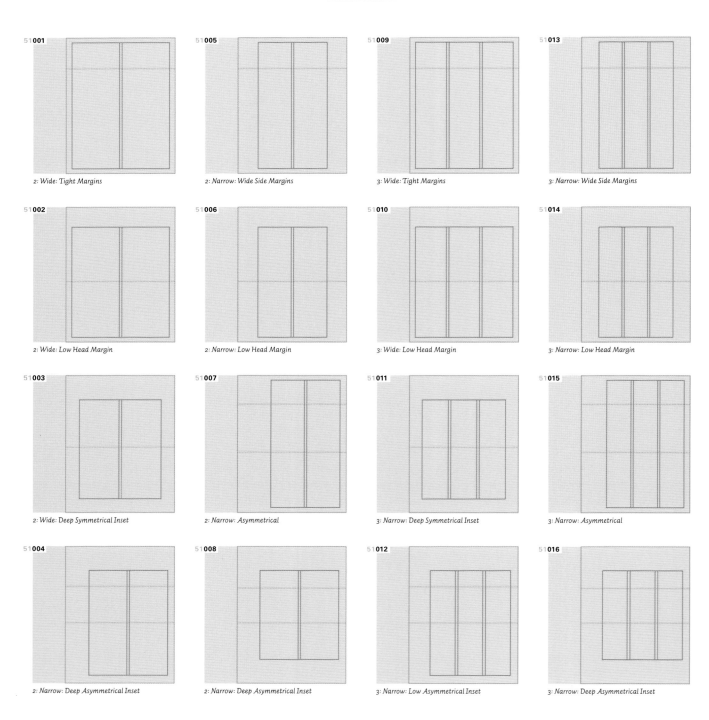

51**001**	51**005**	51**009**	51**013**
2: Wide: Tight Margins	2: Narrow: Wide Side Margins	3: Wide: Tight Margins	3: Narrow: Wide Side Margins
51**002**	51**006**	51**010**	51**014**
2: Wide: Low Head Margin	2: Narrow: Low Head Margin	3: Wide: Low Head Margin	3: Narrow: Low Head Margin
51**003**	51**007**	51**011**	51**015**
2: Wide: Deep Symmetrical Inset	2: Narrow: Asymmetrical	3: Narrow: Deep Symmetrical Inset	3: Narrow: Asymmetrical
51**004**	51**008**	51**012**	51**016**
2: Narrow: Deep Asymmetrical Inset	2: Narrow: Deep Asymmetrical Inset	3: Narrow: Low Asymmetrical Inset	3: Narrow: Deep Asymmetrical Inset

Of all column grids, those with two, three, four, and five columns are the most commonly used. The greatest option for variation in these grids is in their margin measures and, therefore, the symmetry or asymmetry of the individual page. Each grid shown here represents one page of two in a spread. Those which are asymmetrical can be repeated side by side or mirrored over a gutter. Grids with deeply inset columns are shown with flowlines for consideration. Double the number of columns, if greater flexibility and precision are needed.

51**017**
4: Wide: Tight Margins

51**021**
4: Narrow: Wide Side Margins

51**025**
5: Wide: Tight Margins

51**029**
5: Narrow: Wide Side Margins

51**018**
4: Wide: Low Head Margin

51**022**
4: Narrow: Low Head Margin

51**026**
5: Wide: Low Head Margin

51**030**
5: Narrow: Low Head Margin

51**019**
4: Wide: Deep Symmetrical Inset

51**023**
4: Narrow: Asymmetrical

51**027**
5: Wide: Deep Symmetrical Inset

51**031**
5: Narrow: Asymmetrical

51**020**
4: Wide: Low Asymmetrical Inset

51**024**
4: Narrow: Deep Asymmetrical Inset

51**028**
5: Wide: Low Asymmetrical Inset

51**032**
5: Narrow: Deep Asymmetrical Inset

GRIDS *Column: Compound and Hierarchic*

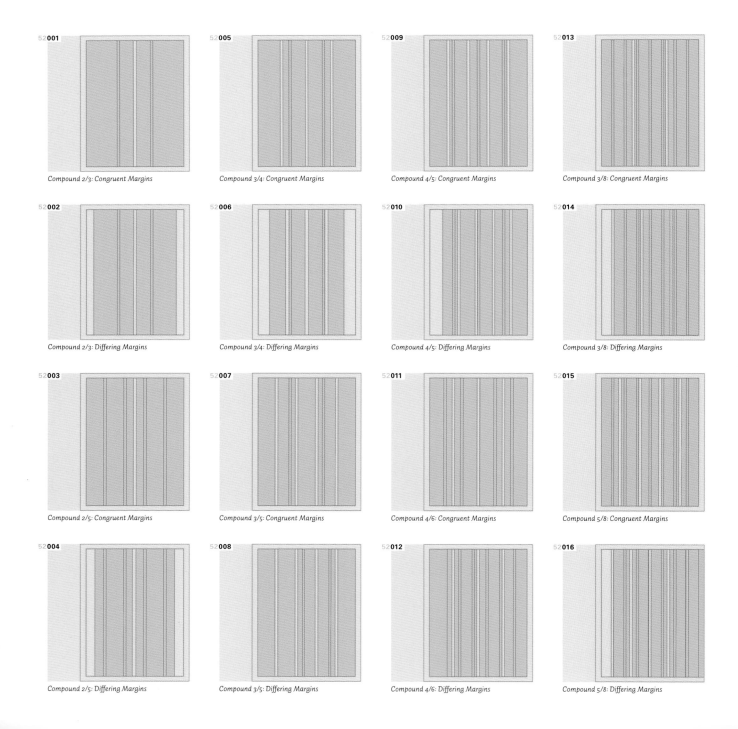

52001
Compound 2/3: Congruent Margins

52005
Compound 3/4: Congruent Margins

52009
Compound 4/5: Congruent Margins

52013
Compound 3/8: Congruent Margins

52002
Compound 2/3: Differing Margins

52006
Compound 3/4: Differing Margins

52010
Compound 4/5: Differing Margins

52014
Compound 3/8: Differing Margins

52003
Compound 2/5: Congruent Margins

52007
Compound 3/5: Congruent Margins

52011
Compound 4/6: Congruent Margins

52015
Compound 5/8: Congruent Margins

52004
Compound 2/5: Differing Margins

52008
Compound 3/5: Differing Margins

52012
Compound 4/6: Differing Margins

52016
Compound 5/8: Differing Margins

Combine grids to exaggerate rhythmic qualities of layouts page by page or section by section. On the left page is a selection of compound grids that overlay commonly used column structures. On the right page are examples of hierarchic structures—columns of different widths defined for specific kinds of content, and structures in which the page is sectioned by different column structures.

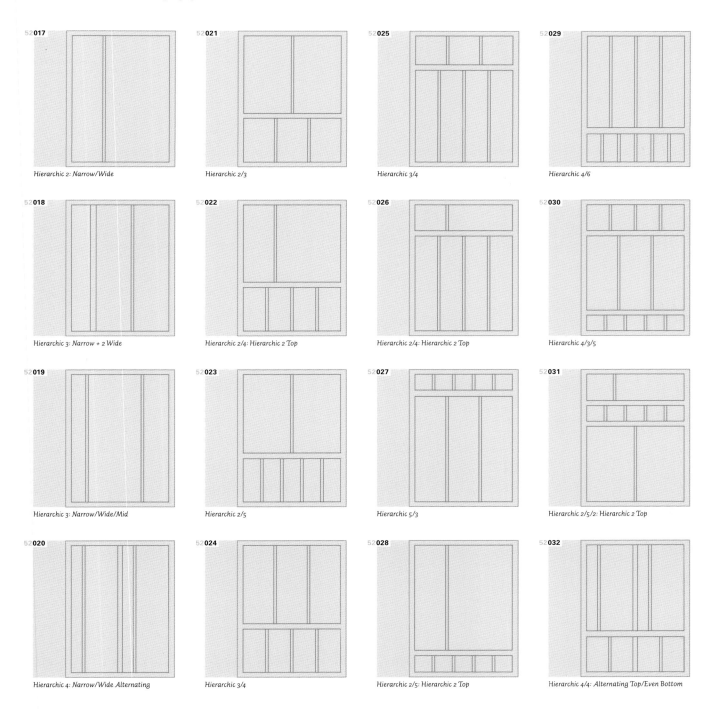

52**017**
Hierarchic 2: Narrow/Wide

52**021**
Hierarchic 2/3

52**025**
Hierarchic 3/4

52**029**
Hierarchic 4/6

52**018**
Hierarchic 3: Narrow + 2 Wide

52**022**
Hierarchic 2/4: Hierarchic 2 Top

52**026**
Hierarchic 2/4: Hierarchic 2 Top

52**030**
Hierarchic 4/3/5

52**019**
Hierarchic 3: Narrow/Wide/Mid

52**023**
Hierarchic 2/5

52**027**
Hierarchic 5/3

52**031**
Hierarchic 2/5/2: Hierarchic 2 Top

52**020**
Hierarchic 4: Narrow/Wide Alternating

52**024**
Hierarchic 3/4

52**028**
Hierarchic 2/5: Hierarchic 2 Top

52**032**
Hierarchic 4/4: Alternating Top/Even Bottom

GRIDS *Modular*

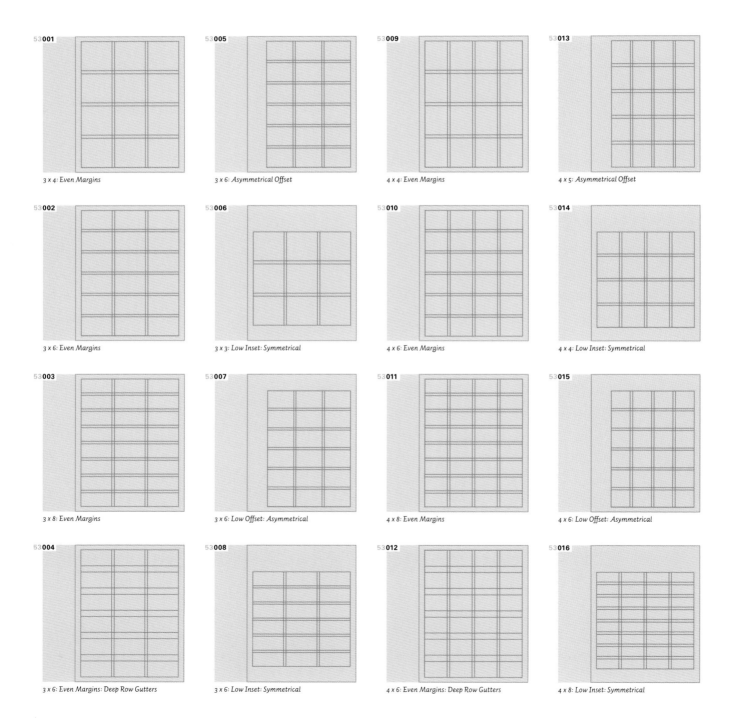

53**001**
3 x 4: *Even Margins*

53**005**
3 x 6: *Asymmetrical Offset*

53**009**
4 x 4: *Even Margins*

53**013**
4 x 5: *Asymmetrical Offset*

53**002**
3 x 6: *Even Margins*

53**006**
3 x 3: *Low Inset: Symmetrical*

53**010**
4 x 6: *Even Margins*

53**014**
4 x 4: *Low Inset: Symmetrical*

53**003**
3 x 8: *Even Margins*

53**007**
3 x 6: *Low Offset: Asymmetrical*

53**011**
4 x 8: *Even Margins*

53**015**
4 x 6: *Low Offset: Asymmetrical*

53**004**
3 x 6: *Even Margins: Deep Row Gutters*

53**008**
3 x 6: *Low Inset: Symmetrical*

53**012**
4 x 6: *Even Margins: Deep Row Gutters*

53**016**
4 x 8: *Low Inset: Symmetrical*

In contrast to regular column grids, the modular grid also provides a set of consistent rows for increased precision. Two-, three-, four-, and five-column structures show varia-tion in the number of rows, module shape, and changes in margin, increasing in complex-ity from left to right. While the needs of most projects can be met with the column-counts presented here, don't hesitate to double the number of columns (e.g., from three to six) if the project demands it.

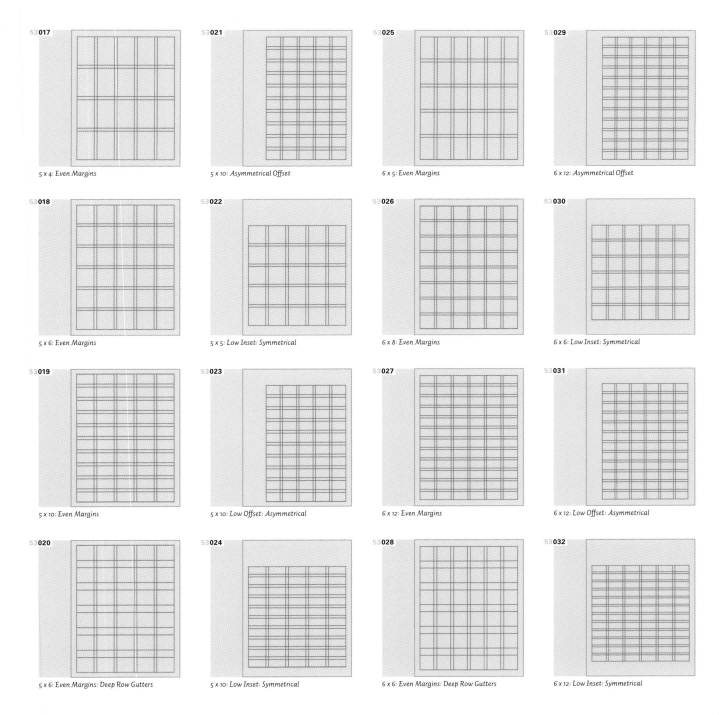

53**017**
5 x 4: Even Margins

53**021**
5 x 10: Asymmetrical Offset

53**025**
6 x 5: Even Margins

53**029**
6 x 12: Asymmetrical Offset

53**018**
5 x 6: Even Margins

53**022**
5 x 5: Low Inset: Symmetrical

53**026**
6 x 8: Even Margins

53**030**
6 x 6: Low Inset: Symmetrical

53**019**
5 x 10: Even Margins

53**023**
5 x 10: Low Offset: Asymmetrical

53**027**
6 x 12: Even Margins

53**031**
6 x 12: Low Offset: Asymmetrical

53**020**
5 x 6: Even Margins: Deep Row Gutters

53**024**
5 x 10: Low Inset: Symmetrical

53**028**
6 x 6: Even Margins: Deep Row Gutters

53**032**
6 x 12: Low Inset: Symmetrical

EDITORIAL STRUCTURE *Folio/Runner Placement*

54

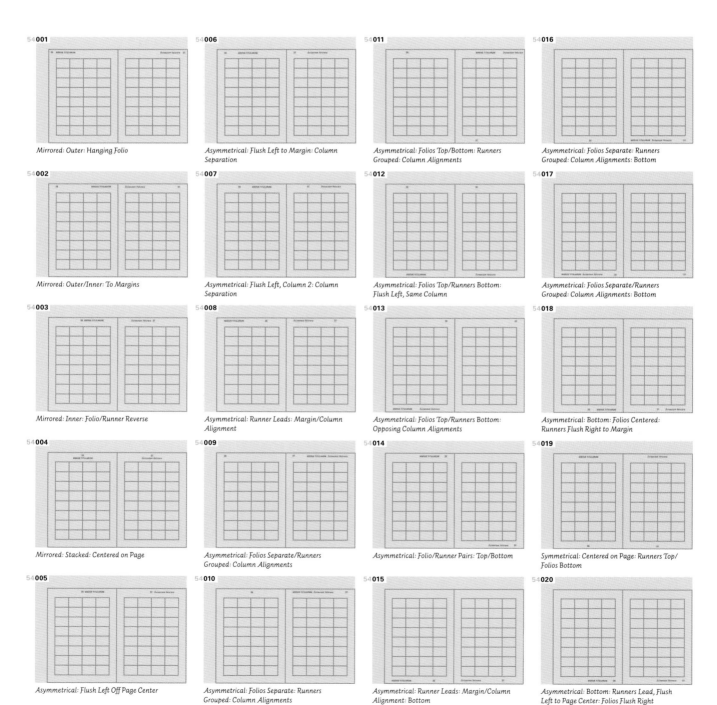

54**001**
Mirrored: Outer: Hanging Folio

54**002**
Mirrored: Outer/Inner: To Margins

54**003**
Mirrored: Inner: Folio/Runner Reverse

54**004**
Mirrored: Stacked: Centered on Page

54**005**
Asymmetrical: Flush Left Off Page Center

54**006**
Asymmetrical: Flush Left to Margin: Column Separation

54**007**
Asymmetrical: Flush Left, Column 2: Column Separation

54**008**
Asymmetrical: Runner Leads: Margin/Column Alignment

54**009**
Asymmetrical: Folios Separate/Runners Grouped: Column Alignments

54**010**
Asymmetrical: Folios Separate: Runners Grouped: Column Alignments

54**011**
Asymmetrical: Folios Top/Bottom: Runners Grouped: Column Alignments

54**012**
Asymmetrical: Folios Top/Runners Bottom: Flush Left, Same Column

54**013**
Asymmetrical: Folios Top/Runners Bottom: Opposing Column Alignments

54**014**
Asymmetrical: Folio/Runner Pairs: Top/Bottom

54**015**
Asymmetrical: Runner Leads: Margin/Column Alignment: Bottom

54**016**
Asymmetrical: Folios Separate: Runners Grouped: Column Alignments: Bottom

54**017**
Asymmetrical: Folios Separate/Runners Grouped: Column Alignments: Bottom

54**018**
Asymmetrical: Bottom: Folios Centered: Runners Flush Right to Margin

54**019**
Symmetrical: Centered on Page: Runners Top/ Folios Bottom

54**020**
Asymmetrical: Bottom: Runners Lead, Flush Left to Page Center: Folios Flush Right

Along with the actual form and styling of these editorial elements—the folio, or page number, and accompanying navigational tag (see **Category 43**, page **128**)—there are myriad possibili ties for their position on a page or page spread. Although the folio and runner conventionally appear together in close proximity, this approach is only one of many. Shown here is but a small sampling of the possibilities for arrangement—all in relation to a conventional 4 x 8 modular grid.

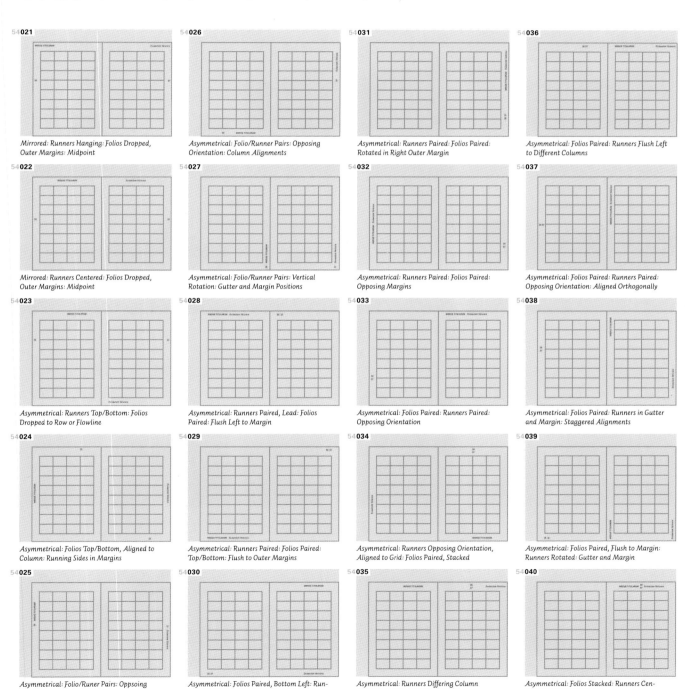

54021
Mirrored: Runners Hanging: Folios Dropped, Outer Margins: Midpoint

54022
Mirrored: Runners Centered: Folios Dropped, Outer Margins: Midpoint

54023
Asymmetrical: Runners Top/Bottom: Folios Dropped to Row or Flowline

54024
Asymmetrical: Folios Top/Bottom, Aligned to Column: Running Sides in Margins

54025
Asymmetrical: Folio/Runer Pairs: Oppsoing Rotation off Page Midpoint

54026
Asymmetrical: Folio/Runner Pairs: Opposing Orientation: Column Alignments

54027
Asymmetrical: Folio/Runner Pairs: Vertical Rotation: Gutter and Margin Positions

54028
Asymmetrical: Runners Paired, Lead: Folios Paired: Flush Left to Margin

54029
Asymmetrical: Runners Paired: Folios Paired: Top/Bottom: Flush to Outer Margins

54030
Asymmetrical: Folios Paired, Bottom Left: Runners Top/Bottom, Flush Left from Center

54031
Asymmetrical: Runners Paired: Folios Paired: Rotated in Right Outer Margin

54032
Asymmetrical: Runners Paired: Folios Paired: Opposing Margins

54033
Asymmetrical: Folios Paired: Runners Paired: Opposing Orientation

54034
Asymmetrical: Runners Opposing Orientation, Aligned to Grid: Folios Paired, Stacked

54035
Asymmetrical: Runners Differing Column Alignments: Folios Paired, Stacked

54036
Asymmetrical: Folios Paired: Runners Flush Left to Different Columns

54037
Asymmetrical: Folios Paired: Runners Paired: Opposing Orientation: Aligned Orthogonally

54038
Asymmetrical: Folios Paired: Runners in Gutter and Margin: Staggered Alignments

54039
Asymmetrical: Folios Paired, Flush to Margin: Runners Rotated: Gutter and Margin

54040
Asymmetrical: Folios Stacked: Runners Centered Left/Right Off Folios

IMAGE CROPPING *Scenes and Objects*

55

55**001**
Aspect Ratio: 35mm Slide: Long Shot
Horizon High: Emphasizes Diagonal Corner to Upper Third

55**002**
Aspect Ratio: 35mm Slide: Mid-Range
Horizon High: Emphasizes Perspective and Square of Format

55**003**
Aspect Ratio: 35mm Slide: Close-Up
Horizon Low: Emphasizes Horizontality and Subject Detail

55**004**
Aspect Ratio: Letterbox: Long Shot
Horizon High: Emphasizes Foreground and Diagonals

55**005**
Aspect Ratio: Letterbox: Mid-Range
Horizon Low: Emphasizes Horizontality, Comparison of Forms

55**006**
Aspect Ratio: Letterbox: Close-Up
Horizon High: Emphasizes Orthogonal Structure and Subject Detail

55**007**
3/4 Vertical: Long Shot
Horizon High: Emphasizes Perspective

55**008**
Tight Vertical: Long Shot
Horizon Low: Emphasizes Negative Space

55**009**
3/4 Vertical: Mid-Range
Horizon High: Emphasizes Diagonals

55**010**
Tight Vertical: Mid-Range
Horizon High: Thirds Subject Detail Centered

55**011**
3/4 Vertical: Close-Up
Horizon Mid-Plane: Emphasizes Halves and Diagonals

55**012**
Tight Vertical: Close-Up
Horizon Mid-Plane: Emphasizes Verticals

55**013**
Square: Long Shot
Horizon Mid-Plane: Centered Subject Detail Emphasizes Sense of Distance

55**014**
Square: Long Shot
Horizon High: Emphasizes Perspective and Symmetry

55**015**
Square: Mid-Range
Horizon High: Emphasizes Triangularity

55**016**
Square: Mid-Range
Horizon Low: Thirds: Asymmetry Emphasizes Scale and Diagonals

55**017**
Square: Close-Up
Horizon High: Emphasizes Square, Triangulation, and Foreground

55**018**
Square: Close-Up
Horizon High: Emphasizes Diagonals and Asymmetry

Cropping photographic images can result in layouts of striking compositional tension, or the alternative—weak, uninteresting arrangements of diminished vitality. The cropping strategies here explore sizing and positioning opportunities for full-frame scenes and silhouetted objects within square, vertical, and horizontal formats of varying proportion. Adjust the proportions to match the single-page or spread proportion of your format, or to correspond to the proportions established by a grid. Try these options to focus attention on a subject's more interesting attributes, dramatize formal qualities, or impart uniqueness in a layout.

55**019**

Aspect Ratio: 35mm Slide: Long Shot: Object Asymmetrical Off Center Axis: Emphasizes Negative Space

55**020**

Aspect Ratio: 35mm Slide: Close Mid-Range: Object Positioned Asymmetrically: Object Contours Emphasize Orthogonal Geometry

55**021**

Aspect Ratio: 35mm Slide: Extreme Close-Up: Object Positioned to Emphasize Format Midline and Irregular Negative Shapes

55**022**

Aspect Ratio: Letterbox: Long Shot: Object Positioned Low: Emphasizes Negative Space and Format's Center Axis

55**023**

Aspect Ratio: Letterbox: Close Mid-Range: Object's Major Vertical Axis Positioned at Format Center Axis: Emphasizes Vertical Rhythm

55**024**

Aspect Ratio: Letterbox: Extreme Close-Up: Object Positioned Asymmetrically: Emphasizes Detail/Identity of Subject and Irregular Shapes of Negative Space

55**025**

3/4 Vertical: Long Shot: Object Positioned Asymmetrically/Low: Emphasizes Surface and Square

55**026**

Tight Vertical: Long Shot: Emphasizes Diagonals

55**027**

3/4 Vertical: Close Mid-Range: Object Positioned Symmetrically: Emphasizes Angle/Curve and Focuses on Detail

55**028**

Tight Vertical: Close Mid-Range: Object Positioned High: Emphasizes Surface

55**029**

3/4 Vertical: Extreme Close-Up: Emphasizes Diagonal/Curve, Scale Difference, and Subject Detail

55**030**

Tight Vertical: Extreme Close-Up: Emphasizes Contours

55**031**

Square: Long Shot: Object Positioned Symmetrically: Emphasizes Solidity

55**032**

Square: Long Shot: Object Positioned Asymmetrically/Low: Emphasizes Weight and Contour

55**033**

Square: Close Mid-Range: Emphasizes Contours, Shape Differentiation

55**034**

Square: Close-Mid-Range: Emphasizes Traingulation

55**035**

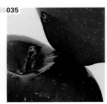

Square: Extreme Close-Up: Emphasizes Corners and Contour Opposition

55**036**

Square: Extreme Close-Up: Emphasizes Mass/Line and Subject Detail

IMAGE CROPPING *Figures and Faces*

56

56**001**

Aspect Ratio: 35mm Slide: Long Shot: Main Axis of Figure Positioned at Format's Center Axis: Emphasizes Subject's Place in Environment and Structure of Angles

56**002**

Aspect Ratio: 35mm Slide: Mid-Range: Figure Positioned Symmetrically: Emphasizes Angle Structure and Dotlike Masses

56**003**

Aspect Ratio: 35mm Slide: Close-Up: Figure Positioned Symmetrically: Emphasizes Face

56**004**

Aspect Ratio: Letterbox: Long Shot: Figure Halves Format: Emphasizes Negative Space and Horizontality

56**005**

Aspect Ratio: Letterbox: Mid-Range: Figure Positioned Symmetrically: Emphasizes Face

56**006**

Aspect Ratio: Letterbox: Close-Up: Figure Positioned Asymmetrically: Emphasizes Confrontation and Subject Details

56**007**

3/4 Vertical: Long Shot: Emphasizes Verticals and Angle Structure

56**008**

Tight Vertical: Long Shot: Rotation of Figure Emphasizes Diagonals

56**009**

3/4 Vertical: Mid-Range: Figure Positioned Asymetrically: Emphasizes Diagonals and Dotlike Mass

56**010**

Tight Vertical: Mid-Range: Figure Positioned Symmetrically

56**011**

3/4 Vertical: Close-Up: Figure Positioned Asymmetrically: Emphasizes Diagonals and Face

56**012**

Tight Vertical: Close-Up: Emphasizes Face

56**013**

Square: Long Shot: Emphasizes Negative Shapes and Diagonals

56**014**

Square: Long Shot: Emphasizes Verticality

56**015**

Square: Mid-Range: Asymmetrical Position Emphasizes Space and Edge Tension

56**016**

Square: Mid-Range: Rotation Emphasizes Diagonals

56**017**

Square: Close-Up: Emphasizes Face and Contours

56**018**

Square: Close-Up: Emphaszies Contours and Diagonals

Images of people—whether those of groups or single portraits—need not be cropped statically, with the subject presented dead center. While the specific composition of such an image may immediately suggest a particular, dynamic crop, it's often true that images of people are composed very neutrally—and designers are just as often wary of chopping into faces and bodies. Always consider a portrait's composition with the same rigor and requirements for dynamism as that of any other image. Shown here are options that will enhance not only a layout, but the liveliness and personality of the subject.

Aspect Ratio: 35mm Slide: Mid-Range: Subject Positioned Symmetrically: Emphasizes Overall Geometry of Composition

Aspect Ratio: 35mm Slide: Close-Up: Subject Positioned Symmetrically: Emphasizes Face and Curvilinear Masses against Negative Spaces

Aspect Ratio: 35mm Slide: Extreme Close-Up: Subject Positioned Asymmetrically with Focal Point Establishing format Center: Emphasizes Expression, Light and Dark Values

Aspect Ratio: Letterbox: Mid-Range: Subject Positioned Asymmetrically with Major Vertical Axis Aligned to Format Center: Emphasizes Horizontality and Light/Dark Progression

Aspect Ratio: Letterbox: Close-Up: Subject Positioned Asymmetrically: Emphasizes Light/Dark Progression and Differentiation of Shapes

Aspect Ratio: Letterbox: Extreme Close-Up: Slight Asymmetry Emphasizes Expression and Interaction of Curvilinear Forms

3/4 Vertical: Mid-Range: Subject Centered: Emphasizes Triangulation

Tight Vertical: Mid-Range: Low Positioning Emphasizes Dotlike Mass and Vertical Spatial Breaks

3/4 Vertical: Close-Up: High Position Emphasizes Vertical Breaks, Diagonals, and Asymmetry of Shadows

Tight Vertical: Close-Up: Emphasizes Subject Detail and Verticality

3/4 Vertical: Extreme Close-Up: Low Position Emphasizes Asymmetry, Rhythm of Curves and Shadows

Tight Vertical: Extreme Close-Up: Emphasizes Expression

Square: Mid-Range: Asymmetrical Position Emphasizes Diagonals and Foreground

Square: Mid-Range: Low, Asymmetrical Position Emphasizes Negative Space

Square: Close-Up: Rotation Emphasizes Format Quadrants and Diagonal Structure

Square: Close-Up: Asymmetrical Position Emphasizes Subject Detail and Light/Dark Progression

Square: Extreme Close-Up: Rotation Emphasizes Curved Forms, Highlight/Shadow, and Subject Detail

Square: Extreme Close-Up: Position Emphasizes Subject Details, Expression, and Diagonals

IMAGE LAYOUT *Compositional Strategies*

57

57001

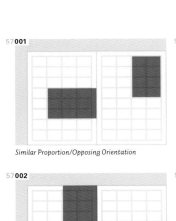

Similar Proportion/Opposing Orientation

57002

Extremes of Scale and Proportion

57003

Extremes of Scale and Proportion: Inset to Margin

57004

Extremes of Scale and Proportion: Inset versus Asymmetrical Bleed

57005

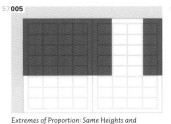

Extremes of Proportion: Same Heights and Alignment: 3/4 Bleed

57006

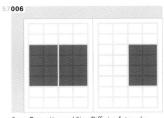

Same Proportion and Size: Differing Intervals: Horizontal Alignment

57007

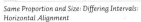
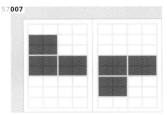

Same Proportion: Modular Configuration

57008

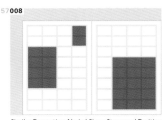

Similar Proportion: Varied Sizes: Staggered Position

57009

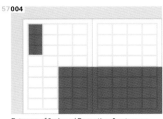

Similar Proportion: Varied Sizes: Differing Intervals: Hanging Alignment

57010

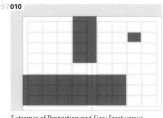

Extremes of Proportion and Size: Inset versus Asymmetrical Bleed

57011

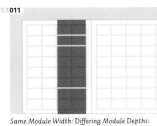

Same Module Width: Differing Module Depths: Vertical [or Horizontal] Alignment

57012

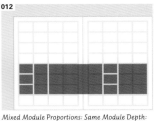

Mixed Module Proportions: Same Module Depth: Vertical [or Horizontal] Alignment

57013

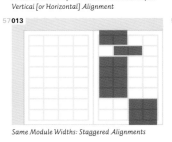

Same Module Widths: Staggered Alignments

57014

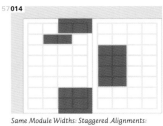

Same Module Widths: Staggered Alignments: Cross-Gutter Arrangement

57015

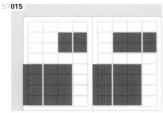

Similar Proportions: Opposing Scale: Staggered Alignments

57016

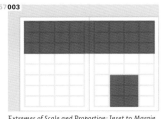

Similar Aspect Ratio Stacking: Opposing Scales: Opposing Positions

57017

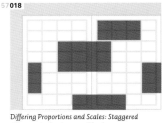

Same Module Depth: Differing Module Widths: Staggered Alignments

57018

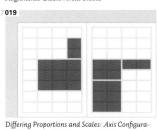

Differing Proportions and Scales: Staggered Alignments: Insets versus Bleeds

57019

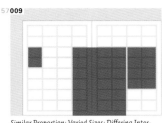

Differing Proportions and Scales: Axis Configuration: Extremes of Depth versus Width

57020

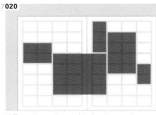

Differing Proportions and Scales: Staggered Alignments: Alternation in Position High/Low

These ingredients offer a multitude of possibilities for arranging square- or rectangle-based images in layouts. With a commonly used grid shown for reference, the strategies provided here progress from simple to complex, and from strictly grid-based to those that ignore the grid in favor of more spontaneous arrangements. Use them as is, or combine approaches from one or more to achieve dynamic pictorial compositions in any medium.

57**021**

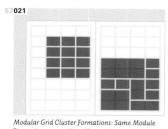

Modular Grid Cluster Formations: Same Module Proportion versus Mixed Proportions

57**022**

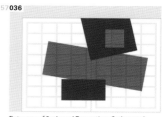

Modular Step Formations: Opposing Scales

57**023**

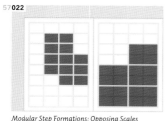

Joined Modular Zones: Step Formations: Simple versus Complex

57**024**

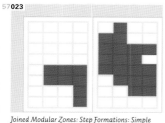

Implied Overlaps/Insets: Gutter Separation

57**025**

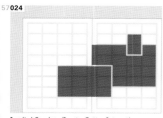

Literal Overlaps/Insets: No Gutter Separation

57**026**

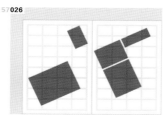

Orthogonal Configuration: Rotated Off Grid

57**027**

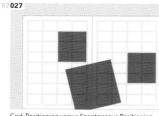

Grid-Positioning versus Spontaneous Positioning

57**028**

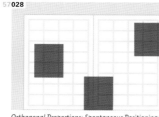

Orthogonal Proportions: Spontaneous Positioning: Same Proportion and Scale

57**029**

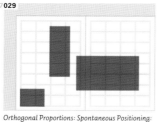

Orthogonal Proportions: Spontaneous Positioning: Differing Proportions and Scales

57**030**

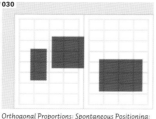

Orthogonal Proportions: Spontaneous Positioning: Depth Variation in Response to Format Horizon

57**031**

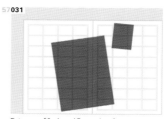

Extremes of Scale and Proportion: Spontaneous Positioning: Opposing Rotation

57**032**

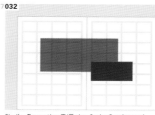

Similar Proportion/Differing Scale: Overlap and Offset: Gutter Bleed

57**033**

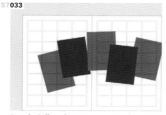

Same [or Different] Proportion: Fan Configuration

57**034**

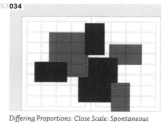

Differing Proportions: Close Scale: Spontaneous Positioning: Collage Formation

57**035**

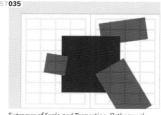

Extremes of Scale and Proportion: Orthogonal Orientation versus Rotation: Overlaps

57**036**

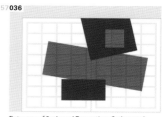

Extremes of Scale and Proportion: Orthogonal Orientation versus Rotation: Overlaps and Inset

57**037**

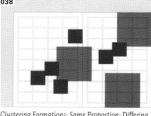

Extremes of Scale and Proportion: Opposing Rotation: Overlap: Asymmetrical Bleed

57**038**

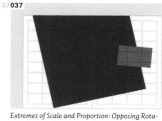

Clustering Formations: Same Proportion: Differing Scale: Insets versus Overlaps and Bleed

57**039**

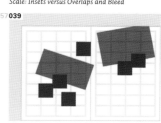

Clustering Formations: Differing Proportions and Scales: Insets versus Overlaps and Bleed

57**040**

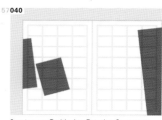

Spontaneous Positioning: Rotation: Inset versus Exterior Bleeds

estion that
asting life—
worldly sensu-
—need not be
ally exclusive
uits.

consectetur felis au
tristique senectus
ac turpis egestas.
a doramus autem
equam erat. Lorem
consectetuis du
velu adipiscing au
ac luctus egeti tel
gilla feugiato vea
vel euismod lacus
volutpat neque ne
elit scelerisque ac
rutrum massa co
egestas quam et i
amet, consectetur
arcu. Pellentesqu
malesuada ut dig

Vivamus vitae au

neque. Suspendiss
imperdiet non, ti
eleifend elit eget

al

e Secular

120 Park Avenue South
At 41st Street

DINNER
MENU

Monday through Saturday
6:00–11:00 p.m.

304 South Franklin Street

HE VANDE
BILTLUX
RYCONDO
INIUMS

At the Grand Central Complex

TIMELESS STYLE
IN THE HEART OF
THE CITY

sential
room
ervice

se

**The Spring
Collections
Are Here**

fa

fir

m

m

Exotically spiced artisanal
chocolates

CELESTIA

Artemis

Rosemary-infused dark
chocolate with almonds and
braised apple slices

ENLY DIFFERENT

**Fiske Market
Consulting**

Investing from
your perspective.

Services | Fund Portfolio | Company Profile | Client Area

How do you see
yourself living in the
next twenty years?

Botanus autem est nunc
et semper ex in gloriosa
equam erat. Lorem ipsum
dolor sit ametiscing elit.
Nam aclectuis eget telus
fringila feugiat urduisar.

nd Conque

but catalyze—with the
botanicals

botanus autem est-nunc et semper ex i
m dolor sit ametiscing elit. Nam ad
bulum vel euismod lacus. Mauris volu
que artimagnificat duis summ

Project Strategies

Examples and
Explorations to
Inspire the
Busy Designer

FIRST IMPRESSIONS

Such simple design applications as covers, ads, and website home pages—often the first glimpse of visual communication that viewers will confront—require the impact provided by strong imagery, color, and type organized in simple, dynamic compositions. As a prelude to the content within, or as ephemeral, stand-alone visual attention-getters, they engage audiences at a glance with the promise of more to come.

Projects in This Section

COVER DESIGN
RESTAURANT MENU

SINGLE-PRODUCT PACKAGING
PHARMACEUTICALS

SIMPLE WEBSITE
HOME PAGE

IMAGE-DRIVEN AD
SINGLE-PAGE FORMAT

COVER DESIGN

RESTAURANT MENU | *Japanese Restaurant*

Project Communication Brief

Convey a sense of the restaurant's cuisine through depiction of typical ingredients and preparation methods.

Communicate the cuisine's cultural context—geography, aesthetic heritage, and political history of Japan.

Visually support concepts related to the restaurant's name, which refers to the decorative art of folded paper.

Text Element Translations

Restaurant name
The Origami House: Hibachi and Sushi Bar

Address
304 South Franklin Street

Supporting Information
Dinner Menu
Monday through Saturday, 6:00–11:00 p.m.

PICTO	
01001	40
01068	41
04013	46
04017	47
06005	50
14007	66
CHROMA	
20017	80
25021	91
TYPO	
37034	117
38029	119
SPATIAL	
49010	142
50004	144

VISUAL PROFILE *Bold • Simple • Fun • Symbolic • Direct •*
Formal Contrast • Integrated • Efficient

PICTO	
01058	41
01068	41
02020	42
03008	44
04020	47
05010	48
09018	57
10018	58
CHROMA	
20032	80
25021	91
TYPO	
37001	116
38023	118
SPATIAL	
49007	142
50038	145

VISUAL PROFILE *Environmental • Subtle Geometry •*
Fluid • Active Surface • Architectural and Cultural References •
Gestural • Spontaneous

PICTO	
01016	40
01028	40
01068	41
09009	56
10031	58
17025	72
CHROMA	
25012	90
TYPO	
33007	108
37030	117
38009	118
SPATIAL	
49061	143

VISUAL PROFILE *Geometric • Handmade • Organic • Symbolic •*
Rhythmic • Detailed • Emphasis on Land • Type and Image Integrated

PICTO	
04001	46
06005	50
13001	64
CHROMA	
19013	78
19019	78
TYPO	
37006	116
38007	118
SPATIAL	
49032	142

VISUAL PROFILE *Concrete Depiction • Flat versus Dimensional •*
Ornamental • Detailed • Elegant • Emphasis on Food

PICTO	
01064	41
01068	41
04017	47
10018	58
CHROMA	
21019	82
TYPO	
33001	108
33007	108
37030	117
38024	118
SPATIAL	
49050	143
50005	144

VISUAL PROFILE *Geometric • Movement • Ambiguous Space • Playful • Type as Image • Dynamic • Clean*

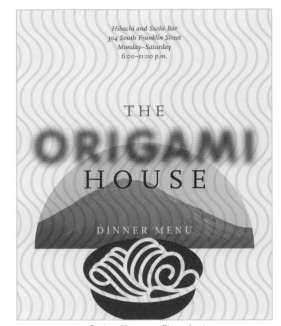

PICTO	
01003	40
02053	42
04002	46
06023	51
15067	69
CHROMA	
29002	98
TYPO	
33031	109
37013	116
38002	118
SPATIAL	
49025	142

VISUAL PROFILE *Tension • Movement • Direct • Iconic • Stately • Historical Color • Hard/Soft Contrast*

PICTO	
01068	41
09015	56
15016	68
CHROMA	
19028	78
29023	99
TYPO	
37018	116
38040	119
SPATIAL	
49009	142
50044	145

VISUAL PROFILE *Allusive • Organic • Handmade • Calligraphic • Fluid • Gestural • Elegant • Suggests Paper, Water, Land*

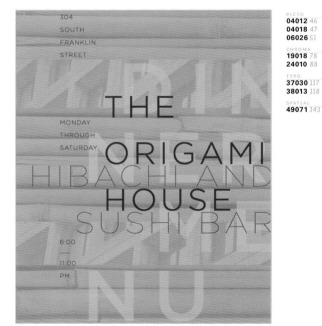

PICTO	
04012	46
04018	47
06026	51
CHROMA	
19018	78
24010	88
TYPO	
37030	117
38013	118
SPATIAL	
49071	143

VISUAL PROFILE *Architectural • Dimensional • Geometric • Rhythmic • Intricate • Strong • Layered • Interactive Forms*

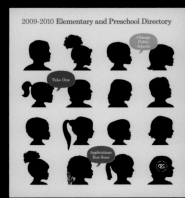

The delicate pencil and watercolor illustration of swans—whose slender necks create a symbolic heart shape—corroborates the romantic, ornamented title treatment and lilting script.

THOMAS CSANO
MONTREAL, QUEBEC | CANADA

Stark black silhouettes are arranged in a fo[...]
school directory cover. This structure's reg[...]
the unique profile contours, asymmetrical[...]
callouts, and dynamic visual texture of the[...]
KYM ABRAMS DESIGN CHICAGO, IL[...]

The cover of this book for a nature preserve evokes the location's lush ecology with a luminous, layered collage of vividly colored plant and animal transparencies. The title[...]

The cover for an annual report (see spreads on page 193) focuses attention on an important financial figure with an asymmetrically configured shape that acts as a window for the image of a sky. A texture making up the large type, as well as crosshair elements and small, sharp text, contrast the neutral color field and bold geometric spatial breaks.

CREUNA OSLO | NORWAY

The "discord" mentioned in the title of this CD cover is evoked in the misaligned meeting of the top and bottom halves of the diagonal line texture. The light, uniform strokes of all-uppercase type restate the pattern's linearity.

THINK STUDIO NEW YORK, NY | UNITED STATES

This cover for a financial service firm's brochure uses a subtle visual metaphor to support the title concept; a rich palette of analogous and complementary colors underscores the concept's focus on the unique.

IDEAS ON PURPOSE NEW YORK, NY | UNITED STATES

The designers of these covers for poetry books explore the allusive quality of form, situating a reserved titling treatment over sensuous, ornamental patterns. The swirling, decorative motifs provide a contemplative, literary quality, as well as evoke the fluid, metaphorical aspects of poetic writing. Austere, limited palettes bring warmth and contemporaneity.

PEOPLE DESIGN
GRAND RAPIDS, MI | UNITED STATES

The book covers in this series are unified through the use of a single serif type family and silhouetted, high-contrast images derived from treated photographs—as well as through a humble, textured, craft-paper cover stock.

THOMAS CSANO
MONTREAL, QUEBEC | CANADA

For the cover of this annual report, graphical depictions of browser interfaces overlap black-and-white photography (some of which is textured with a coarse dot screen) washed with color.

CREUNA OSLO | NORWAY

SINGLE-PRODUCT PACKAGING

PHARMACEUTICALS | *Over-the-Counter Cold Remedy*

Project Communication Brief

Communicate the product's concept: a two-part remedy that provides relief and energy during the day, and comfortable restful sleep at night— suggested by the product's brand name, invented by combining the words relax and maximize.

Convey ideas of rest, energy, and health.

Suggest the efficacy of the product.

Text Element Translations

Product Brand Name
Relaximize Day and Night
Multisymptom 24-hour cold remedy

Tagline
Nondrowsy for daytime, helps you sleep through the nigh

PICTO	
14018	66
CHROMA	
19001	78
19016	78
TYPO	
37031	117
38025	119
38043	119
SPATIAL	
49027	142

VISUAL PROFILE *Complementary •
Direct • Abstract • Rhythmic • Ordered •
Energetic • Simple*

PICTO	
01028	40
01055	41
14018	66
CHROMA	
19037	79
23028	87
TYPO	
36028	115
38013	118
45014	132
SPATIAL	
49025	142
50013	144

VISUAL PROFILE *Diagonal Movement •
Transition • Direct • Strength • Reliability •
Ambiguous Space • Metaphorical*

PICTO	
01014	40
02089	43
15013	68
15043	68
CHROMA	
19016	78
19025	78
TYPO	
36027	115
38042	119
SPATIAL	
49007	142
49018	142
50028	144

VISUAL PROFILE *Transition • Integrated •
Complementary • Cool and Warm • Radial
Geometry • Time • Rhythmic*

PICTO	
01028	40
01035	40
02084	43
04019	47
05017	49
CHROMA	
21045	83
TYPO	
37029	117
38043	119
SPATIAL	
49009	142

VISUAL PROFILE *Allusive • Pictorial
Reference • Linear • Efficient • Direct*

PICTO	
01021	40
01028	40
02113	43
CHROMA	
19049	79
20038	81
20066	81
TYPO	
37043	117
38002	118
SPATIAL	
49049	143

VISUAL PROFILE *Juxtaposition of Abstract
and Iconic • Work • Relaxation • Contrast in
Energy • Strong*

PICTO	
01001	40
04020	47
12069	63
CHROMA	
21033	83
25005	90
TYPO	
34025	111
37043	117
38037	119
38039	119
SPATIAL	
49008	142

VISUAL PROFILE *Playful • Youthful •
Accessible • Montage • Vibrant • Contemporary •
Pill/Steel Equivalence*

PICTO	
01057	41
08005	54
CHROMA	
25010	90
TYPO	
37029	117
38048	119
SPATIAL	
49003	142

VISUAL PROFILE *Stylized • Systematic •
Bold • Abstract • Effervescent • Energetic*

PICTO	
01020	40
01021	40
04003	46
06005	50
06021	51
CHROMA	
19038	79
25001	90
TYPO	
34009	110
37027	117
38025	119
SPATIAL	
49056	143
50007	144

VISUAL PROFILE *Juxtaposition of Realism
and Stylization • Narrative • Dreamlike • Comfort •
Energy • Soft/Hard Contrast*

PICTO	
04001	46
CHROMA	
21003	82
TYPO	
37029	117
38038	119
SPATIAL	
49008	142

VISUAL PROFILE *Pictorial • Primary •
Vivid • Narrative • Everyday • Personal*

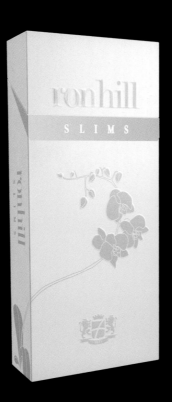

Neoclassical serif typefaces, with their pronounced stroke contrast, visually restate the thins and thicks of the iconic illustration, as well as impart a sense of luxury. The curling flower images position the product as refreshing and natural, while their compositional aspects suggest a cloud of smoke.

BRUKETA & ZINIC ZAGREB │ CROA

In this cover for a songwriter's compilation CD, classic jazz-album typography is supported by a toned photograph; line and dot elements visually connect to the details in the image.

COMPASS 360 DESIGN
TORONTO, ONTARIO │ CANADA

An economical label, as simple as it seems, nonetheless transforms this from a mere snack to an inviting experience through bold, sunny color, a friendly (almost schoolbook) slab serif, and cleverly subtle pictorial detail.

RED CANOE
DEER LODGE, TN │ UNITED STATES

The tall, perky proportion of this juice packaging provides a tense, linear contrast to the collection of dotlike photographic forms. The images are lush and concrete, but organized to form a landscape, enhanced by illustrative elements that transform the scene into an engagingly surreal experience.

BRUKETA & ZINIC
ZAGREB | CROATIA

The dramatic complementary relationship of red-orange and blue-violet, enriched with black and an intense blue-green, acts as a compelling backdrop to the contrasting angular form and supporting, stylized flower images arranged in a loose, collage-like composition. The shapes, color, and abstracted floral forms allude to the dynamic experience of storytelling, the subject of this CD's package.

MARY DOMOWICZ
NEW YORK, NY | UNITED STATES

A subtle palette of blue hues—one intense, one desaturated and slighlty darker in value—mutes the dramatic graphic quality of the abstract form language applied to this shopping bag. The logotype, a customized sans serif, contrasts the dots' mass

SIMPLE WEBSITE

HOME PAGE | *Financial Services Consultants*

Project Communication Brief

Communicate the client's primary service, banking and investment consulting.

Position the client as an advocate for their customers' lifestyle planning.

Convey the client's competency in their field of expertise.

Differentiate the client through visual language that suggests they are forward-thinking.

Text Element Translations

Client Name
Fiske Market Consulting

Promotional Headlines
Investing from your perspective.
How do you see yourself living in the next twenty years? We see it, too.

Navigational Elements
Company Profile/Investor Services/Fund Portfolio/Client Area

PICTO	
01059	41
04001	46
04016	46
CHROMA	
19051	79
26001	92
TYPO	
36025	115
38005	118
46022	134
SPATIAL	
49007	142
52017	149
56004	156

VISUAL PROFILE *Strong • Financial • Credible • Competent • Focused • Narrative • Planning versus Goal • Vibrant*

PICTO	
01068	41
04002	46
04005	46
05018	49
14022	66
CHROMA	
19051	79
26001	92
TYPO	
37025	117
38018	118
46044	135
SPATIAL	
53022	151
56006	156

VISUAL PROFILE *Ordered • Mathematical • Rational • Linear • Dimensional • Fluidity • Responsive • Serious • Reliable*

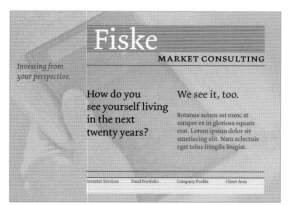

PICTO	
04012	46
05004	48
CHROMA	
19057	79
26001	92
TYPO	
37001	116
38036	119
46045	135
SPATIAL	
52018	149

VISUAL PROFILE *Distinctive • Neutral • Classical • Structured • Competent • Bookish • Textural • Reserved • Sophisticated*

PICTO	
01052	41
04008	46
04017	47
CHROMA	
21028	83
26002	92
TYPO	
37025	117
38006	118
46049	135
SPATIAL	
53022	151
56006	156
56023	157

VISUAL PROFILE *Simple • Organized • Direct • Mosaic • Part-to-Whole • Comprehensive • Progressive • Integrated*

PICTO	
04001	46
06005	50
06019	51
06031	51
CHROMA	
29017	99
TYPO	
37040	117
38027	119
46047	135
SPATIAL	
52023	149

VISUAL PROFILE *Personalized • Customer-Focused • Direct • Honest • Reliable • Clean • Metaphorical*

PICTO	
01054	41
01068	41
04001	46
06005	50
06009	50
06031	51
10001	58
CHROMA	
19018	78
26002	92
TYPO	
33031	109
37025	117
38025	119
46023	134
SPATIAL	
49056	143

VISUAL PROFILE *Symbolic • Intangible • Aspirational • Concrete • Accessible • Youth into Retirement • Collage • Integrated*

A promotional website organizes closely cropped images and text in
a sliding, letter-boxed viewing area. Content is grouped according to
conceptual headings listed in the minimal navigation above the band.

PEOPLE DESIGN GRAND RAPIDS, MI │ UNITED STATES

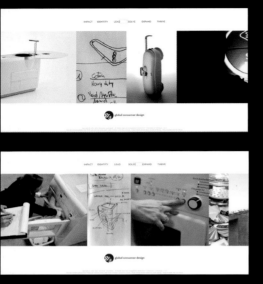

This elegant site groups thumbnail
grid navigation and text content
into a foreground box area, quietly
supported by muted color fields and
subtle patterns.

FORM LONDON │ UNITED KINGDOM

Relatively extensive informational text is cleanly organized on a hierarchic grid that provides distinct zones for branding, navigation, and imagery. Reversing the proportion of the geometric page breaks between zones adds movement. A selection of gothic sans serif and ornamental all-cap serif typefaces evokes the colonial period, as does the updated engraved line illustration of the map.

THINK STUDIO
NEW YORK, NY | UNITED STATES

The portfolio area of this design studio's website is accessed through a grid of intricate geometric patterns, each revealing a snapshot of a particular project case study upon rollover. The remaining navigation is clustered neatly to the left of the main texture grid.

BASE ART CO.
COLUMBUS, OHIO | UNITED STATES

This website for a manufacturer of hiking boots organizes images and navigation in a photographic scrapbook-style collage. Earthy colors and a background of tree bark reinforce the rustic message.

999 DESIGN
LONDON | UNITED KINGDOM

PICTO	
04031	47
04032	47
06022	51
08022	55
16025	70
CHROMA	
29023	99
TYPO	
34038	111
37025	117
38047	119
41017	125
46031	135
46036	135
SPATIAL	
49037	143
56008	156
56010	156
56030	157

VISUAL PROFILE *Eclectic ● Geometric ● Mixed Narratives ●
Presentational ● Dimensional ● Constructing ● Fluid*

PICTO	
01029	40
04018	47
06005	50
10032	58
17042	73
CHROMA	
25001	90
26002	92
TYPO	
37017	116
38040	119
39031	121
46006	134
SPATIAL	
50017	144
52030	149

VISUAL PROFILE *Thematic ● Romantic ● Storybook ● Dimensional ●
Interactive ● Detailed ● Dream versus Concrete ● Metaphorical*

PICTO	
01028	40
02010	42
13042	65
18012	74
CHROMA	
29017	99
TYPO	
37042	117
38048	119
46002	134
SPATIAL	
49007	142
53014	150

VISUAL PROFILE *Eclectic ● Narrative ● Symbolic ● Delicate ● Nostalgic ●
Comfortable ● Reserved*

PICTO	
04022	47
12064	63
CHROMA	
29023	99
TYPO	
37045	117
38038	119
46047	135
48069	138
48101	138
48118	138
48122	138
SPATIAL	
53031	151

VISUAL PROFILE *Contemporary ● Clean ● Professional ●
Subtle Ornamentation ● Organized ● Environmental Reference*

PICTO	
01068	41
02018	42
02104	43
06005	50
07032	53
17026	72
CHROMA	
29030	99
TYPO	
33016	108
37044	117
38044	119
38047	119
46004	134
SPATIAL	
49004	142
49049	143

VISUAL PROFILE *Illustrative ● Narrative ● Gestural ● Personal ●
Dimensional ● Spontaneous ● Playful*

PICTO	
01057	41
CHROMA	
21003	82
24022	89
TYPO	
37030	117
38018	118
38043	119
46044	135
SPATIAL	
53027	151

VISUAL PROFILE *Efficient ● Informational ● Rigorous ● Sophisticated ●
Neutral ● Geometric ● Systematic ● Edgy ● Technological*

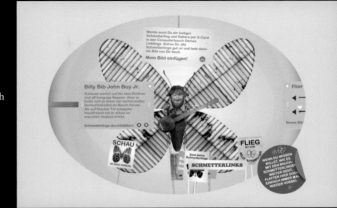

A free-form collage of photographic elements allows users to navigate through the content of this promotional website.

MAURICE REDMOND/FEUER
MUNICH | GERMANY

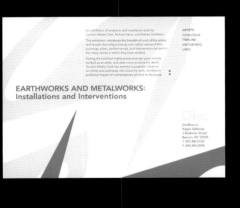

This website template articulates text and inset images, along with an interactive timeline, over a three-column hierarchic grid; abstract forms derived from the featured art activate the austere white space of the background, their color used to highlight navigational links.

FRANCESCA SCIANDRA
NEW YORK, NY | UNITED STATES

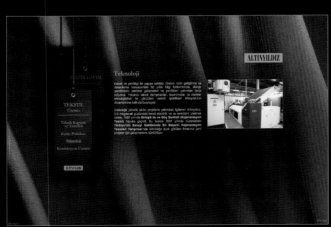

Text, images, and navigation, organized in a hierarchic column grid, are supported by a full-screen backdrop of sensuously lit fabric in this site for an apparel manufacturer. The navigation is classically typeset on a photographic clothing tag.

2FRESH ISTANBUL | TURKEY,
LONDON | UNITED KINGDOM

IMAGE-DRIVEN AD

SINGLE-PAGE FORMAT | *Lifestyle Products*

Project Communication Brief

Identify the brand and purpose of the product.

Establish an understanding of the product's organic, botanical qualities.

Evoke the product's effectiveness as a result of advanced scientific manufacture.

Convey a sense of improved hygiene, health, and energy.

Communicate the product's potential to improve long-term health.

Text Element Translations

Client
Nutria Bath and Body System

Headline and Deck
Revive and Conquer! Don't simply clean, but catalyze—
with the science of organic botanicals.

Tagline
Science makes the difference.

Body copy is represented by dummy text
in this project.

PICTO	
02025	42
04001	46
06024	51
10011	58
CHROMA	
19029	78
25010	90
TYPO	
36028	115
38031	119
SPATIAL	
49008	142
50003	144
56036	157

VISUAL PROFILE *Iconic ● Botanical ● Scientific ● Authoritative ●
Natural ● Clean ● Direct ● Refreshing*

PICTO	
01028	40
02005	42
09030	57
CHROMA	
25010	90
TYPO	
34024	110
36028	115
37025	117
SPATIAL	
49040	143

VISUAL PROFILE *Invigorating ● Clean ● Metaphorical ● Elemental ●
Imaginative ● Organic ● Sensuous*

PICTO	
01028	40
01067	41
04001	46
06023	51
08020	55
10022	58
CHROMA	
19029	78
25007	90
TYPO	
36029	115
37025	117
38007	118
38038	119
39011	120
SPATIAL	
49010	142
50040	145

VISUAL PROFILE *Scientific ● Source versus Use ● Botanical ●
Molecular ● Analytical ● High-End ● Personalized*

PICTO	
01025	40
01028	40
02033	42
06005	50
11042	61
CHROMA	
20039	81
26008	92
TYPO	
34048	111
36030	115
38008	118
SPATIAL	
49005	142
50003	144
50045	145

VISUAL PROFILE *Empowered ● Clean ● Aspirational ● Scientific ●
Botanical ● Classical ● Strong ● Simple ● Health-Conscious*

PICTO
04001 46
06005 50
13004 64
17009 72
CHROMA
28001 96
29006 98
TYPO
37047 117
38035 119
38040 119
40017 123
40030 123
SPATIAL
49002 142
49011 142

VISUAL PROFILE *Editorial • Classical • Victorian • Sensuous •*
Experiential • Detailed • Suggests Indulgence

PICTO
01013 40
01018 40
02084 43
07022 53
18008 74
18013 74
CHROMA
19002 78
25016 90
28002 96
TYPO
37025 117
38029 119
38031 119
45025 133
SPATIAL
50056 145

VISUAL PROFILE *Joyous • Illustrative • Dimensional • Active •*
Healthy • Everyday • Youthful Lifestyle • Vibrant

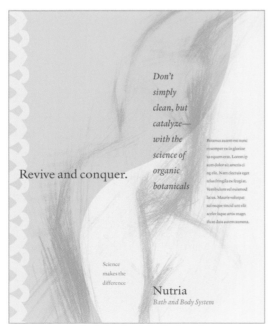

PICTO
01068 41
07002 52
17046 73
CHROMA
19014 78
28002 96
TYPO
37002 116
38007 118
44016 130
SPATIAL
49012 142
50044 145

VISUAL PROFILE *Emphasis on Female Health • Energetic •*
Illustrative • Botanical Allusion • Personal • Handmade

PICTO
01018 40
01028 40
01057 41
04001 46
06005 50
06021 51
13048 65
14019 66
CHROMA
21021 82
21043 83
TYPO
37030 117
38041 119
44019 130
45024 133
SPATIAL
49009 142
50043 145

VISUAL PROFILE *Subtle • Gradual • Enhancing • Molecular •*
Modern Science versus Romantic Experience • Effective • Beauty

The designer characterizes the family-friendly performan[ce] of an iconic symphonic work with a charming, simplified illustration style and stylized script titling elements. A rich, analogous color palette suggests the narrative's rural settin[g].

999 DESIGN LONDON | UNITED KINGDOM

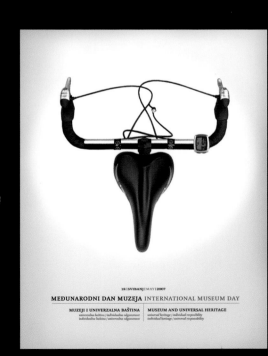

This poster for a lecture by typographic innovator Philippe Apeloig mixes hand-drawn icons with dimensional and abstract type treatments characteristic of his work. An intricate layout grid alludes to the designer's process and precision.

DURRE DESIGN RANCHO PALOS VERDE, CA | UNITED STATES

This poster ad promotes art's timelessness through an ima[ge] that evokes the iconic messages of cave painting while riffi[ng] an iconic, modern sculpture by Pablo Picasso. Careful cont[rol] visual contrast among elements introduces rhythm and ten[sion] that enhances the symmetrical composition.

BRUKETA & ZINIC ZAGREB | CROATIA

...irling spiral of multicolored, woven texture ...s the eye to its asymmetrically placed focal ...t—a block of information set all uppercase ... organized by line elements.

TICAL MAGIC
...PHIS, TN │ UNITED STATES

The grid used to organize product images withi[n]
of a jewelry catalogue (see page 193) appears in [a]
ment of boxes on the catalog cover.

SUNG SOO SONG
NEW YORK, NY | UNITED STATES

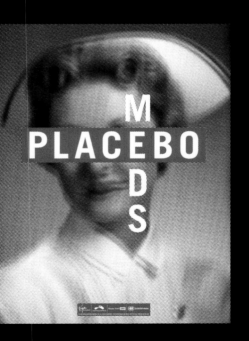

Overprinting the same coarse dot-screen image in
complementary red and green—usually associated with
3D images—evokes a disoriented state of mind in need
of conceptual medication.

STEREOTYPE DESIGN
NEW YORK, NY | UNITED STATES

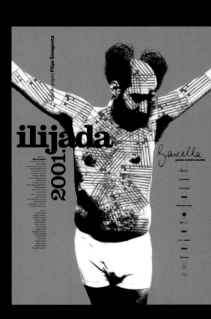

The central image of this theater poster
combines a high-contrast, posterized photo
with overprinted diagram images. The slab
serif titling responds to the forms in the figure
with its heavy dot elements and contrasting
stroke weights.

STUDIO CUCULIĆ ZAGREB | CROATIA

ETTING THE STAGE

is category of project's serves to transition between
e introductory impact of a visual communication and
main message, or as a lead-in to more complex proj-
ts of a serial or sequential nature. Type plays a greater
e in these communications—storefront displays,
torial page spreads, and advertising campaigns—but
agery remains a strong component.

Projects in This Section

SIMPLE EDITORIAL PAGES
NEWSLETTER/MAGAZINE FEATURE

RETAIL DISPLAY
STOREFRONT WINDOW PROMOTION

POSTER/AD CAMPAIGN
KIOSK OR SINGLE-PAGE FORMAT

SIMPLE EDITORIAL PAGES

NEWSLETTER/MAGAZINE FEATURE | *Nonprofit Organization*

Project Communication Brief

....

Communicate the financial subject of the feature article.

Organize the editorial content with images and the newsletter's table of contents.

Refer to the client's core activities: building low-income housing, refurbishing neglected properties, and developing public green spaces and gardens.

Indicate the publication's seasonal period.

Text Element Translations

....

Article Headline
Welcome to the Jungle: Navigating the Nonprofit Venture Capital Market

Article Deck
In today's volatile economy, many venture capital firms are delaying investment until they see the prospect of a good return—often preventing early initiatives that could ensure such certainty.

Article Callout
"We have to look rational, but part of the equation is passion."
Walter Rosegarten, Venture Capitalist

Newsletter Masthead
Urban Hope Quarterly / October 2012 / Volume 5, Issue 02

Body copy and contents listing elements in this project are represented by dummy text.

VISUAL PROFILE

Geometric ● Ordered ● Simple ●
Clean ● Academic ● Formal ●
Rigorous ● Ecological ● Urban ●
Journalistic

PICTO	
04017	*47*
04019	*47*
04029	*47*
06005	*50*

CHROMA	
20047	*81*
20064	*81*

TYPO	
37048	*117*
38017	*118*
40002	*122*
41001	*124*
42012	*126*
44017	*130*
46011	*134*

SPATIAL	
49046	*143*
49048	*143*
51017	*147*
57002	*158*

VISUAL PROFILE

Complex ● Accessible ●
Layered ● Graphing Reference ●
Iconic ● Constructing ●
Organized ● Financial Emphasis ●
Sophisticated ● Formal

PICTO	
02090	*43*
02104	*43*
04017	*47*
04030	*47*
18049	*75*

CHROMA	
21046	*83*

TYPO	
37038	*117*
38034	*119*
41027	*125*
42008	*126*
44017	*130*
46010	*134*

SPATIAL	
52011	*148*
57004	*158*

VISUAL PROFILE

Dynamic Color ● Dimensional ●
Physical ● Icon Detailing ●
Organized ● Industrial ●
Journalistic ● Subtly Playful

PICTO	
02030	*42*
04012	*46*
04032	*47*

CHROMA	
21022	*82*
21023	*82*

TYPO	
37048	*117*
38025	*119*
39026	*121*
40002	*122*
40020	*123*
40029	*123*
41005	*124*
42019	*127*
46045	*135*

SPATIAL	
53017	*151*
57003	*158*

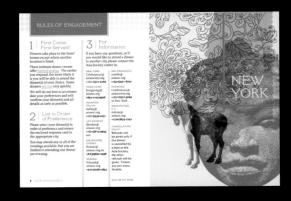

These pages from an event invitation show a rich combination of illustrative elements—colorized photographs, ornamental patterns, and border treatments—supported by detailed typography that uses line rules, patterns, initial numerals, and colored text.

IDEAS ON PURPOSE
NEW YORK, NY | UNITED STATES

Using a common, stylized icon of the female form as a primary image in this brochure—for the cover, as part of a photographic illustration, and as the basis for charts—underscores statistical information and reinforces a projection of female worker identity.

KYM ABRAMS DESIGN
CHICAGO, IL | UNITED STATES

An exciting mix of such illustrative elements as vector silhouettes, scribbles, arrows, icons, and grids combines with a soft, neutral sans serif to create an engaging publication for students.

FORM LONDON | UNITED KINGDOM

This quarterly newsletter mixes a variety of illustration styles—high-contrast photography, vector objects, and engraving—with contemporary sans serif faces and Victorian layout and text detailing to evoke the hip, yet timeless, character of the dive bar billiards enthusiast.

JASEN D. ROLFE LEXINGTON, MA | UNITED STATES

Starkly defined spatial divisions across the width of this magazine page spread establish a strong compositional geometry which the various elements alternately complement and contrast. The boundary between image and negative space is crossed by the deck, but repeated by the text block. The architectural qualities of the layout are contrasted by the roundness of the title form, yet the tree's arc is repeated in by the accented lowercase e. Diagonals, differing line weights, and scale within the image are restated by the sizes, weights, and positioning of the typographic elements.

JOSEPH CASERTO
ART DIRECTION AND DESIGN
BROOKLYN, NY | UNITED STATES

VISUAL PROFILE
*Metaphorical • Illustrative •
Inviting • Diverse • Personal •
Metaphorical • Narrative •
Hierarchic • Navigable*

PICTO
04001 46
04019 47
06022 51
07009 52
07015 52

CHROMA
20003 80
20025 80
20035 80

TYPO
37048 117
38038 119
38043 119
40009 122
41029 125
42024 127
44017 130
44019 130
46026 135

SPATIAL
49008 142
53026 151

VISUAL PROFILE
*Modular • Precisely Organized •
Dramatic Depth • Textural •
Gritty • Businesslike • Urban
Interactive • Confrontational*

PICTO
04026 47
05022 49
17069 73

CHROMA
19026 78
25002 90

TYPO
33021 108
34028 111
37025 117
38007 118
38017 118
40005 122
41009 124
42004 126
44012 130
46012 134

SPATIAL
49052 143
53026 151
55007 154
56021 157

VISUAL PROFILE
*Geometric • Hierarchic •
Journalistic • Ecological •
Urban • Architectural •
Businesslike*

PICTO
04001 46
04009 46
04032 47
06005 50

CHROMA
21039 83
25002 90

TYPO
37038 117
38017 118
38038 119
40009 122
41009 124
44002 130
44026 131
46013 134

SPATIAL
52022 149
56003 156
56027 157
57006 158

144

For a product catalog, jewelry is presented in varying layouts on a consistent grid structure, with page colors responding to the particular metal used in the work.

SUNG SOO SONG

NEW YORK, NY │ UNITED STATES

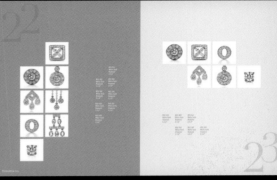

22

23

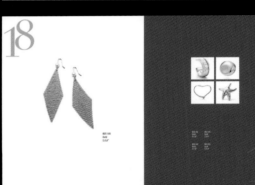

18

19

Basic geometric shapes frame text columns, integrating them in the compositional spaces of dramatically cropped color photographs. Typographic callouts are treated with a linear pattern.

CREUNA OSLO │ NORWAY

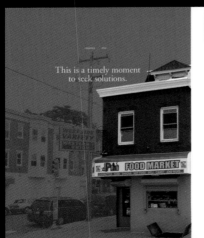

This is a timely moment to seek solutions.

If Beverly Davis can get back on her feet, she wants to enroll her daughter Alyla in dance class or gymnastics.

This sleek layout for a report related to urban poverty juxtaposes stately, almost bookish, typography—in a quiet mix of serif and sans serif faces—with selectively toned images in which focal points are silhouetted in vivid color.

IDEAS ON PURPOSE

NEW YORK, NY │ UNITED STATES

Geometric forms, abstracted from furniture, architecture, and science diagrams, compose the section-opener pages in this furniture brochure. Offsetting their cold linearity is the fact that they were drawn by hand. Overprinted colors in muted, complementary palettes enrich the chromatic experience. The typography alternates between hard-edged sans serif display and sharply elegant serif text.

PEOPLE DESIGN GRAND RAPIDS, MI | UNITED STATES

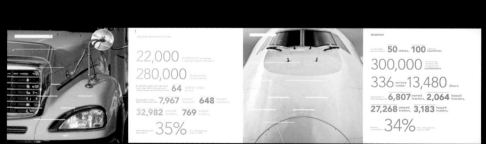

This annual report is unconventionally formatted as an accordion-fold booklet. One side presents upper-level messaging—an overview of business performance integrated with texture-treated slices of photography—while the other shows saturated, full-bleed photographs alternating with large typographic highlights. The financial tables are bound in as a saddle-stitched booklet, continuing the linear elements established in the other pages.

ANN IM SUNWOO
NEW YORK, NY | UNITED STATES

This season brochure for a dance company features closely cropped black-and-white photographs of dancers, overlaid with colored cutouts derived from the shapes within the images. A neutral typographic structure offsets the images' dynamism.

SURFACE FRANKFURT AM MEIN | GERMANY

RETAIL DISPLAY

STOREFRONT WINDOW PROMOTION
Home Decor and Housewares Store

Project Communication Brief

....

Establish the nature of the client's business: retail home furnishings.

Communicate the range of product styles offered.

Appeal to style-conscious, upwardly mobile customers and interior designers.

Convey the aesthetic and production qualities of the furnishings.

Announce the featured sale on lighting.

Allude to the season of the promotion.

Text Element Translations

....

Client Logotype
The Home Store

Promotional Headline
Essential Room Service: Fancy and Fine to
Mod and Minimal

Deck
The Spring Collections Are Here

Sale Announcement
For a limited time: 30% off all lighting fixtures

Listing Elements
Chairs / Sofa / Sectionals / Credenzas /
Ottomans / Divans / End Tables / Shelving /
Stools / Display Cases / Lamps / Sconces

VISUAL PROFILE
Dimensional • Kinetic •
Contemporary • Concrete •
Rich • Stylish • Eclectic •
Layered • Constructed •
Geometric • Detailed

PICTO
02059 42
02064 42
04001 46

CHROMA
28006 96

TYPO
37003 116
37031 117
38038 119
38043 119
46041 135

SPATIAL
49037 143

VISUAL PROFILE
Eclectic • Ambiguous Space •
Seasonal • Fresh • Fun •
Decorative • Vibrant •
Contemporary • Pop

PICTO
01016 40
01020 40
04009 46
04029 47
06005 50
10032 58
12026 62
13013 64
14004 66

CHROMA
25029 91
28005 96

TYPO
33025 109
33030 109
37029 117
38027 119
46048 135

SPATIAL
49010 142
49040 143
49055 143

VISUAL PROFILE
Pattern Against Solid •
Linear • Geometric •
Urban • Quirky •
Lifestyle • Objects and
Spaces • Dimensional •
Customizable

PICTO
01019 40
01056 41
04011 46
04024 47
04030 47
06005 50
10022 58
13051 65
13052 65
13064 65
14011 66
14031 66
16126 71

CHROMA
25002 90

TYPO
36047 115
37030 117
38038 119
46022 134

SPATIAL
52013 148

VISUAL PROFILE
Geometric • Structured •
Architectural • Sensuous •
Eclectic • Edgy • Modern •
Kinetic • Decorative

PICTO
08022 55
13042 65
13064 65
13067 65
CHROMA
25017 91
29023 99
TYPO
33009 108
37028 117
38042 119
38048 119
SPATIAL
49019 142
49035 142

VISUAL PROFILE
Illustrative • Luminous •
Sleek • Stately • Formal •
Diagrammatic • Composed •
Contrast of Activity •
Contemporary

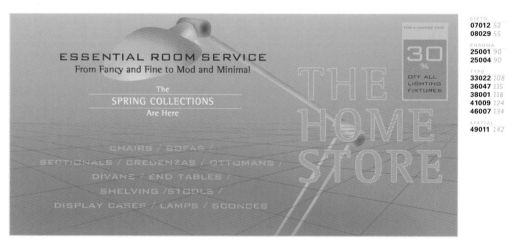

PICTO
07012 52
08029 55
CHROMA
25001 90
25004 90
TYPO
33022 108
36047 115
38001 118
41009 124
46007 134
SPATIAL
49011 142

VISUAL PROFILE
Continuity • Integrated •
Flow • Modular • Spatial
Progression • Lifestyle •
Narrative • Seasonal •
Layered • Rhythmic

PICTO
04032 47
CHROMA
22013 84
23027 87
TYPO
37030 117
38018 118
38042 119
41009 124
44017 130
SPATIAL
52011 148
56011 156
56028 157
57006 158

The graphic power of physical forms and materials—stone, glass, metal, textured paper—is evidenced by the bold environment created for this restaurant. A palette of neutrals is punctuated by a vivid orange wall, while the linearity of the wall pattern and seating areas gets a pop of contrast from giant, shiny dots: pendant lamps and grid-mounted mirrors.

KUHLMANN LEAVITT DESIGN

SAINT LOUIS, MO | UNITED STATES

In this exhibition design, compositional layering of photographic, textural, and physical elements creates dimensional, vignetted compositions. Considering multiple viewing angles, the effects of light and transparency, and color relationships between fabrication materials and the content of the display affords a design experience similar to that of a retail display or even a printed application.

ATELIER BRÜCKNER

STUTTGART | GERMANY

Branded construction barricades designed around various type-textured C forms provide visual relief from storefront renovation and create expectation for the future potential of the street-level display.

ADAMSMORIOKA

BEVERLY HILLS, CA | UNITED STATES

POSTER/AD CAMPAIGN

KIOSK OR SINGLE-PAGE FORMAT | *Men's Fragrance*

Project Communication Brief

Introduce and visually brand an upscale Italian fragrance.

Convey the product's masculine focus.

Express notions of mystery and surrealism; evoke the sensuality of fragrance, creating a sensory experience.

Create provocative narratives, suggesting the taboo nature of diverse sexuality among men.

Equate the fragrance with an aspired-to lifestyle of adventure, intrigue, power, and pleasure.

Text Element Translations

Ad Headlines
It takes one to know one. (1)
Maybe you do, maybe you don't. (2)
One door closes, another opens. (3)

Product Brand and Positioning Statement
Mistero: There's a little mystery in every man

Tagline
The new fragrance for men who know better

*Body copy is represented by dummy text
in this project.*

VISUAL PROFILE
Smoky ● Fluid ●
Languorous ● Elegant ●
Sensuous ● Rich ●
Body-Conscious ●
Strong ● Nebulous

PICTO	
04007	*46*
09014	*56*
11040	*61*

CHROMA	
25013	*90*
25014	*90*

TYPO	
37025	*117*
38031	*119*
45005	*132*
45032	*133*

SPATIAL	
49001	*142*
50044	*144*
50045	*145*

VISUAL PROFILE
Illustrative ● Sharp ●
Narrative ● Obscuring
and Revealing ●
Intrigue ● Power ●
Counterintuitive

PICTO	
01007	*40*
02014	*42*
02024	*42*
02027	*42*
02060	*42*
02090	*43*
02122	*43*
02125	*43*
07025	*53*
18010	*74*
18013	*74*
18039	*75*

CHROMA	
20013	*80*
23015	*86*

TYPO	
37026	*117*
38008	*118*
38038	*119*
45014	*132*

SPATIAL	
49008	*142*
50015	*144*

VISUAL PROFILE
Sensuous ● Tactile
Ambiguous Space ●
Fluid ● Elegant ●
Powerful ● Hidden ●
Interior and Exterior
Life ● Emotional

PICTO	
04007	*46*
05026	*49*
06031	*51*
09030	*57*

CHROMA	
28010	*96*
28023	*97*

TYPO	
37039	*117*
38023	*118*
45024	*133*

SPATIAL	
49007	*142*
50044	*145*
56030	*157*

Interconnected compositions of dots and lines directly
unify the four posters in this series; radically altering the
overprints of process colors differentiates each poster.
SHINNOSKE, INC.   OSAKA │ JAPAN

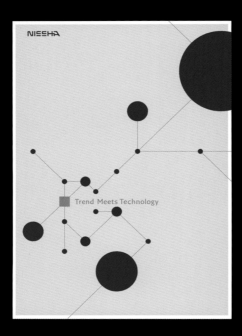

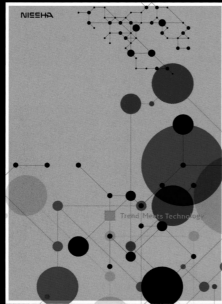

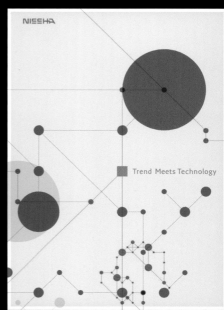

Each poster predicates the type arrangement on the photographic element, here reduced to nearly pure geometry and richly illuminated. A rhythmic mix of serifs and sans serifs alternates weights, cases, and spacing.

PAONE DESIGN ASSOCIATES
PHILADELPHIA, PA | UNITED STATES

This ad campaign for children's furnishings creates surreal and dynamically composed environments with color coding; each ad mixes analogous values and temperatures of a predominant color, accented by tiny amounts of complements.

PEOPLE DESIGN
GRAND RAPIDS, MI | UNITED STATES

VISUAL PROFILE
Iconic ● Symbolic ● Industrial ● Urban ● Edgy ● Electronic ● Pop-Culture Environment ● Trendy ● Dominating ● Confrontational

PICTO	
02082	43
02084	43
02087	43
03019	45
08005	54
18031	75
18036	75
18037	75

CHROMA	
20006	80
21021	82

TYPO	
36044	115
37029	117
38006	118
38007	118
44026	131

SPATIAL	
49008	142
49010	142

VISUAL PROFILE
Illustrative ● Kinetic ● Ambiguous Masculine Sexuality ● Symbolic ● Collage ● Retro ● Multilayered

PICTO	
05002	48
05012	48
17025	72

CHROMA	
25008	90
28014	96

TYPO	
37034	117
38016	118
45016	132

SPATIAL	
49033	142

VISUAL PROFILE
Animal and Natural Allusions ● Suggests the Irrational ● Intimate ● Seductive Gaze ● Confrontation

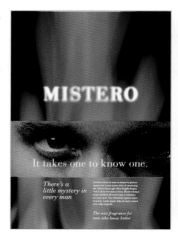

PICTO	
04001	46
04023	47
06026	51
10006	58
10041	59
10043	59

CHROMA	
20018	80
25002	90

TYPO	
34036	111
37009	116

SPATIAL	
49015	142
56024	157

The deadpan quality of these ad headlines is echoed by cut-and-paste, photocopied imagery. Contributing to the dry sense of imperfection, the headlines are drawn in marker. A full-bleed texture softens the compositional geometry.

MAURICE REDMOND / FEUER
MUNICH | GERMANY

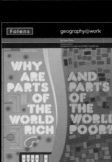

Much like an ad campaign, this series of educational book covers uses a graphic headline treatment to propose provocative questions related to social issues. The unified graphic language of vector illustrations and a soft, yet industrial, pseudo-stencil font is supported by a limited palette based on maps.

FORM LONDON | UNITED KINGDOM

OFF THE
ROAD AGAIN.

ENDURO
PARK
HECHLINGEN

Powered by BMW Motorrad

High-contrast, posterized photography, supported by the dynamic texture of hand-generated ink spatter, works in tandem with neutral, all-uppercase text that has also been textured. The complementary colors vary in saturation and value to increase the poster's dimensionality.

MAURICE REDMOND / FEUER
MUNICH | GERMANY

A series of promotional flyers mixes textured, woodcut-like illustrations in varying combinations with a supporting abstract texture. An analogous color scheme in each flyer is accented by a complementary hue.

THOMAS CSANO
MONTREAL, QUEBEC | CANADA

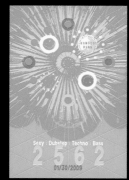

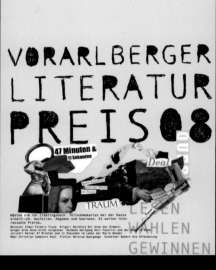

3

THE HEART OF THE MATTER

Illustrated here are approaches to the larger, more substantial visual communication projects incorporating and structuring large amounts of information, such as text-heavy editorial and web publishing, and visual branding systems for multicomponent product packaging. Well-chosen imagery and complex typographic structure are combined into layouts that will satisfy the most demanding client.

Projects in This Section

PACKAGING SYSTEM
LUXURY SWEETS

COMPLEX WEBSITE
E-COMMERCE CATALOGUE

BOOK DESIGN
TRADE BOOK

PACKAGING SYSTEM

LUXURY SWEETS | *Artisanal Flavored Chocolates*

Project Communication Brief

Communicate the unique features of the product: unusually flavored, richly crafted chocolates.

Evoke the history and sensuality of chocolate.

Differentiate and express the individual flavor profiles of each product type.

Visually support the brand's mythological, narrative concept.

Allude to the geographical context of each product type.

Text Element Translations

Brand Name, Positioning, and Tagline
Celestia
Exotically spiced artisanal chocolates
Heavenly Different

Product Names and Descriptors
Vishnu (1)
Garam masala-infused milk chocolate with goat's milk praline chunks

Quetzalcoatl (2)
Jalapeño-infused white chocolate with turmeric-encrusted golden raisins

Artemis (3)
Rosemary-infused dark chocolate with almonds and braised apple slices

VISUAL PROFILE *Sensuous •*
Exotic • Ornamental • Detailed •
Finely-Crafted • Victorian • Sweet •
Sumptuous • Narrative

PICTO
04012 46
04029 47
05021 49
09014 56
17052 73

CHROMA
25012 90
29006 98

TYPO
35021 112
35022 112
37023 116
38001 118
38030 119
39008 120
48259 139
48280 139
48303 139

SPATIAL
49010 142

VISUAL PROFILE *Sensuous •*
Organic • Tactile • Languid •
Dreamlike • Restive • Quirky •
Stylized

PICTO
04032 47
10010 58
15078 69

CHROMA
22042 85
25012 90

TYPO
33043 109
37001 116
45024 133
45032 133

SPATIAL
49007 142
50044 145

VISUAL PROFILE *Cultural*
Context • Contemporary • Clean •
Luxurious • Narrative • Concrete •
Depiction • Flat versus Dimensional

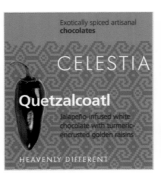

PICTO
04001 46
06005 50
13015 64
13064 65
13068 65

CHROMA
32003 104

TYPO
37031 117

SPATIAL
49008 142
49011 142

VISUAL PROFILE *Mythic •*
Sculptural • Narrative • References •
Cultural Aesthetics • Symbolic •
Majestic • Magical • Rich

PICTO
01041 41
01049 41
01060 41
04029 47
06005 50

CHROMA
25017 91
25019 91
25024 91

TYPO
37021 116

SPATIAL
49008 142

VISUAL PROFILE *Abstract • Unexpected Color • Edgy • Innovative • Experimental • Hip or Trendy • Unconventional • Sophisticated • Bold • Exciting • Systematic*

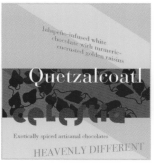

PICTO	
02027	42
02030	42
02031	42
CHROMA	
19039	79
31010	102
TYPO	
35046	113
37010	116
45020	133
SPATIAL	
49008	142
50008	144

VISUAL PROFILE *Delicate • Illustrative • Classical Styling • Old-World • Decorative • Sophisticated • Cultured • Reserved • Earthy • Handmade • Symbolic*

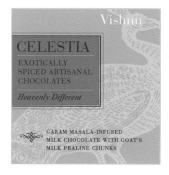

PICTO	
07009	52
17009	72
CHROMA	
30014	100
TYPO	
37010	116
38006	118
48303	139
SPATIAL	
49026	142
49027	142

VISUAL PROFILE *Opulent • Classical • Formal • Crisp • Precision • Luxurious • Exclusivity • Unexpected Color • Environmental Context • Hint of Edginess • Artsy*

PICTO	
04019	47
12003	62
12039	63
12044	63
17013	72
CHROMA	
19039	79
19050	79
19053	79
TYPO	
37020	116
38043	119
SPATIAL	
49026	142

VISUAL PROFILE *Layered • Contemporary • Energetic • Vibrant • Sensuous • Abstract • Fluid Rhythm • Formal*

PICTO	
15070	69
15077	69
15085	69
CHROMA	
19039	79
32011	104
TYPO	
37035	117
SPATIAL	
49009	142

A series of promotional tote bags for a fairy-tale festival supports a family of black-and-white creature illustrations with a rainbow of vivid hues. A contemporary serif, used for the type elements, visually relates to the thins and thicks in the drawings.

STUDIO CUCULIĆ ZAGREB │ CROATIA

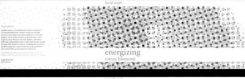

Electric hues and sharply stylized illustrations of insect pests convey the potency of these repellent sprays. Consistency among illustrative treatments, type styles and arrangement, positioning of the primary insect subject relative to the titling and background areas, and secondary hue identities provides immediate product family recognizability.

BRUKETA & ZINIC ZAGREB │ CROATIA

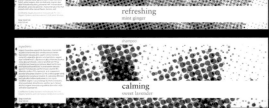

Wraparound labels of abstracted, dot-patterned photographs bring energy and a contemporary edge to this packaging system for a line of toiletries. The choice of a classical serif brings detail and organicism to the otherwise hard-edged presentation.

FRANCESCA SCIANDRA NEW YORK, NY │ UNITED STATES

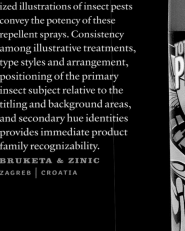

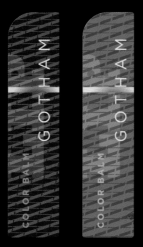

For a funky, sophisticated cosmetics line, the designer evokes the energy and architecture of an urban environment with a variety of geometric patterns. A two-level palette brands the overall line and color codes products for day or evening. Added drama and contrast are supplied by the mix of typefaces: a sleek sans serif family and a chunky slab serif.

STIM VISUAL COMMUNICATION
BROOKLYN, NY | UNITED STATES

The immediacy and variability of narrative inherent in public storytelling announce themselves in this vibrant packaging system for a set of archive CDs produced by a storytelling organization. A family of vivid primary hues underpins the packages; each cover's layout combines several elements whose subjects change from CD to CD, but whose visual treatments remain consistent. Formal attributes from within the images inform the selection of type styles to help unify the visual language.

MARY DOMOWICZ
NEW YORK, NY | UNITED STATES

Shopping bags for a delicatessen of regional Croatian specialties show a range of hand-drawn illustrations that evoke the area's rich heritage of textile design.
STUDIO CUCULIĆ ZAGREB | CROATIA

A painterly composition of the continents on the cover of this CD, "Beats on Canvas," metaphorically links art making and drumming. Inside the case, a grid of paint daubs, an inscription on the reverse of a stretched canvas, and an array of paint-covered brushes (arranged to evoke long, vertical drips) continue the metaphor. The CD surface itself suggests a "paint-by-numbers" idea.

THOMAS CSANO MONTREAL, QUEBEC | CANADA

Brilliantly colored typographic pictorializations of each fruit wine's primary ingredient describe the products and how to enjoy them.

BRUKETA & ZINIC ZAGREB | CROATIA

COMPLEX WEBSITE

E-COMMERCE CATALOG PAGE
Eco-Conscious Apparel and Home Fashions

Project Communication Brief

Communicate the site's product offering: organic clothing—produced using eco-friendly, sustainable production methods—that doesn't sacrifice style.

Evoke a sense of luxury and convey the materiality and workmanship of the products.

Convey the seasonality of the current collection.

Provide catalog functionality for browsing products and exploring selected items in greater detail.

Text Element Translations

Client/Website Name
Sew Ready: Responsible Outfitters

Positioning Line
Organic apparel for the couture-conscious

User's Browser Focus
Fall 2010 Collection / Womens / Evening Dresses / Silk

Navigation Elements
Collections: Mens / Womens / Kids
Accessories
Home Fashions
About Sustainable Fashion
Company Profile
Shopping Cart / Checkout

Product labels and description are represented
by dummy text in this project.

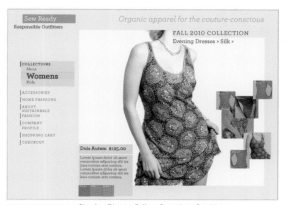

PICTO	
01004	40
01016	40
01067	41
04001	46
04008	46
CHROMA	
24009	88
TYPO	
37013	116
38025	119
42011	126
46021	134
46050	135
SPATIAL	
52017	149

VISUAL PROFILE *Simple • Direct • Collage Browsing • Intuitive •*
Personal • Contemporary • Friendly • Fresh • Light

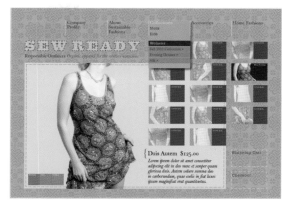

PICTO	
04001	46
04017	47
13028	64
17031	72
CHROMA	
24014	88
28032	97
TYPO	
33022	108
37019	116
46013	134
46043	135
46044	135
SPATIAL	
53032	151

VISUAL PROFILE *Modular • Organized • Thumbnail Grid Browsing • Layered •*
Embroidery Allusion • Well-Made • Detailed • Sophisticated

PICTO	
01006	40
01069	41
04001	46
04029	47
10061	59
CHROMA	
24018	89
25002	90
TYPO	
33025	109
37030	117
42029	127
45014	132
46039	135
SPATIAL	
50009	144

VISUAL PROFILE *Geometric • Collage Browsing • Kinetic Size Progression •*
Cutout • Weave Reference • Chic • Urban • Exclusive

PICTO	
04001	46
12004	62
17037	73
17061	73
17069	73
CHROMA	
19063	79
21045	83
TYPO	
36044	115
37028	117
38026	119
42003	126
46008	134
46036	135
SPATIAL	
49010	142
51017	147

VISUAL PROFILE *Textural • Page-Turn Browsing • Diversity • Look-Book/*
Editorial Allusion • Tactile • Eclectic • Pop • Glamorous

PICTO	
04001	46
06005	50
14010	66
14115	67
15114	69
17031	72
17032	72
CHROMA	
28032	97
TYPO	
33022	108
37030	117
46044	135
46045	135
SPATIAL	
52031	149

VISUAL PROFILE *Simple • Geometric • Movable Strip Browsing •*
Weave Reference • Fabric Edges • Patterning

PICTO	
04001	46
22032	85
TYPO	
37013	116
42009	126
46041	135
SPATIAL	
49033	142
51017	147

VISUAL PROFILE *Neutral • Minimal • Clean • Chic • Large Thumbnail*
Browsing • Informational • Direct • Reserved

screen to screen. The deep, saturated color and sleek sans serif typeface contribute to the sense of the client's competency.

STIM VISUAL COMMUNICATION
BROOKLYN, NY | UNITED STATES

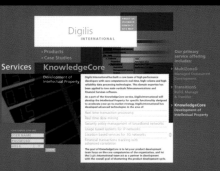

Sharp, vector-based, illustrative animations in the header combine with icons and geometric details to

PICTO
04001 46
06005 50

CHROMA
20007 80
25031 91

TYPO
37001 116
42001 126
42009 126
46043 135

SPATIAL
52019 149

VISUAL PROFILE *Collage • Button/Text Browsing • Subject Context • Rich • Seasonal Color • Dimensional • Image/Navigation Form Similarity*

PICTO
02032 42
04001 46
04015 46
04030 47
05024 49
06005 50
09003 56

CHROMA
25012 90
28032 97

TYPO
33047 109
37039 117
38042 119
42019 127
46017 134

SPATIAL
53030 151

VISUAL PROFILE *Modular • Staggered, Large Thumbnail Browsing • Ecological • Rich • Interaction with Nature • Collage • Illustrative • Textural*

PICTO
01014 40
02032 42
03016 44
04001 46
04011 46
05022 49
06005 50
07031 53

CHROMA
25009 90
25031 91

TYPO
33039 109
37013 116
42009 126
42027 127

SPATIAL
53032 151

VISUAL PROFILE *Bold • Ordered • Pop • Kitschy Glamour • Street • Fresh • Vivacious Energy • Large Thumbnail Browsing • Illustrative Detailing*

PICTO
04001 46
06005 50

CHROMA
20047 81
20070 81

TYPO
37031 117
38042 119
46018 134
46044 135

SPATIAL
53032 151

VISUAL PROFILE *Modular • Thumbnail Grid Browsing • Ordered • Neutral • Architectonic • Constructed • Utilitarian • Warm • Responsible*

PICTO
01045 41
02075 43
04001 46
06008 50
09031 57
18014 74

CHROMA
20034 80
23023 87

TYPO
33009 108
37048 117
41018 125
46050 135

SPATIAL
52017 149

VISUAL PROFILE *Collage Browsing • Intuitive • Fabric and Thread Allusions • Textural • Populist • Responsible • Concrete versus Abstract*

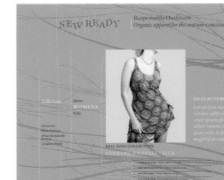

PICTO
01023 40
04001 46
06005 50
09011 56

CHROMA
23016 86

TYPO
33032 109
37048 117
42004 126
46017 134

SPATIAL
52013 148

VISUAL PROFILE *Soft • Text/List Navigation • Rhythmic • Ecological • Reserved • Formal • Sophisticated • Dimensional • Weather Allusion*

BOOK DESIGN

TRADE BOOK | *Cultural/Historical Subject*

Project Communication Brief

Create a complex editorial layout structure for a coffee-table book titled
The Garden of Dark Delights:
Confronting Passion and Morality in the Vampire Legend.

Visually evoke legendary aspects of the vampire: undead state, sleeping in earth, shape-shifting, drinking of blood, superhuman movement, rising at night, death and decay, mysteriousness, the ethereal, animal sensuality, earthly pleasure, heightened sensory experience, sharpened teeth and nails, paleness, alienation, religious excommunication.

Suggest the spiritual context of the vampire with regard to religion and notions of good and evil.

Convey feelings of sensuality, pleasure, mystery, darkness, anxiety, horror, lust, sacrifice, and power.

Text Element Translations

Titling
Chapter 4
*The Spiritual and the Secular: Embracing
the Afterlife on Earth*

Introductory Paragraph
Acknowledging the Victorian struggle between a desire for spiritual redemption and a newfound zeal for physical gratification, the figure of the vampire titillates with the suggestion that everlasting life—and worldly sensuality—need not be mutually exclusive pursuits.

Callout Head
*Eternity in Heaven or Endless Living?
Comparing Symbolic Iconography*

VISUAL PROFILE *Classical •*
Renaissance • Historic • Aged • Sinister •
Formal • Manuscript • Artifact •
Treasure • Sensual • Metaphorical

VISUAL PROFILE *Contemporary •*
Iconic • Medieval References • Rich •
Jewel-like Color • Illustrative •
Dimensional • Emphasis on Symbolism

VISUAL PROFILE *Timeless •*
Elegant • Ethereal • Narrative • Light •
Decorative • Elusive • Relatively
Neutral • Spiritual • Contemplative

VISUAL PROFILE *Earthy ● Dark ● Contemporary ● Rich ● Illustrative ● Supernatural ● Theatrical ● Emphasis on Legend ● Edwardian ● Historical ● Presentational ● Haunting*

PICTO	
04009	46
04016	46
07009	52
17061	73
17068	73

CHROMA	
20006	80
25012	90
25014	90

TYPO	
35014	112
35015	112
37035	117
40002	122
41031	125
42021	127
43091	128
44013	130
44047	131

SPATIAL	
52014	148
54027	153
57028	159
57037	159

VISUAL PROFILE *Geometric ● Ordered ● Contemporary ● Dynamic Image Proportion ● Bold ● Clean ● Neutral ● Direct ● Informational*

PICTO	
01068	41
04001	46
04009	46
04026	47
17069	73

CHROMA	
21003	82
22014	84

TYPO	
37028	117
40011	122
41009	124
42022	127
43124	129
43159	129
44019	130

SPATIAL	
53027	151
54034	153

VISUAL PROFILE *Academic ● Journalistic ● Light ● Open ● Historical ● Neutral ● Slightly Embellished ● Contemporary ● Quiet ● Typographic Emphasis ● Imagery Minimized ● Restrained Color ● Structural*

PICTO	
04009	46
07010	52
17009	72

CHROMA	
29002	98

TYPO	
37019	116
40017	123
41007	124
42002	126
43020	128
44011	130

SPATIAL	
51027	147
54005	152
57001	158

A six-column grid, used in a classical mirrored format, organizes a rich mix of text and illustrations for this book about sea travel. Gothic drop caps lead the paragraphs of serif-set text, while alternating page colors and textural details bring contrast and rhythm to the page sequence.

SUTHERN DESIGN
MADISON, NJ | UNITED STATES

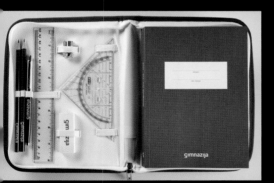

Actual objects—pencils, protractor, pencil sharpener, eraser, and ruler—become companion images to the printed photographs in this unusual monograph for a progressive school, bound inside a student's pencil case. Duotoned images, limited type style, and linear elements underscore the academic quality of the piece.

BRUKETA & ZINIC ZAGREB | CROATIA

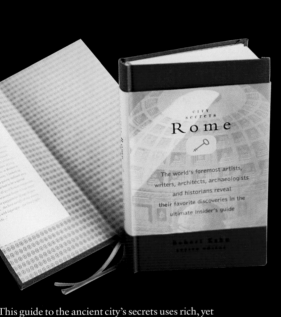

This guide to the ancient city's secrets uses rich, yet restrained, color, delicate patterning, and exquisitely crafted text typography folded neatly into an intimate size. A light, sepia-toned photograph provides a sense of the city's historical weight.

RED CANOE DEER LODGE, TN | UNITED STATES

The text spreads in this book organize content on an eight-column grid, staggering text and images across the spread in a rhythmic bounce of proportions. This movement contrasts the focused, horizontal band that governs the chapter openers; both share a limited vocabulary of typeface, delicate floral color, and decorative geometric motifs.

JULIE SHIM
NEW YORK, NY | UNITED STATES

Summer

In the page spreads of a book for a nature preserve, precise and delicate typographic structure provides a quiet, analytical counterpoint to the vibrancy of color images. Section openers are graced with lush, layered collages of transparent plant silhouettes, while interior pages display super-saturated photographs of actual plants. Colored bands code the sections, corresponding to locations in the preserve.

PAONE DESIGN ASSOCIATES

PHILADELPHIA, PA | UNITED STATES

Simple and Satisfying Entertainment

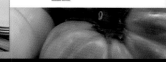

Black Cod with Snow Peas

"I went to the woods because I wished to live deliberately, to front only the essential facts of life, and see if I could not learn what it had to teach, and not, when I came to die, discover that I had not lived."
—Henry David Thoreau, Walden

68

Forest Pond and Pond Edge

The straightforward, four-column structure and presentation of photographic imagery is enlivened through a mix of strongly-contrasted type styles, bold color fields, dramatic cropping, and visually interesting page breaks. Silhouetted images contrast those framed in rectangles, while smaller, overlapping insets and variations in positioning provide tremendous bounce across the spreads. Informational details set in color bring the rich chromatic quality of the images into the type.

BTD:NYC

NEW YORK, NY | UNITED STATES

Joe Pye Weed
Eupatorium purpureum

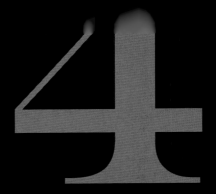

LETTER-PERFECT
Purely Typographic Solutions

No less complex than approaches that integrate imagery, this selection of projects explores the possibilities of letters and text alone—whether casual and light, strong and simple, or rich and textural. The projects here present type's fascinating design potential as a visual image unto itself, the perfect way to round out a varied and nuanced selection of design approaches.

the only ones
in luxurious coats
this season.

and see
some real bling...
Ice, ice, baby

Projects in This Section

COVER DESIGN
MARKETING BROCHURE

PACKAGING SYSTEM
LIGHTING HARDWARE

POSTER/AD CAMPAIGN
TOURISM

SIMPLE WEBSITE
HOME PAGE

EDITORIAL PAGES
ANNUAL REPORT
MESSAGING SECTION

COVER DESIGN

MARKETING BROCHURE
Real Estate Marketing

Project Communication Brief

....

Establish a connection between the heritage of a historic building, located close to New York City's Grand Central Terminal, and its contemporary renovation.

Convey the upscale nature of the property.

Evoke the energy of the urban environment and of the train station itself.

Promote the significance of the new architecture.

Invite prospective buyers to participate in a prestigious lifestyle.

Text Element Translations

....

Property Name
The Vanderbilt
At the Grand Central Complex
Luxury Condominiums

Address
120 Park Avenue South
At 41st Street

Tagline
Timeless style in the heart of the city

This series of financial books is "packaged" und a gigantic visual device—an ampersand cropped across the covers. Contrasting the continuity of the punctuation mark, the color of each cover changes, as does the linear, geometric pattern that creates the ampersand.

FORM   LONDON | UNITED KINGDOM

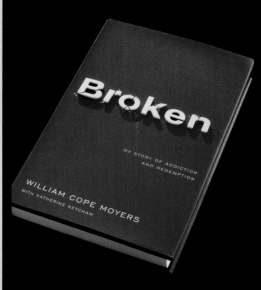

A rich red field creates a backdrop for the three-dimensional typographic treatment of the title on this book cover.

THINK STUDIO
NEW YORK, NY | UNITED STATES

PICTO	
01053	41
17002	72
CHROMA	
29014	98
TYPO	
37009	116
38048	119
SPATIAL	
49004	142
49010	142

VISUAL PROFILE *Classical • Exclusive • Majestic • Sharp • Historic • Precise • Timeless*

PICTO	
17052	73
CHROMA	
21030	83
25002	90
TYPO	
34002	110
37024	116
38046	119
39024	121
SPATIAL	
49002	142
49049	143

VISUAL PROFILE *Expressive • Gestural • Urban • Architectural Detail • Historic • Aesthetic Quality • Decorative*

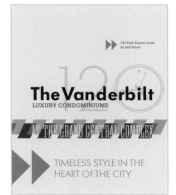

PICTO	
02089	43
18025	74
CHROMA	
26016	92
TYPO	
33016	108
37040	117
38038	119
SPATIAL	
49011	142
49019	142

VISUAL PROFILE *Iconic • Transit Heritage • Historic • Urban Culture • Detailed • Metaphorica • Ambiguous Space*

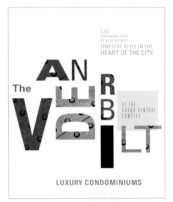

PICTO	
12069	63
CHROMA	
25002	90
TYPO	
33007	108
37028	117
38046	119
45007	132
SPATIAL	
49009	142

VISUAL PROFILE *Bold • Architectural Allusion • Geometric • Progressive • Vibrant • Cultured • Integrated*

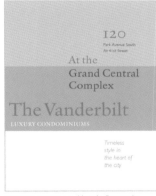

PICTO	
NA	
CHROMA	
25015	90
TYPO	
37002	108
37026	117
38017	118
38043	119
SPATIAL	
49008	142
49049	143

VISUAL PROFILE *Muted • Reserved • Elegant • Nostalgic • Geometric • Historic • Contemplative*

PICTO	
10001	58
CHROMA	
29023	99
TYPO	
33007	108
37028	117
38024	118
38043	119
SPATIAL	
49012	142
49033	142

VISUAL PROFILE *Skyline Allusion • Visionary • Sophisticated • Pictorial Metaphor • Architectural • Expansive • Aspirational*

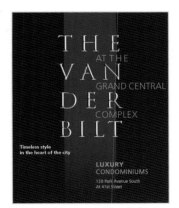

PICTO	
NA	
CHROMA	
26002	92
TYPO	
34035	111
35007	112
37028	117
38032	119
SPATIAL	
49002	142
49011	142

VISUAL PROFILE *Aggressive • Challenging • Majestic • Classical • Luxury • Confidence • Urban Canyon Allusion • Privileged*

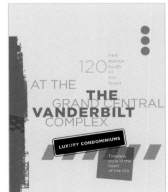

PICTO	
01001	40
01015	40
01068	41
17037	73
17069	73
18046	75
CHROMA	
19017	78
25002	90
TYPO	
34034	111
37030	117
38007	118
38023	118
41009	124
SPATIAL	
50021	144

VISUAL PROFILE *Collage • City Allusions • Multilayered • Expressive • Artsy • Spontaneous*

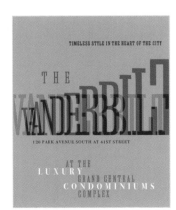

PICTO	
01068	41
01069	41
CHROMA	
19003	78
19067	79
TYPO	
37023	116
38041	119
SPATIAL	
49007	142
50004	144

VISUAL PROFILE *Rhythmic • Columnar • Structural • Grandiose • Eclectic • Transit • Rush-Hour • Movement*

Large-scale, elegant serif type against crisp, white backgrounds brings a refreshing, no-nonsense appeal to the packaging of these day-to-day bath products.

KYI SUN LEE NEW YORK, NY | UNITED STATES

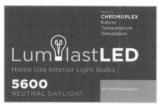

PICTO
18011 74

CHROMA
20003 80
20025 80
20033 80

TYPO
33016 108
37030 117
38042 119

SPATIAL
49011 142

PICTO
NA

CHROMA
21025 83
21027 83
32029 105

TYPO
33043 109
34004 110
36032 115

SPATIAL
49019 142

PICTO
01028 40

CHROMA
19051 79
27029 95

TYPO
37009 116
38025 119

SPATIAL
49020 142

VISUAL PROFILE *Geometric • Concrete Depiction • Sharp • Clear • Efficient*

VISUAL PROFILE *Radiant • Augmented Color • Hi-Tech • Vibrant • Geometric*

VISUAL PROFILE *Austere • Economical • Efficient • Ordered • Systematic • Responsible*

PICTO
NA

CHROMA
19040 79
21048 83

TYPO
33021 108
34048 111
37028 117
38041 119

SPATIAL
49056 143

PICTO
01028 40

CHROMA
32010 104

TYPO
34024 110
37001 116
38031 119

SPATIAL
49033 142

PICTO
01069 41
15006 68

CHROMA
19037 79
21027 83
32017 105

TYPO
33010 108
37030 117

SPATIAL
49072 143

VISUAL PROFILE *Montage • Metaphorical Augmentation • Ecological • Responsible • Long-Term • Direct*

VISUAL PROFILE *Organic • Luminous • Transition • Enlightened • Augmentation • Ecological • Illustrative Detailing • Humanistic*

VISUAL PROFILE *Concrete • Grounded • Radiant • Straightforward • Utilitarian • Bold • Contemporary • Colorful*

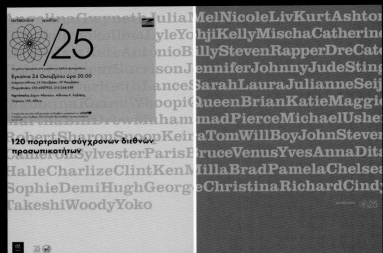

This two-sided celebrity event poster wraps the first names of various famous personages front to back in a large scale, slab serif typeface set in a vivid process blue. The large text's varying color relationship to its background, along with transparent box elements and contrasting sans serif type elements, contribute to an edgy, yet elegant, layered dimensional quality.

PAARPILOTEN DÜSSELDORF | GERMANY

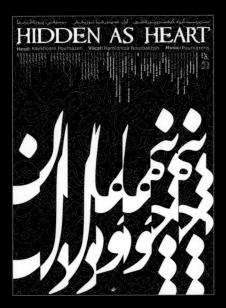

A study in textural scale, this performance poster pitches enormous, vertically emphatic script elements—themselves spliced into a secondary rhythm—against a textured, horizontal Roman headline, staggered, rotated text elements, and a delicate, linear pattern.

CASSRA STUDIO
TEHRAN | IRAN

VISUAL PROFILE
Abstracted Space •
Colorful • Bold •
Layered • Weather
and Flag Allusions

PICTO
01057 41
14007 66
14008 66

CHROMA
21001 82
25028 91

TYPO
37028 117
38023 118
38031 119

SPATIAL
49008 142

VISUAL PROFILE
1930s Americana •
Iconic • Streamline •
Transportation •
Exploration • Crisp •
Industrial • Abstract

PICTO
01057 41
14008 66

CHROMA
29012 98
29015 98

TYPO
37023 116
37029 117
38032 119

SPATIAL
49025 142

VISUAL PROFILE
Sense of Expectation •
Vertical Emphasis •
Grandeur • Focused •
Bigger than Life •
Dimensional • Cold

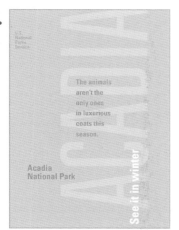

PICTO
NA

CHROMA
25028 91

TYPO
37028 117
38031 119
38048 119

SPATIAL
49027 142
49029 142

VISUAL PROFILE
Direct • Fresh •
Neutral • Emphasis
on Environment •
Contemporary •
Expansive • Under-
stated • Elegant

PICTO
04030 47
10017 58
10020 58
10038 59

CHROMA
23023 87
32006 104

TYPO
33007 108
37046 117
38017 118
38018 118

SPATIAL
49046 143

VISUAL PROFILE
Geometric • Iconic •
Pristine • Grandeur •
Experiential • Dynamic
Scale • Cinematic

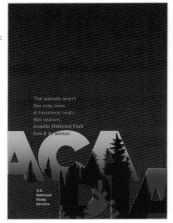

PICTO
01028 40
02009 42
02010 42
02011 42

CHROMA
19039 79
19049 79
25032 91

TYPO
33037 109
37030 117
38043 119

SPATIAL
49035 142

VISUAL PROFILE
Mid-Century Modern •
Nostalgic • Family
Activity • Ambiguous
Space • Iconic •
Emphasis on Train
Travel • Vernacular •
Stylized

PICTO
01028 40
02093 43
03031 45
14005 66

CHROMA
26014 92
29017 99

TYPO
33016 108
37047 117
38027 119

SPATIAL
49040 143

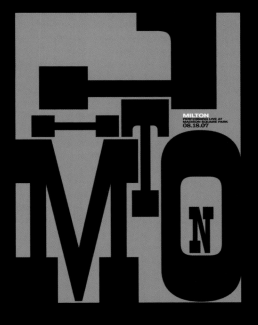

Old wood-type slab serif capitals are rearranged in playful configurations from poster to poster in this series to promote a band. Stark black-and-white text elements are set off by a different vibrant hue in each poster.

STEREOTYPE DESIGN
NEW YORK, NY | UNITED STATES

SIMPLE WEBSITE

HOME PAGE
Cultural Institution: Performing Arts

Project Communication Brief

·······································

Communicate the concept of operatic performance, evoking its rich history and cultural significance.

Establish the organization's contemporary, nontraditional artistic direction.

Allude to the grand themes of opera and of the current season; introduce the performance currently on stage.

Convey the organization's context in a rural environment.

Text Element Translations

·······································

Client
The animals aren't the only ones in luxurious coats this season.
Acadia National Park (1)

Titling
Love, Death, and Everything in Between: The 2010 Season

Featured Content
On Stage Now: The Magic Flute
Wolfgang Amadeus Mozart
A surrealist adaptation set in the decade prior to World War I

Navigation Elements
Performance Calendar
Capital Campaign
People and Programs
Subscriptions

This home page uses modular grid elements, size changes, and sharp, angular rules to provide richness of detail; the shift of elements left and right, and the varied intervals of space around them, impart rhythm against the geometric solidity of the structure.
PAONE DESIGN ASSOCIATES
PHILADELPHIA, PA │ UNITED STATES

Updating and abstracting typographic language commonly associated with printed newspapers, this online political journal and blog captures the spirit of hard-nosed, credible journalism and nostalgia of the physical inspiration and translates it to speak to a current, techologically-savvy audience.
STIM VISUAL COMMUNICATION   BROOKLYN, NY │ UNITED STATES

PICTO	
14004	66
CHROMA	
19023	78
25013	90
TYPO	
34001	110
37045	117
46017	134
48001	138
48201	139
48292	139
SPATIAL	
49014	142
50043	145

VISUAL PROFILE *Romantic • Sensuous • Musical • Rigorous • Ornamental • Ambiguous Space • Rhythmic • Classical*

PICTO	
02019	42
10028	58
CHROMA	
19070	79
24018	89
TYPO	
33007	108
33016	108
36023	114
37001	116
38040	119
46002	134
SPATIAL	
49056	143

VISUAL PROFILE *Simple • Rural Environment • Rustic • Organic • Natural Color • Timeless • Decorative Detailing*

PICTO	
01002	40
02037	42
17028	72
17056	73
18013	74
18021	74
18034	75
CHROMA	
19032	78
19041	79
19049	79
TYPO	
33016	108
33037	109
36042	115
37001	116
38025	119
46050	135
SPATIAL	
49068	143

VISUAL PROFILE *Vernacular • Eclectic • Geometric • Constructed • Narrative • Symbolic • Delicate • Nostalgic • Iconic • Collage • Symbolic*

PICTO	
NA	
CHROMA	
19006	78
29006	98
TYPO	
37022	116
38045	119
38046	119
39015	120
46008	134
48193	139
48208	139
48214	139
48265	139
48291	139
SPATIAL	
49046	143

VISUAL PROFILE *Classical • Victorian • Eclectic • Rural Environment • Nostalgic • Romantic • Organic • Ornamental • Direct*

PICTO	
NA	
CHROMA	
24013	88
TYPO	
37026	117
38014	118
38018	118
38043	119
46020	134
48018	138
48089	138
48114	138
48181	139
SPATIAL	
49009	142
52018	149

VISUAL PROFILE *Contemporary • Clean • Professional • Subtle Ornamentation • Organized • Efficient • Informational • Rigorous • Sophisticated • Neutral • Quiet*

PICTO	
01001	40
01025	40
01029	40
CHROMA	
19038	79
24001	88
TYPO	
36042	115
37026	117
38007	118
46040	135
SPATIAL	
49003	142
50043	145

VISUAL PROFILE *Eclectic • Geometric • Presentational • Thematic • Interactive • Informational • Systematic • Fluid*

Supported by an equally dramatic three-color palette, extremes of spatial proportion and scale among element are enriched by a contrast in serif and sans serif faces, opposing structural logic, areas of bold simplicity, and a myriad of finely detailed informational elements.

ADAMSMORIOKA BEVERLY HILLS, CA | UNITED ST

EDITORIAL
PAGES

ANNUAL REPORT
MESSAGING SECTION
Industrial Chemical Manufacturing

Project Communication Brief

. . . .

Communicate the client's core products and services: developing and distributing chemical compounds for industrial and technological manufacture.

Convey the general idea of chemistry

Establish the client's expertise and credibility within their field.

Visualize the page spread's primary message in an accessible, dynamic way.

Establish a sense of accomplishment and the client's aspirations.

Text Element Translations

. . . .

Client/Project
*Chemokore Industrial Group
2010 Annual Report*

Spread Title
More than simple growth: A new formula for research and development efficiency

Deck
This past year saw the implementation of a dramatic new centrifuge system and informatics systems that not only shorten the development schedule by half, but open up new avenues of exploration

Diagram Head
Change in financial performance relative to development time

PICTO	
01001	40
01004	40
18049	75
CHROMA	
20037	81
26012	92
TYPO	
36030	115
40003	122
40004	122
43055	128
44017	130
44018	130
45002	132
SPATIAL	
53006	150
54005	152

VISUAL PROFILE *Chemical • Bold • Abstract • Allusive • Complex • Diagrammatic • Scientific • Ambiguous Space • Kinetic*

PICTO	
01001	40
01028	40
18050	75
CHROMA	
20025	80
26011	92
TYPO	
34048	111
36030	115
38030	119
40003	122
40009	122
40021	123
43057	128
44013	130
44028	131
48070	138
48146	138
SPATIAL	
51009	146
54002	152

VISUAL PROFILE *Classic Editorial Structure • Linear • Integrated • Progression • Efficient • Transformation • Molecular • Industrial*

PICTO	
01018	40
01028	40
CHROMA	
19004	78
26013	92
TYPO	
33006	108
36032	115
37029	117
38014	118
40023	123
43119	129
43144	129
44021	130
44022	130
47001	136
SPATIAL	
52008	148
54011	152

VISUAL PROFILE *Systematic • Vibrant • Energetic • Innovative • Dimensional • Sequential • Chemically-Altered • Rotated Graph • Layered*

PICTO	
01001	40
01067	41
CHROMA	
20062	81
26012	92
TYPO	
34032	111
37028	117
43016	128
43142	129
43153	129
44042	131
44049	131
SPATIAL	
52008	148
54025	153

VISUAL PROFILE *Symbolic • Abstract • Rotational Movement • Liquid • Psychedelic • Chemical • Augmentation • Complex Organization • Edgy*

PICTO	
01004	40
18048	75
CHROMA	
19049	79
23027	87
TYPO	
37028	117
39011	120
40001	122
43013	128
44015	130
44047	131
SPATIAL	
53026	151
54008	152

VISUAL PROFILE *Geometric • Translucent • Ordered • Technological • Part-to-Whole Interaction • Innovative • Clean • Analytical • Competent*

PICTO	
18025	74
CHROMA	
24012	88
TYPO	
37028	117
43042	128
44016	130
SPATIAL	
53029	151
54014	152

VISUAL PROFILE *Precision • Analytical • Efficient • Metaphorical • Dynamic • Graph as Image • Rhythmic • Horizontal Emphasis • Dimensional*

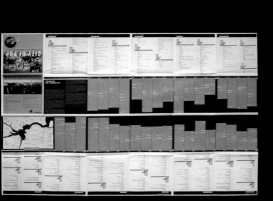

Vivid orange sets off the text-heavy informational panels in this foldout brochure/poster enumerating the pop-culture history and places of interest within a city. A tight column structure is given movement through staggered-height boxes, and kitschy display caps add fun and texture.

DESIGNLIGA

MUNICH | GERMANY

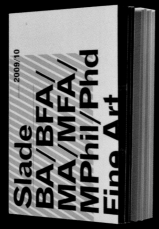

A chunky, grotesk sans serif, supported by near-primary colors and a diagonal line pattern, creates a bold, fresh, almost un-designed identity for an art school. Contrast is achieved through extreme scale and weight changes, along with carefully proportioned spatial intervals such as margins and paragraph separations.

PAARPILOTEN

DÜSSELDORF | GERMANY

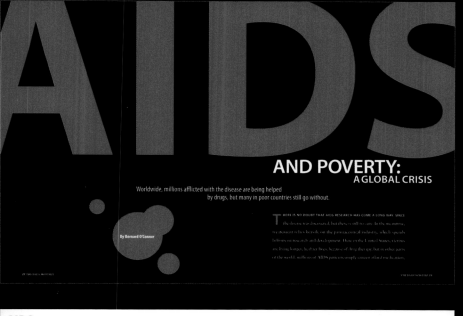

AND POVERTY:
A GLOBAL CRISIS

Worldwide, millions afflicted with the disease are being helped
by drugs, but many in poor countries still go without.

By Bernard O'Connor

Typography need not be considered limited strictly to letters, numbers, and punctuation: the components of the alphabet—dots, lines, and planes—also count. In these editorial pages, the dot assumes a primary role not only as a structural and visual contrast to the linear word and text forms, but bcomes an evocation of the article's subject, being read both as blood and the molecules of a virus. Tremendous scale shifts and contrast between block and linear forms in the opener give way to a more rigid, tightly justified configuration on the jump spread. Expansive margins provide focus on the columns—as well as a pristine, credible, literary feel—and, in concert with carefully positioned callouts and text subheads, help relieve the texture of the primary reading area.

JOSEPH CASERTO
ART DIRECTION AND DESIGN
BROOKLYN, NY | UNITED STATES

Index *by Subject*

Note: Page numbers in grayscale indicate figures.

Directory of Contributors

2 FRESH
Pages 179, 218
Beybi Giz Plaza · Kat 26
Maslak 34396 Istanbul · Turkey
....
1 Liverpool Street
London EC2M 7QD · United Kingdom
www.2fresh.com

999 DESIGN
Pages 177, 183
91 Great Eastern Street
London EC2A 3HZ · United Kingdom
www.999design.com

ADAMSMORIOKA, INC.
Pages 199, 238
8484 Wilshire Blvd., Suite 600
Beverly Hills, CA 90211 · USA
www.adamsmorioka.com

ATELIER BRÜCKNER
Page 199
Krefelderstrasse 32
Stuttgart · Germany 70376
www.atelier-brueckner.de

BASE ART CO.
Page 177
17 Brickel Street
Columbus, OH 43215 · USA
www.baseartco.com

BRUKETA & ZINIC
Pages 172, 173, 183, 213, 215, 223
Zavrtnica 17
Zagreb · Croatia 10000
www.bruketa-zinic.com

BTD:NYC
Page 225
611 Broadway, Room 511
New York, NY 10012 · USA
www.btdnyc.com

**JOSEPH CASERTO
ART DIRECTION AND
DESIGN**
Pages 191, 241
238 7th Avenue, No. 4R
Brooklyn, NY 11215-3435 · USA
www.josephcaserto.com

CASSRA STUDIO
Page 232
Unit 11, No.5 · 4th Golestan Alley ·
Golestan Street · Marzdaran Blvd.
Tehran · Iran
www.cassraabedini.com

**COMPASS 360 DESIGN
AND ADVERTISING**
Page 172
11 Davies Avenue, Suite 200
Toronto, Ontario · Canada M4M 249
www.compass360.com

CREUNA
Pages 168, 169, 193, 195
Karenslyst Allé 9B
0278 Oslo · Norway
www.creuna.no

THOMAS CSANO
Pages 167, 169, 206, 215
3655 Boulevard St. Laurent · No. 202
Montréal, Quebec · Canada H2X 2V6
www.thomascsano.com

DESIGNLIGA
Pages 20, 240
Erzgiessereistrasse 4
Munich, Bavaria · Germany 80335
www.designliga.com

MARY DOMOWICZ
Pages 173, 214
New York, NY · USA
www.domowicz.com

DURRE DESIGN
Page 183
26440 Birchfield Avenue
Rancho Palos Verde, CA 90275 · USA
www.durredesign.com

FORM
Pages 176, 190, 205, 228
47 Tabernacle Street
London EC2A 4AA · United Kingdom
www.form.uk.com

GROW CREATIVE
Page 20
107 SE Washington St., Suite 251
Portland, Oregon 97214 · USA
www.grow-creative.com

IDEAS ON PURPOSE
Pages 190, 193
307 Seventh Avenue, Suite 701
New York, NY 10001 · USA
www.ideasonpurpose.com

KYM ABRAMS DESIGN
Pages 167, 190
213 West Institute Place, Suite 608
Chicago, IL 60610 · USA
www.kad.com

**KUHLMANN LEAVITT
DESIGN**
Page 199
7810 Forsyth Boulevard, 2 West
Saint Louis, MO 63105 · USA
www.kuhlmannleavitt.com

KYI SUN LEE
Page 230
480 Second Avenue, No. 27F
New York, NY 10016 · USA
www.kyisunlee.com

LSD SPACE
Page 184
San Andreas 36, 2° 6
28004 Madrid · Spain
www.lsdspace.com

PAARPILOTEN
Pages 232, 240
Wasserstrasse 2
40213 Düsseldorf · Germany
www.paarpiloten.com

**PAONE DESIGN
ASSOCIATES**
Pages 16, 167, 203, 225, 236
240 South Twentieth Street
Philadelphia, PA 19043 · USA
www.paonedesign.com

PEOPLE DESIGN
Pages 21, 169, 176, 194, 203
648 Monroe Ave. NW, Suite 212
Grand Rapids, MI 49503 · USA
www.peopledesign.com

RED CANOE
Pages 172, 224
347 Clear Creek Trail
Deer Lodge, TN 37726 · USA
www.redcanoe.com

**MAURICE REDMOND/
FEUER**
Pages 179, 205, 206
Herzogstrasse 32
80803 Munich · Germany
www.mauriceredmond.com

JASEN D. ROLFE
Page 191
1 Loring Road
Lexington, MA 02421 · USA
www.thebambieffect.com

**SÄGENVIER DESIGN-
KOMMUNIKATION**
Page 207
Sägerstrasse 4
6850 Dornbirn · Austria
www.saegenvier.at

**FRANCESCA
SCIANDRA**
Pages 179, 213
38 Hope Street
Providence, RI 02903 · USA
www.fsciandra.com

JULIE SHIM
Page 224
211 West 58th Street · No. 8
New York, NY 10019 · USA

SHINNOSKE, INC.
Pages 173, 202
2-1-8 Tsuriganecho, Chuoku,
6th Floor
Osaka 540-0035 · Japan
www.shinn.co.jp

STEIN ØVRE
Page 21
Grensefaret 23C
1341 Slependen · Norway
www.steinovre.com

**STEREOTYPE
DESIGN**
Pages 185, 235
39 Jane Street, No. 4A
New York, NY 10014 · USA
www.stereotype-design.com

**STIM: VISUAL
COMMUNICATION**
Pages 31, 215, 218, 236
238 South 3rd Street, No. 4
Brooklyn, NY 11211 · USA
info@visual-stim.com

STUDIO CUCULIĆ
Pages 185, 213, 214
Bukovačka 218 A
Zagreb · Croatia 10000
www.studio-cuculic.hr

SUNG SOO SONG
Pages 185, 193
820 Avenue A
Bayonne, NJ 07002 · USA
designurban@hotmail.com

SURFACE
Page 195
Peterstrasse 4
60433 Frankfurt am Main ·
Germany
www.surface.de

SUTHERN DESIGN
Page 223
37 Alexander Avenue
Madison, NJ 07940 · USA
sutherndesign@gmail.com

ANN IM SUNWOO
Page 194
214 East 24th Street, No. 6
New York, NY 10010
swik0929@gmail.com

TACTICAL MAGIC LLC
Page 184
1460 Madison Avenue
Memphis, TN 38104 · USA
www.tacticalmagic.com

THINK STUDIO, NYC
Pages 168, 177, 228
16 Beaver Street
New York, NY 10004 · USA
www.thinkstudionyc.com